Making Australian Foreign Policy

In a tense and dangerous international environment, this book looks at the important question of how Australia deals with the outside world. It describes the role of the government departments and intelligence organisations that support the government's policy-making, and the thinking of the people who make it, in more detail than ever before. The book discusses the processes, institutions, actors and calculations involved in foreign policy making in Australia, and how these have changed under the impact of globalisation. It draws on an extensive survey – the first ever – of how Australian foreign affairs officials think about the world, and includes case studies of four recent Australian foreign policy initiatives. It concludes by speculating on the challenges ahead for Australian foreign policy making.

This is essential reading for all of those who are interested in Australian foreign policy, and for politics students in international relations and foreign policy courses.

Allan Gyngell has had a long career in making, advising on and implementing foreign policy. He headed the International Division of the Department of Prime Minister and Cabinet, and has been posted to many countries since joining the Department of Foreign Affairs in 1969. He was foreign policy adviser to former Prime Minister Paul Keating from 1993 until 1996. He is Executive Director of the Lowy Institute for International Policy.

Michael Wesley is Senior Lecturer in Politics and International Relations, University of New South Wales.

Making Australian Foreign Policy

ALLAN GYNGELL

Lowy Institute for International Policy

MICHAEL WESLEY

University of New South Wales, Sydney

CAMBRIDGE
UNIVERSITY PRESS

PUBLISHED BY THE PRESS SYNDICATE OF THE UNIVERSITY OF CAMBRIDGE
The Pitt Building, Trumpington Street, Cambridge, United Kingdom

CAMBRIDGE UNIVERSITY PRESS
The Edinburgh Building, Cambridge CB2 2RU, UK
40 West 20th Street, New York, NY 10011–4211, USA
477 Williamstown Road, Port Melbourne, VIC 3207, Australia
Ruiz de Alarcón 13, 28014 Madrid, Spain
Dock House, The Waterfront, Cape Town 8001, South Africa

http://www.cambridge.org

First published 2003

Printed in Australia by Ligare

Typeface Times New Roman 10/13 pt.   *System* QuarkXPress®   [PK]

A catalogue record for this book is available from the British Library

National Library of Australia Cataloguing in Publication data
Gyngell, Allan.
    Making Australian foreign policy.
    Includes index.
    ISBN 0 521 83234 9.
    ISBN 0 521 53997 8 (pbk.).
    1. Australia – Foreign relations. I. Wesley, Michael.
    II. Title.
327.94

ISBN 0 521 53997 8 paperback
ISBN 0 521 83234 9 hardback

Contents

Preface

This book began its life over a late-night beer in a hotel in Taiwan in 1997. We two authors – one a political scientist with a background in international relations theory, the other a former diplomat and policy-maker – discovered that we were each interested from our different perspectives in the same questions. Why do international relations theorists and foreign policy practitioners see the process of making foreign policy in such different ways? Why has so little of the writing about foreign policy in Australia successfully reconciled the theoretical approaches to the subject with the actual, erratic, contingent way in which foreign policy making takes place?

In contrast with other areas of public policy – microeconomic or social policy, for example – the gap between foreign policy academics and practitioners is large. They speak different languages. Empirical to their bootstraps, foreign policy practitioners tend to regard theory as an artificial template imposed on an uncertain world. For their part, international relations theorists consider practitioners dangerously limited by their failure to understand, or to have regard for, the broader patterns shaping international events. We consider some of the reasons for this gap in Chapter 1. One important objective of this book is to clear away some of the dust and to help practitioners and theorists see each other more clearly.

Foreign policy is a subject worth taking seriously. If it is conceived and implemented effectively, foreign policy delivers to a country benefits as tangible and significant as those produced by good economic policy. If it is done badly, the consequences are frequently serious and can eventually be calamitous. So both authors believe that understanding how foreign policy is made in Australia, how the key institutions operate, and how the structures and mechanisms are changing are matters of more than simply academic interest.

We are not concerned in this book with the important public-policy question of what particular foreign policy Australia should pursue. We hope, however, that by investigating the modalities of foreign policy making in Australia we can help frame and give more precision to that vital debate.

For the most part, Michael Wesley conceived and wrote the first drafts of the chapters on theory and the internal and external environment. Allan Gyngell did the same for the chapters on the institutions of foreign policy making and the case studies. We then argued about, edited and rewrote the text until we were each comfortable with the result. The work was completed in early 2003.

We have many people, inside government and outside, to thank for help in writing the book and shaping our ideas. Their contributions – some on the record, some off – will be apparent from the text, although the responsibility for the content is entirely ours.

Among those we would like to thank specifically are the Australian Foreign Minister, Alexander Downer, and his predecessor, Gareth Evans. Dr Ashton Calvert, the Secretary of the Department of Foreign Affairs and Trade, was generous in giving us access to the department and in agreeing to distribute the questionnaire on how DFAT policy officers think about their jobs. In two different positions – as head of Corporate Services and later as Deputy Secretary – Alan Thomas was of great assistance. So, too, in Australia and overseas, were John Dauth, Ian Kemish, Dennis Richardson, Richard Smith, Allan Taylor, Michael Thawley and Hugh White. Michael Costello, Michael Keating and Stuart Harris gave us the benefit of their extensive experience in government and outside it. Over five years while we were working on this book, a number of other people patiently gave us their views on their involvement with the foreign policy process, in structured interviews and informal conversations: we thank Ron Bonighton, Bill Bowtell, Laurie Brereton, Paul Comfort, Wendy Craik, Jane Drake-Brockman, Peter Drysdale, Geoff Forrester, Glenda Gauci, Genta Hawkins Holmes, Bill Hayden, Joanna Hewitt, Cavan Hogue, Mitch Hooke, Lyle Howard, Greg Hunt, Jeremy Jones, Miles Jordana, Paul Kelly, Miles Kupa, Michael L'Estrange, Geoff Miller, Kevin Rudd, Nick Warner, Mack Williams and Kyle Wilson.

For their generosity in reading and commenting on parts of the manuscript, or for providing helpful suggestions on literature and approaches, we thank Chris Black, Glyn Davis, Stephen FitzGerald, Kath Gelber, Geoff Levey and Marc Williams. Michael Wesley tested much of the theoretical framework of this book over the course of a number of seminars held at the Asia–Australia Institute, the School of Politics and International Relations at the University of New South Wales (UNSW), and at the Australian Institute of International Affairs – our thanks to all of the participants in those contexts who responded with useful comments to the papers presented. The theoretical framework was also tested as the course material for the subject "Diplomacy and Foreign Policy Analysis", a second-year unit in the School of Politics and International Relations at UNSW: many thanks to the students in that subject who participated in lively tutorial discussions and asked often-demanding questions at the lectures.

Shah Eshan Habib translated the results of the DFAT survey into meaningful statistics with the patience and humour of one accustomed to dealing with the mathematically challenged. The staff of the ASIO, DFAT and UNSW libraries provided wonderful professional help.

Thanks in particular are due to Paul Keating for his longstanding support and the opportunities he opened up, and to David Kwon for his support.

We are grateful to all the staff members of the Department of Foreign Affairs and Trade who took the time to complete the questionnaire on which some of our conclusions are based.

Cambridge University Press, especially Kim Armitage, Amanda Pinches and David Barrett, were a pleasure for the authors to deal with.

Above all, for all their forbearance, support and patience, we thank Catherine Gyngell and Sheridan Hume.

CHAPTER 1

Introduction

It still seems to me to be a shortcoming in Australian public discussion that so many commentators who profess political expertness look only at personalities, parties and doctrines and obviously know very little about political institution or the processes of public administration. "Who did it?" becomes the centre of interest. "How was it done and why" are seldom considered.

Sir Paul Hasluck[1]

In February 1997 Australian intelligence agencies picked up the first clear indications that the Papua New Guinea (PNG) Government was recruiting mercenary fighters to help it recapture the island of Bougainville. In Bougainville's dense jungles, an intractable rebellion had been under way for nearly a decade, forcing the closure of the island's copper mine and causing extensive death and suffering. Intelligence reports confirmed that the PNG Government had signed a $36 million contract with the British company Sandline International to supply arms, training and former South African fighters to destroy the Bougainville Revolutionary Army and reopen the copper mine.[2] News of the Sandline contract immediately became a foreign policy issue of major importance to Australia. Papua New Guinea is Australia's closest neighbour, the recipient of $300 million annually in civil aid and $12 million in defence aid. It is an important element in Australia's security planning. Up to 10,000 Australian citizens were thought to be in PNG.

The initial fragmentary intelligence reports had already been discussed by the Strategic Policy Coordination Group, the small group of senior officials from the departments of Defence, Foreign Affairs and Trade (DFAT) and Prime Minister and Cabinet (PM&C) charged with the day-to-day coordination of strategic policy within the public service. By 18 February, the intelligence had become firmer, and on that day the government's principal analytical intelligence organisation, the Office of National Assessments (ONA), briefed the Prime Minister, senior ministers including the Foreign Minister, Alexander Downer, and their staff about the news. The briefings confirmed that a giant Russian-built AN-124 transport aircraft and a smaller AN-12, believed to have delivered men and equipment, were now sitting on the ground at the Port Moresby airport.

Prime Minister John Howard took charge of the Australian response. He had experienced assistants and advisers. His foreign policy adviser, Michael

Thawley, had previously headed areas responsible for PNG in both DFAT and PM&C. Howard summoned ministers and senior officials to a meeting in his Parliament House office. The basic outlines of the Australian policy response were resolved at that meeting. The Australian position would be that the introduction of mercenaries into PNG would set a dangerous precedent in the South Pacific, a region where several other states were facing internal fractures, and would not lead to a settlement of the long-running conflict on Bougainville. Australia's policy aim was twofold: first, to stop the mercenaries who were training in Wewak from deploying to Bougainville; and second, to get them out of the country. It was also going to be important, through all of this, to secure Australia's policy aims at the least possible cost to the important Australian relationship with PNG.

Australia's diplomatic machinery swung into action. Howard telephoned the PNG Prime Minister, Sir Julius Chan, directly about the reports. Chan would concede only that he had hired foreigners to provide special training to the PNG armed forces. By chance, Foreign Minister Alexander Downer was to leave on the following day on an official visit to PNG. In Port Moresby he raised Australian concerns about the reports during his meeting with Chan. Chan again replied that the package involved no more than training. Downer told Chan that even if that were so (and privately Australia knew that it was not), Australia was opposed to the precedent and would be particularly outraged if the forces were used on Bougainville. Downer reported the unsatisfactory response back to Howard, who again telephoned Chan to reinforce the Foreign Minister's message.

Meanwhile, in an effort to increase the pressure on the PNG Government, the Australian High Commissioner in Port Moresby, David Irvine, was instructed to brief United States, British and New Zealand diplomats on what Australia knew about arms shipments and Sandline involvement, and to show them photographs of ammunition boxes and crates of AK-47s. An experienced Australian journalist, Mary-Louise O'Callaghan, had already picked up many aspects of the story. Downer met her at a reception at the Australian High Commission on the night of 19 February. The Foreign Minister wanted to get the story into the public domain, presumably in part to further raise the stakes for Chan and his government. He directed Foreign Affairs officials to confirm O'Callaghan's story and provide her with additional background. After further inquiries, O'Callaghan broke the story three days later, on 22 February. It generated a storm of media and public interest. At the same time, a senior International Monetary Fund (IMF) official, Stanley Fischer, was visiting Canberra. After discussions with the Australian Government, he hinted to the media that IMF and World Bank aid packages to PNG might be reviewed if there was any interference with agreed budget spending projections as a result of these developments.

The Defence Department and the Australian Defence Force (ADF) had been heavily involved in the policy process from the beginning. The initial intelligence focus was on finding out where the Sandline forces were and keeping them under observation. The RAAF played an important role in this, flying surveillance flights over Wewak, where the majority of the Sandline personnel were located. On 18 February the Commander of the ADF, General John Baker, instructed the Assistant Chief of Operations to develop options for any response that might be required from the ADF. Ten days later, at a routine annual meeting, the Australian and New Zealand defence ministers, representing the two largest military powers in the South Pacific, issued a communiqué describing the mercenaries as unwelcome. The Australian Defence Minister, Ian McLachlan, said that Australia would look at all avenues, including financial and defence cooperation, to influence PNG to reverse its decision on employing mercenaries. "We will do everything we can to make sure they go away", he said.

By this time the "Sandline Affair" had become a prominent public issue in Australia. Newspapers, radio and television – the last of these looking principally for colourful footage – were giving wide coverage to events in PNG and were often getting it wrong. Even serious media like the Melbourne *Age* newspaper and the AAP press agency provided highly inaccurate accounts of developments on Bougainville. As one of the most experienced Australian reporters about PNG, Sean Dorney, later commented, releases from the office of the Bougainville Revolutionary Army "found a ready and gullible audience amongst generally ill-informed Australian and New Zealand journalists suddenly given the task of covering the … unfamiliar story". Within Parliament, opposition parties began trying to influence policy, or at least public attitudes. In the House of Representatives, ALP foreign affairs spokesman Laurie Brereton called on the government to give PNG the six months' notice of cancellation required under the bilateral aid treaty. The Australian Senate passed a motion moved by a Greens Senator calling for a comprehensive review of all Australian aid to PNG, including defence cooperation.

Australian intelligence agencies continued to monitor the situation in PNG. The National Security Committee of Cabinet met to consider intelligence assessments of the situation and to discuss Australia's options if PNG rejected Australia's advice. Because, contrary to Australia's hopes, Chan seemed determined to press ahead with the operation, the high-level diplomacy between the two prime ministers continued. On Sunday, 9 March, Howard and Chan held a secret meeting for four and a half hours at Kirribilli House, the Australian Prime Minister's Sydney residence. The main Australian aim at the meeting was to prevent the deployment of the Sandline forces to Bougainville. Howard told Chan that Australia remained "very strongly opposed to the use of mercenaries on Bougainville and that, if the use of the mercenaries took place, there would be consequences of a serious kind so far as the relationship between Australia and PNG was concerned".[3] He offered something in return: changes to the Defence Cooperation Program, including improved training for the PNG Defence Force (PNGDF) and extra non-military aid for Bougainville. Chan, however, wanted Australia to buy the mercenaries out. The media knew of the secret meeting by the same afternoon.

Then, on 17 March, the affair took a startling turn. In an event whose specifics were unforeseen by the Australian intelligence agencies and government,[4] officers under the direction of the Commander of the PNGDF, Brigadier General Singirok, launched an operation codenamed *Rausim Kwik.* They arrested Sandline's chief in PNG, a British national, and demanded the resignation of the Prime Minister, Deputy Prime Minister and Defence Minister. The police force, however, decided to throw its support behind the government, and by midafternoon Singirok had been sacked by the government and a replacement sworn in. Nevertheless, elements of the army remained loyal to their sacked commander, and unrest spread in Port Moresby. Crowds milled outside military headquarters at Murray Barracks, and students demonstrated in support of the general.

However much the aim of the PNG army's action was in line with Australian policy objectives, it had about it elements of an attempted military coup in Australia's nearest neighbour, a longstanding Australian security fear. There were other concerns also. With thousands of Australian citizens in PNG, a potential consular crisis was looming. One large Australian company, BHP, evacuated its employees and their families.

In Canberra, Prime Minister Howard made a statement to the House of Representatives on 18 March, expressing Australia's support for the elected government of PNG but reiterating its opposition to the use of mercenaries. He also expressed Australia's "primary concern" as being the safety of Australian citizens in PNG. He said the government was monitoring the situation closely.[5]

Australian troops in Townsville had already been placed on alert for possible movement to PNG to assist with the evacuation of Australian citizens. As order broke down among elements of the PNGDF, the question of whether the ADF should be sent to help the PNG Government restore order was raised. Aware of large-scale US and Australian military exercises under way in the

Northern Territory, Chan sounded out the Australian High Commissioner about possible Australian help. The High Commissioner agreed to refer the matter to Canberra but left Chan with the impression that Australia would not get involved. No formal response was provided to the PNG Government. According to officials who participated in the decision-making, the diplomatic aims were complex: to leave Chan with the impression that Australia would not intervene with forces, but Singirok, who was in contact with the Australian Defence Attaché, with the impression that it might if the situation became uncontrollable.[6]

Howard again telephoned Chan on 19 March to assure him that his sacking of the Defence Commander had Australian support and to ask whether he would receive a personal emissary. Apparently thinking that the new situation might give him more leverage with Australia over the Sandline contracts, Chan agreed. The "emissary" turned out to be a three-member delegation led by the Secretary of DFAT, Philip Flood, with a Deputy Secretary from Defence, Hugh White, and the head of the International Division of PM&C (and a former High Commissioner to PNG), Allan Taylor. They left Canberra on an RAAF VIP Falcon jet in midafternoon and arrived in Port Moresby about 8.20 that night.

The delegation, accompanied by the High Commissioner, met Chan on the following day. Carrots were proffered and sticks brandished. Chan was told politely but firmly that if he did not abandon the idea of using mercenaries in Bougainville, Australia would take "dramatic and drastic measures that would harm PNG". These measures would involve both the $300 million aid program and the $12 million Defence Cooperation Program. Chan was offered additional aid if he walked away from the Sandline deal, including a significant expansion of defence aid. Chan tried to bargain – perhaps Australia might pay Sandline's $30 million bill? He was told firmly that this was not possible. Chan said later that the commander's revolt was not discussed, despite his hope that events on the ground would change the Australian views of the situation. The meeting broke up with the Australians unsure of the outcome. Chan said he would see the delegation again on the following morning. That night, Chan advised the High Commissioner, and announced in a news release, that he was suspending the Sandline contract while he set up a judicial inquiry into the affair. At his meeting with the Australians the following day, Chan told them that the mercenaries were leaving on a chartered Air Niugini aircraft to fly to Hong Kong. The Sandline Affair was over. The announcement did not end the tension and uncertainty in Port Moresby, which bubbled on until Chan's resignation as Prime Minister on 26 March, but the immediate crisis had passed.

As a foreign policy issue for Australia, the Sandline Affair was unusual. In the first place, Australia was a major player, able to bring considerable leverage of its own to bear in support of its diplomacy. The number of countries involved was limited, so the variables were reduced. The crisis had a more or less clear beginning and came to a sort of end. It was over quickly and the policy aims the Australian Government had set at the beginning were achieved: the mercenaries were withdrawn; PNG's constitutional integrity was maintained; and, in the longer run, opportunities were opened up to address the Bougainville situation peacefully. Not all of these outcomes were attributable to Australian foreign policy alone, but it is safe to say that a different set of Australian policies would almost certainly have led to a different result.

Our consideration of the outlines of Australian foreign policy in the Sandline Affair raises a number of questions about foreign policy making in Australia. What makes some events (such as the arrival of mercenaries in PNG) major foreign policy issues and others not? Why did the Australian Government set those particular policy objectives, and outline them in that particular way? How did each participant, from the Prime Minister down, contribute to the formulation, execution and evaluation of policy? How were the vast array of Australian Government activities, from monitoring to decision-making to diplomacy, coordinated? Was the outcome typical of Australian policy and influence in foreign affairs?

These are questions that are not easily answered by existing accounts of Australian foreign policy. On the one hand, the academic literature on Australian foreign policy offers very blunt instruments. The vast majority of this literature examines the content rather than the process of Australian foreign policy, and can be divided into either broadly historical studies of Australian foreign policy,[7] or thematic treatments of Australian foreign policy in relation to specific countries, geographic regions, issues and events.[8] There are some studies that consider certain impacts on foreign policy making, such as culture and society,[9] or politics between the political parties.[10]

A few studies devote chapters or sections of chapters to foreign policy making; however, these accounts are impressionistic and brief because the books that contain them are focussed primarily on other aspects of Australian foreign policy. As a result, Evans and Grant[11] focus heavily on the work of the Foreign Minister, while Smith, Cox and Burchill[12] briefly discuss the ministers, the bureaucracy, Parliament and pressure groups. Some accounts of policy-making are downright misleading. Stewart Firth argues that

> Departments compete for influence over foreign policy. Their competition is an enduring characteristic of the policy-making process. Government departments have different priorities and different constituencies ... Bureaucrats like their own

departments to win, whatever the merits of the case, because winning departments earn status which itself is a source of influence in the next battle over policy. In part, then, foreign policy is the outcome of bureaucratic politics.[13]

Russell Trood agrees:

[DFAT and the departments of Defence, Prime Minister and Cabinet, Immigration, Primary Industry, Treasury, Environment and Education have their] own administrative mandate and distinctive departmental culture and sometimes their interests clash, threatening both the coherence of the policy-making process and the quality of its decisions. In the face of these dangers, maintaining the integrity of the policy-making system, both in terms of its overall coherence and policy outcomes is a major challenge for the government.[14]

As we will demonstrate in subsequent chapters, these conceptions of bureaucratic conflict in foreign policy making are particularly inappropriate to the Australian experience, which is overwhelmingly collegial. They demonstrate the dangers of importing US models of foreign policy making into the Australian context, or observations from other areas of the Australian bureaucracy into the foreign policy realm.

Nor are our questions adequately answered by the accounts of participants or eyewitnesses. Most such accounts, whether published memoirs or verbal recollections, tend to concentrate on the personalities involved, their calculations at the time, and the specific circumstances of the policy.[15] It is difficult from these accounts alone to draw more general conclusions about the way that Australian foreign policy is made across a range of issues and contexts.

Academics and practitioners: The two worlds of foreign policy

Our questions appear to fall into the gap between the academic and practitioner foreign policy communities. Indeed, this reflects a more general situation in Australia, summed up by a longstanding foreign policy practitioner, that there is no field of politics or policy in which research and practice have less mutual impact than international relations (IR). There seem to be a number of reasons for this. On the academic side, as IR cements its position within Australian universities, it has succumbed to the common tendency for academic disciplines to privilege theoretical over applied inquiry as they seek to consolidate their positions and build respect within the academic world.[16] In the process, the attention of the academic IR community has become increasingly focussed inwards. Debates among IR academics have singularly failed to arouse the attention or interest of any but the IR community; and measures of professional esteem largely seem to be internally set.

For its part, the practitioner community seems to have grown increasingly uninterested in the results of academic research, thinking it lacks much relevance to the real world. Many are unconvinced of the value of critiques of realism, which for the majority of DFAT staff continues to provide simple, powerful signposts about the nature of their trade. The more critical IR theory questions the normative bases of the international status quo – be it from neo-Gramscian, postmodernist or cosmopolitan traditions – the more the work of IR academics seems to criticise practitioners and their world, and the more distance and contempt become the predominant reactions. Those in the academic world who have influenced Australian foreign policy and had their views sought out in the past two decades have been figures not from IR but from economics, strategic studies and specialist-area studies. Less and less have retired practitioners been able to maintain the links between the two worlds in the ways that John Burton, Hedley Bull or Coral Bell were able to. Many retired practitioners find it hard to relate to and gain acceptance from the increasingly rarefied world of academic IR.

Partly, the separation is also the result of the very different worlds occupied by academics and practitioners. The practitioner's view of foreign policy is of a world of complex detail and incessant demands on time, attention and resources. The policy field of the practitioner resists simple solutions and evades summary or generalisation: "The reality lies in the detail and in the interaction of detail lies the policy".[17] Practitioners look for exceptions to general statements about foreign policy issues. Their experience of trying to implement policy in the difficult, wilful, resistant world of IR makes them sceptical of high-sounding schemes and principles, as well as the moral simplicity and unqualified solutions offered by academics and public alike. In contrast, the academic's world is one of abstraction and generalisation, of post-hoc analysis and probabilistic prediction. Detail, caveats, and information falling outside of general trends are obstacles and pedantic irritations that detract from the more instructive "big picture" and from the explanatory power of the theory. Logical consistency, analytical rigour and innovations of inference are the standards of success for academics; for practitioners, effectiveness consists in standards of fine, verifiable detail and knowledge of the dispositions of key people in both the policy and organisational environments.

This book is a result of the belief of its authors that the results of research and theory-building in international relations can be combined to great effect with the experience of foreign policy practitioners. It seeks to answer the questions of the type asked above, as well as a number of others. What do we mean when we talk about foreign policy? How does it differ from diplomacy? How is it made in Australia? Who is it made by? Who influences it?

We deal principally in this book with foreign policy, not foreign relations or diplomacy. Put simply, *foreign policy* is that dimension of public policy that deals with the outside world. Its job, in the words of John Lewis Gaddis, is to create "an international environment conducive to the nation's interest".[18] It is not the same as *foreign relations*, which is the outcome of the foreign policy process; the objective relationship at any given time between sovereign states. And it is different from *diplomacy*, which is the tool used to implement the policy: the means to the end.

The book then looks forward to another set of issues. How are the deep changes in society and in the international system, driven in part by technological developments, influencing the way foreign policy is made, and where are these changes likely to lead? What is the impact of the shrinking space between domestic and foreign policy as globalisation transforms the nature of economic and social transactions between governments? Are we seeing the first signs of the death of foreign policy, at least in the traditional way we have thought about it?

This is a book about foreign policy making, investigated by way of an Australian case study. It makes a number of points about the process of foreign policy making – an activity performed by every state – that can be generally applied. On the other hand, Australia, like all other countries, makes unique demands on its foreign policy making machinery, and many of the observations made in other chapters are relevant to Australia and its situation alone. It is important at the outset to consider Australia's situation in the world, in order to set the stage for our consideration of Australian foreign policy making.

Australia *sui generis*

Australians comprise less than one-third of 1 per cent of the world's population. This is a slightly higher proportion than the one-fifth of 1 per cent at the end of the Second World War, but about the same proportion that is projected for the year 2050. This tiny fraction of humanity lives on an island continent comprising just over 5 per cent of the earth's land surface. It shares a land border with no other country: its 36,735-kilometre coastline is bordered by vast expanses of ocean. Its east coast, along which live more than two-thirds of its population, is washed by the earth's largest ocean, all 165 million square kilometres of the Pacific. Its west coast looks onto the earth's third-largest body of water: the 73-million-square-kilometre Indian Ocean. To the south are the frozen expanses of the Antarctic; to the north, first the island archipelagos and then the vast landmass of Asia, closer, but so different in history, language, culture, society, economy and politics.

Despite its isolation, Australia is and always has been deeply involved in world politics. It has become involved in nearly every major military conflict that has occurred since 1901. At federation, Australian troops were serving in the Boer War in South Africa. Australia was an original belligerent in both world wars. It was also quick to become involved in two of the major conflicts of the Cold War, the Korean War and the Vietnam War. Since the end of the Cold War, Australian troops have been sent to both Gulf Wars, to Afghanistan and to Iraq. There are few wars in the Western Pacific, whether major, like Korea and Vietnam, or minor, like the Malayan Emergency or Indonesia's *Konfrontasi*, insurgencies on Bougainville or in Irian Jaya, in which Australian troops have not become involved. Australians commanded the only two United Nations peacekeeping missions in the region: Cambodia, 1992–93, and East Timor, 1999 to 2001. War has been central to the development of the Australian identity; its major national holiday commemorates a military action. Australia's economy is enmeshed extensively with the global economy, with its trade dependency ratio, or the size of its foreign trade as a proportion of the size of its economy, at 34 per cent, compared with single-figure ratios for countries like Japan or the US. Australia was a founding member of the League of Nations and the UN, and is heavily involved in a range of international and regional organisations.

Despite such an extensive series of involvements, it is hard to pinpoint Australia's "place in the world" with any precision. Its strategic environments are Southeast Asia and the South Pacific. Its major strategic ally, however, is in North America, 12,000 kilometres away. Its major trading partners lie in Northeast Asia, 8,000 kilometres as the Boeing flies. The historical and cultural roots of the largest proportion of its population lie in Europe, on the other side of the globe.

Australians are prone to watch the world around them apprehensively. "More fluid" is a perennial refrain in Australian strategic and foreign policy speeches. Foreign Minister W.M. Hughes mused in 1937:

> The present international situation is one of anxiety and complexity, and under modern conditions with the increasing application of science and invention to all phases of social and economic life, and with the constant speeding up of communications, the interdependence of all nations is such that no country can afford to devote its attention solely to its domestic problems.[19]

"Instead of living in a tranquil corner of the globe, we are now on the verge of the most unsettled region of the world", said R.G. Casey in 1955.[20] "We live in a world of change of an unprecedented rate and degree which makes great demands on all our human and natural resources", wrote the DFAT Secretary, Alan Renouf, in 1974.[21] The DFAT Annual Report for 1984–85 claimed that, "The world is in a profound era of transition with significant shifts taking place in the dispersal of power, both military and economic".[22] A decade later it said, "the pace of change in the international arena continued to be unrelenting in security and economic matters". "The most important features of this environment during the 2000–2002 period are likely to be ... [a] fluid and uncertain security situation, both in the region and globally", proclaimed the DFAT Corporate Plan in 2000,[23] while Prime Minister John Howard in 2002 claimed that, "Not since the early 1960s have we faced a more complex and uncertain region".[24]

This sense of uncertainty about the country's international environment is one of the things that impels Australian policy-makers in the direction of activism. Australian foreign policy frequently has about it a sense that the country needs to shape or be shaped. "Unless we are foreign policy makers, we will end up as foreign policy takers", as Paul Keating put it.[25] At the same time, the security of distance has helped give Australia a looseness and confidence in foreign policy making; it provides Australia with the psychological capacity to take risks with fewer consequences than for others. Australian foreign policy making has about it a tinkering quality, a sense that things can be tried without exposing the country to too many obvious dangers. In the words of Alexander Downer, Australia seems to be "irrepressibly activist", a quality he sees as born out of the country's national interest: "We are a middle power with the capacity to influence events. We have to make our way in the world in a way other countries don't".[26] This quality may be more noticeable because in the environment in which Australia principally operates – Asia – culture and history (or, rather, culture shaped by history) impose a more cautious, incremental approach to foreign policy. At its best (for example, the Cambodia settlement; see case study, page 88), the distinctive tone of Australian diplomacy leads to a useful stimulatory interchange. Less successfully, it can simply annoy as Australia's neighbours try to dodge or deflect yet another initiative from Canberra.

Australia's capacity to influence the outside world has been classified by many as that of a middle power. That is, Australia is large enough to have quite specific interests in global issues such as a healthy multilateral trading system or control of weapons of mass destruction, but it lacks the capacity of a great power to impose its will. Like other middle powers, it is forced into coalition-building diplomacy. The Secretary of DFAT, Ashton Calvert, summed Australia's situation up this way:

> Because Australia does not belong to a natural grouping we are not in a position to rely on the efforts of others in protecting and advancing our interests in international affairs. If, for example, we were a country of comparable population and economic weight located somewhere in Western Europe, we might be tempted to rely on the efforts of bigger powers around us to look after our stake in the international system. But, given where we are located, Australia does not have that luxury. We have to rely more directly on our own efforts to protect and advance the considerable security and economic interests we have engaged in the international system.[27]

This is not to imply, however, that all governments and political ideologies have a similar vision for Australian foreign policy. The most enduring divide in Australia's foreign policy lies between those who believe that Australia's interests will best be advanced by building and reinforcing ties with what Robert Menzies famously described as "our great and powerful friends", and an alternative view, summed up in Paul Keating's phrase that "Australia must find its security in Asia, not from Asia". A related but slightly different division exists between an emphasis on the centrality of bilateral relations and a "selective approach" to the multilateral agenda advanced most clearly in the Howard Government's 1997 and 2003 foreign policy White Papers, and a more internationalist view of Australian foreign policy. The latter, articulated most prominently by Labor Party leaders like H.V. Evatt and Gareth Evans, asserts that Australia's future is best secured by support for a robust multilateral system that enables middle powers to build coalitions of support for their interests.[28]

This debate has taken different forms at different times in Australia's history: it lay behind the decision-making on most of Australia's overseas military deployments, including Vietnam, as well as behind the effort Australia put into the development of regional institutions like APEC.

These divisions are not found exclusively within or between individual political parties. Any Australian government finds it necessary to deal effectively with both the United States and Asia, and to use international forums to achieve its goals. A strong liberal internationalism guided Malcolm Fraser's foreign policy on issues such as Africa and the Third World, while Labor leaders like John Curtin, Bob Hawke and Kim Beazley have been tenacious supporters of the US alliance. And, not least for reasons of political caution, most Australian governments make rhetorical nods in all directions.

Still, it is clear that the first approach has been the most powerful point of departure in thinking about foreign policy for Coalition governments and the latter for Labor governments.

These elements shape the context in which Australian foreign policy is made from day to day. But the personalities, structures and processes of its foreign policy machinery are also important. And the impact of globalisation on all of these factors needs to be assessed. These issues are the primary focus of this book.

Plan of the book

Our argument in the chapters ahead is that while foreign policy making in Australia has similarities to foreign policy making in other countries, there are specific attributes of Australia, its situation in the world, and the nature of its foreign policy institutions that require a specific focus on the Australian situation. Readers who are less interested in the specific institutions of foreign policy making in Australia, and more interested in foreign policy making generally, may wish to concentrate their reading on chapters 2 and 3, and Chapter 10 if they are interested in foreign policy and globalisation. Those who are interested in Australia-specific material can concentrate on chapters 4 to 9, but should be warned that chapters 2 and 3 provide crucial context to the material in the chapters on institutions and contexts.

Chapter 2 seeks to define foreign policy as the process of monitoring and anticipating disturbances in a given policy "space". In defining foreign policy as a process that occurs simultaneously across four levels – the strategic, the contextual, the organisational and the operational – it is an explicit rejection of most common models of foreign policy making that characterise it as a fairly constant and enclosed set of regular processes. Complementing this is Chapter 3, which focusses on the foreign policy process. It examines how the institutions and actors in the foreign policy machinery are constituted, and divided according to functional, hierarchic and authority/responsibility criteria, and how they relate to each other. It develops a theory of influence, based on the work of Michel Foucault, to examine the patterns of involvement and influence of various actors in the policy process. It also develops a model of communication within the policy process.

Chapters 4 to 7 are devoted to the foreign policy institutions and actors in Australia. Chapter 4 examines the bureaucracy. It initially focusses on DFAT: its history, its policy routines and processes, its departmental cultures and the world views of its staff. It then addresses the other internationally involved departments, and the processes of coordination of all of these. Chapter 5, on the executive, examines the role of elected members of the foreign policy making process – the Prime Minister, the ministers for Foreign Affairs and Trade – as well as the roles of their ministerial staff. It also examines some of the lesser understood processes of Cabinet deliberation and consideration of foreign policy issues. A portrait of Australia's network of diplomatic posts and the ways in which it contributes to foreign policy is examined in Chapter 6. It includes an examination of the formal functions of diplomats, with details about diplomatic procedures and protocols, as well as observations about the diplomatic culture and styles of Australia's overseas representatives. Chapter 7 surveys Australia's important intelligence organisations. This chapter outlines the various institutions and arrangements through which Australia gathers and analyses covert and open-source information about the outside world. It also deals with the inherent foreign policy problems of information selection and the unpredictability of the international environment.

Chapters 8 and 9 survey the two policy landscapes in which and for which foreign policy is made. Chapter 8, on the domestic landscape, surveys the domestic factors that impact on foreign policy making. It assesses the roles of Parliament, the media, interest groups, business and the general public. Chapter 9 considers the international policy landscape. It provides a detailed survey of the international system from the point of view of Australian foreign policy. It looks at what parts of the world are important to Australian foreign policy makers and why, as well as emerging threats, opportunities, changes and continuities in the international landscape.

The conclusion examines the effects of globalisation thus far on Australian foreign policy making. It critically appraises current writing that foretells the decline of the state under the pressures of globalisation. This chapter finds that, while some of the evidence is mixed, foreign policy institutions continue to play critical roles for Australia, even if these roles have changed somewhat. This chapter also advances some conclusions about the nature of foreign policy making more generally, which have implications for international relations and its study beyond Australia.

Interspersed through the book are four case studies that examine recent issues in Australian foreign policy. Two of them – the Sandline Affair, which opens this chapter, and the response to the Bali bombings – are studies in policy response. In the case of the Bali bombings, a catastrophic event had already taken place, and the critical issue for Australian policy-makers was how to respond quickly, and in the absence of full information. We describe this as a crisis of response. The Sandline Affair, which we characterise as a crisis of prevention, presented a different problem. An event – the deployment of mercenary soldiers to Bougainville – that would have had harmful consequences for important Australian interests was known to be about to take place. The question for Australian policy-makers was how to prevent it. The two remaining cases are studies of policy development. In the cases of the Cambodia Peace Process and the development of APEC Leaders' Meetings, actions by the Australian Government drove outcomes that would not otherwise have taken place, at least not in the form or at the time they did.

Notes

1 Sir Paul Hasluck, *Diplomatic Witness: Australian Foreign Affairs, 1941–1947*, Melbourne: Melbourne University Press, 1980, p. 21.

2 Separate accounts of the Sandline Affair and its aftermath have been published by two experienced Australian reporters, Sean Dorney and Mary-Louise O'Callaghan. This account draws heavily on their excellent books. It is supplemented by interviews with some of the principal Australian participants. See Sean Dorney, *The Sandline Affair,* Sydney: ABC Books, 1998; Mary-Louise O'Callaghan, *Enemies Within: Papua New Guinea, Australia and the Sandline Crisis*, Sydney: Doubleday, 1999.

3 *CPD, House of Representatives*, 18 March 1997, p. 2263.

4 ibid., p. 2264.

5 ibid., p. 2263.

6 Personal interviews.

7 For example T.B. Millar, *Australia in Peace and War: External Relations 1788–1977*, Canberra: Australian National University Press, 1978; E.M. Andrews, *A History of Australian Foreign Policy: From Dependence to Independence*, Melbourne: Longman Cheshire, 1979; I.M. Cumpston, *A History of Australian Foreign Policy, 1901–1991*, Canberra: Union Offset, 1995.

8 For example, James Cotton and John Ravenhill (eds), *The National Interest in a Global Era: Australia in World Affairs 1996–2000*, Melbourne: Oxford University Press, 2002.

9 See, for example, J.A. Camilleri, *An Introduction to Australian Foreign Policy*, Brisbane: Jacaranda Press, 1973; Altman, "Internal Pressures on Australian Policy" in Gordon McCarthy (ed.), *Foreign Policy for Australia: Choices for the Seventies*, Sydney: Angus & Robertson, 1973.

10 See, for example, Henry S. Albinski, *Australian External Policy under Labor: Content, Process and the National Debate*, Brisbane: University of Queensland Press, 1977.

11 Gareth Evans and Bruce Grant, *Australia's Foreign Relations: In the World of the 1990s*, 2nd ed., Melbourne: Melbourne University Press, 1995.

12 Gary Smith, Dave Cox and Scott Burchill, *Australia in the World: An Introduction to Australian Foreign Policy*, Melbourne: Oxford University Press, 1997.

13 Stewart Firth, *Australia in International Politics*, Sydney: Allen & Unwin, 1999, pp. 57–8.

14 Russell Trood, " Bureaucratic Politics and Foreign Politics" in F.A. Mediansky (ed.), *Australian Foreign Policy: Into the New Millennium*, Melbourne: Macmillan, 1997, p. 33.

15 See, for example, R.G. Casey, *Australian Foreign Minister: The Diaries of R.G. Casey 1951–60*, London: Collins, 1972; F.W. Eggleston, *Reflections on Australian Foreign Policy*, Melbourne: F.W. Cheshire, 1957; Sir Percy Spender, *Exercises in Diplomacy: The ANZUS Treaty and The Colombo Plan*, Sydney: Sydney University Press, 1969.

16 William Wallace, "Truth and Power, Monks and Technocrats: Theory and Practice in International Relations", *Review of International Studies*, Vol. 22, No. 3, 1996, p. 303.

17 Roy E. Jones, *Analysing Foreign Policy: An Introduction to Some Conceptual Problems*, London: Routledge and Kegan Paul, 1970, p. 14.

18 John Lewis Gaddis, "Setting Right a Dangerous World" in Strobe Talbott and Nayan Chanda (eds), *The Age of Terror and the World After September 11*, New York: Basic Books, 2002.

19 W.M. Hughes, Minister for External Affairs, in *Annual Report of the Department of External Affairs*, 1936–37, p. 5.

20 R.G. Casey, *Friends and Neighbors: Australia, the US and the World*, East Lansing, MI: Michigan State College Press, 1955, p. 87.

21 Alan Renouf, "New Challenges in Foreign Policy Administration", *Australian Outlook*, Vol. 28, No. 2, August 1974, p. 109.

22 Department of Foreign Affairs and Trade Annual Report, 1984–85, p. 3.

23 Department of Foreign Affairs and Trade Corporate Plan 2000–2002, p. 4.

24 John Howard, "Strategic Leadership for Australia: Policy Directions in a Complex World", speech to Committee for Economic Development of Australia (CEDA), 20 November 2002.

25 Paul Keating, "John Curtin's World and Ours", Curtin Prime Ministerial Library Anniversary Lecture, 5 July 2002.

26 Interview with Alexander Downer, 1999.

27 Ashton Calvert, "Secretary's Speech: The Role of DFAT at the Turn of the Century", address to the Canberra Branch of the Australian Institute of International Affairs, 4 February 1999.

28 For an extended reflection on Labor attitudes, see David Lee and Christopher Waters, *Evatt to Evans: the Labor Tradition in Australian Foreign Policy*, Sydney: Allen & Unwin, 1997.

CHAPTER 2

Conceiving Foreign Policy

Foreign policy and diplomacy have always seemed resistant to rational investigation and broad public understanding. Partly this is a function of the inherently secretive and executive nature of the activity; even the most public diplomacy tends to originate in the private calculations of foreign ministries. Partly it is a function of generally held perceptions about the nature of statecraft, which is considered to be a realm of complex gambits and intricate strategy. The origins of modern diplomacy, in Renaissance Italy, saw the development of the popular view of the diplomat as a highly cultured practitioner in an elaborate game of oratorical manoeuvre, cunning and deception. The diplomatic coups of Richelieu, Talleyrand, Metternich and Bismarck have been admired as feats of original genius, to be studied *sui generis*, defying attempts to understand them by investigating their mechanisms of policy-making or policy thinking. But once we penetrate under these popular conceptions, we reach the real difficulty confronting attempts to understand the nature of the process of foreign policy making: the sheer complexity and seeming anarchy of the activities commonly conceived of under its rubric.

This chapter is an attempt to construct an account of the nature of foreign policy making that is both understandable and accurate. It begins by surveying the declining field of foreign policy making studies, concluding with the contention that a new approach is needed in conceiving the nature of such policy-making. The middle section of the chapter advances a different conception of the nature of foreign policy making, presenting it as an activity responding to two sets of priorities: the goals and values of government and society, and the daily flow of events that impact on the goals and values deemed to be the responsibility of the foreign policy machinery. The last section of the chapter advances a characterisation of foreign policy making as a process occurring simultaneously across four levels: strategic, contextual, organisational and operational. This basic conception of the nature of foreign policy making serves as the foundation for the discussion of the specific mechanisms considered in the remaining chapters in this book.

The difficulties of foreign policy analysis

When writing about foreign policy and the process of its formulation, one confronts a range of difficulties. Perhaps the most basic challenge is to develop an account that is at the same time comprehensible, reliable and broadly applicable, but which also provides an authentic description of the great complexities and variations that attend the practice of foreign policy. Most writing on foreign policy has been unable to reconcile these aspirations, providing either detailed memoirs of negotiations or initiatives, with little indication of whether they are typical of the broader policy process, or highly general schemas providing little guidance on the nature of the actual dynamics of foreign policy making. In many ways, academic writing on foreign policy making still betrays the influence of the subfield's origins within the behaviouralist revolution in US political science.[1] During the 1950s and 1960s, foreign policy analysis was seen as a new frontier, the basis for constructing a rigorous and unified theory of international relations that would develop into an empirically testable, cumulative corpus of social scientific knowledge.[2] The drive for abstraction, generalisation and internal logical consistency has since been powerful, producing a range of general foreign policy making models ever more divorced from actual foreign policy processes.[3] Other attempts to factor in all possible variables affecting foreign policy have tended to become bewilderingly complex and analytically unwieldy.[4]

Further difficulties are posed by the nature of the topic itself. Foreign policy analysis contains its own version of the "agent–structure problem" that confronts most social theory, challenging theorists to account for the extent to which a foreign policy action is attributable to individual volition and initiative, against how much is determined by the constraints and demands of the international system and bureaucratic structures.[5] The precipitous decline in foreign policy analysis since the late 1970s is mostly attributable to the charges of "reductionism" levelled against agent-level theory by structural international relations theorists, and by the continuing dominance of structural theorising in the field.[6] The way in which the Cold War ended, however, should have resulted in a much greater discrediting of structural realism; while it continues to be surprising that the startling role played by agency – particularly the initiative and volition of Gorbachev – in ending that conflict has not led to a resurgence in agent-level theorising about international relations. Perhaps the closest attempts have been by those theorists who have tried to combine structure and agency by drawing on Giddens's structuration theory.[7] There is also the problem of determining how much each particular foreign policy initiative contributes to an international "event", as international events are usually the product of the interacting foreign policies of several states, plus a number of other factors. Disentangling individual foreign policies from ensuing international events becomes particularly important when evaluating foreign policy initiatives.

The assault against the beleaguered subdiscipline was renewed from a different angle in the 1990s, as postmodern theorists began to critique the "given" understandings of foreign policy as "the external deployment of instrumental reason on behalf of an unproblematic internal identity situated in an anarchic realm of necessity".[8] For these theorists, foreign policy was as much a part of the social world as any other realm of human action, and was thus no less a sociolinguistic and intertextual product than the others.[9] Foreign policy making, for Roxanne Doty, is a process of asserting a linguistic construction of reality in order to maintain a "discursive space" including decision-makers, bureaucrats, academics and the general public, and thereby perpetuating certain actions and discursive practices.[10] James Der Derian has defined diplomacy as a set of discursive practices mediating human estrangement, legitimating some forms of foreign policy discourse while rejecting others as threatening to ordered global interaction.[11] For David Campbell, foreign policy provides a "discourse of danger and otherness" that constitutes the state and its identity.[12] Many of these postmodern critiques of traditional foreign policy studies make very important and appropriate points. Indeed, our own discussion of the policy process in Chapter 3 is sympathetic to some postmodern accounts of power and communication in foreign policy. But in the final analysis, postmodern writing on foreign policy provides little guide for those who are curious about how foreign policy is made, who is involved, and how it is coordinated. It is also doubtful whether intertextual and discourse analysis can account for the vast range of activities that comprise the foreign policy process.

For its part, most writing on foreign policy by practitioners or former practitioners has supplied a wealth of contextual detail about specific foreign policy issues or crises, without providing a general account of the operation of the processes of the foreign policy machinery. Often practitioners understandably place great emphasis on their own role and the parts played by their colleagues and interlocutors in a particular foreign policy situation, at the expense of other crucial contextual factors. While some former practitioners, such as most recently Sir John Coles,[13] have set down general impressions and experiences of the foreign policy process, these are not placed in a broader framework of explanation about how the policy process works.

The nature of foreign policy itself makes characterising the policy process extremely difficult. It is a policy domain that has become occupied by an increasing variety of issue areas over time, many of which have historically been seen as domestic policy issues (for example, health, policing), and others which have previously not been policy issues at all (for example, the environment). Unlike other public-policy analysis, the field of foreign policy studies cannot rely on an inherent "logic" of a particular issue area to inform its study, as it may have once been able to do when foreign policy was mainly about security, trade and prestige. Posing perhaps the greatest conceptual problems is the fact that foreign policy analysis must confront the sovereign and conceptual boundary between domestic and international politics. Any account of foreign policy must reconcile the logic of an anarchic international system and the politics of a hierarchic domestic system in the same account, a challenge that has inspired a significant amount of writing since the 1960s.[14]

Defining foreign policy

These difficulties confronting foreign policy analysts are serious, but they cannot justify the current paucity of writing on the process of foreign policy making. (In fact, in his 1987 survey of the field, Steve Smith does not even mention study of the foreign policy making process within his four approaches, although conceivably they would fall into his category of "Middle-Range Theory".)[15] The majority of published material on Australian foreign policy has been concerned with the specific content of Australian foreign policy; if the process of policy-making is discussed, it is as a brief prelude to the more detailed discussion of actual policy stances.[16] Before developing our own characterisation of foreign policy making, it is necessary to define clearly what the subject of foreign policy is. While perhaps Roy Jones's pessimism about defining this particular subject matter is overstating the case, it does suggest that the process of definition is difficult, but is also a necessary preliminary to any writing on the subject:

> an attempt at an acceptable, and an acceptably brief, definition of foreign policy would be to invite ridicule. The nature of foreign policy is not agreed, and one is tempted to believe that in political societies it never will be agreed.[17]

There will inevitably be disagreements with our definition. Our purpose in defining our subject matter is to signal the boundaries of our own study of the foreign policy making process, rather than to impose yet another all-purpose definition on a contested field.

In the first place, our study of foreign policy making will only be concerned with the actions taken on behalf of the state by its government, bureaucrats and accredited representatives. While other parts of society hold interests and undertake actions outside the borders of the state, these will only become the subject of our analysis when they impact on state policy. Second, foreign policy cannot be defined by a particular issue or set of issues for which it is responsible: as stated above, a range of issue areas have become the subject of foreign policy. Potentially, any area of state policy has the capacity to become the subject of foreign policy if it develops attributes that affect or are affected by situations outside Australia's borders. The boundaries of the field must therefore be defined by the "situations [the policy is] designed to affect".[18] In this study, foreign policy will refer to all actions of state directed in whole or part outside of the boundaries of the state. Third, our definition of "policy" attempts to include all parts of the policy process, from the identification of foreign policy issues, through formulation, to implementation and evaluation. Therefore, "policy" is taken across its range of possible connotations: as a general undertaking or commitment of state; as an ideal of a coherent plan of action against which behaviour can be evaluated; and as the specific actions taken by state representatives in certain situations to influence certain states of affairs.

The nature of foreign policy making

Most accounts of the foreign policy process either directly or implicitly draw on the metaphor of the foreign policy apparatus as a self-contained system that reacts to stimuli in the external environment, consumes resources, and produces actions and decisions as outputs back into an external environment.[19] This is, once again, an enduring influence of the behaviouralist revolution in US political science, and in particular the work of David Easton.[20] Systems theory uses a biological analogy of a political structure as an enclosed system that needs to perform certain functions to survive, which functions are in turn produced by certain internal structures. While the systems approach offers certain advantages for simplifying a complex subject area, it also has several serious drawbacks. First, it is not clear of what the "environment" external to the system consists, and how "inputs" from the different parts of the external environment (rest of government, domestic society, international context) may differ and affect each other. Second, it implies that a foreign policy apparatus can be clearly differentiated from a surrounding "environment", and that it is composed of the same actors and component parts over time. Third, it suggests that all "stimuli" to which the system responds originate from outside of the foreign policy apparatus, and that all actions of the apparatus are directed outside of the apparatus itself. None of these implications is sustainable. The foreign policy apparatus relates in different ways to governmental, domestic and international pressures; its boundaries and internal components are seldom fixed; and some issues and objectives of foreign policy remain within the apparatus itself.

Another problem with some existing accounts of foreign policy making is that they tend to break up the process into what appear to be separate and sequential activities: agenda-setting, policy-making, implementation and monitoring (or some variation on that basic theme). While all of these activities are present in the foreign policy process, most foreign policy practitioners agree that characterising it as invariably a rational, sequential process is deeply misleading. The reality for the vast majority of practitioners is that the foreign policy process is profoundly anarchic: for some, even using the inevitable phrase "foreign policy making" is to risk reifying a highly complex and variable set of activities. The nature of foreign policy, the breadth of issues with which it must deal and between which it must coordinate, and the deep complexity and unpredictability of the international system that forms its policy context defies such clear-cut, sequential characterisations. The nature of foreign policy often makes it difficult to unravel the start and finish of any one policy; to distinguish where one policy is distinct from another; to adjudicate with any finality between a foreign policy goal and foreign policy means; or to isolate a definitive foreign policy "choice" from surrounding processes of issue definition, implementation and monitoring. Individual decisions may be identifiable, but they are seldom distinct and autonomous from surrounding policy activities.

In advancing an alternative conception of the foreign policy making process, it is necessary to begin with a definition of policy and policy-making. We define policy as the promotion and protection of given social values within the boundaries of state responsibility by agents of the state. Each department of government is assigned responsibility for monitoring a certain policy "space", which can be conceived of as a flow of events impacting to a greater or lesser extent on a given section of the society's values (health, education, law and order, employment, communications). Each department of government monitors its policy space according to certain defined limits of quietude and disturbance – disturbance meaning either a threat to social values or an opportunity to promote them. Policy-making involves responding to issues that introduce disturbance into the policy space, by trying to limit the adverse impact of an event on social values, by manipulating a situation to advance social values, or by taking advantage of an opportunity to alter expectations regarding the

promotion or protection of a social value. Yet this is not to imply that governments are simply reactive, that they sit inertly awaiting disturbances to policy
spaces. Governments are highly risk-averse; they are particularly concerned to
avoid large and unforeseen policy disturbances. Therefore much of the activity
of monitoring the policy space is active, trying to anticipate policy disturbances into the future and trying to avoid or pre-empt them, or to develop
coping mechanisms for when they may occur. So pronounced is the systemic
risk-aversion of most governments that they will tolerate and even create minor
disturbance in the current policy space in order to avoid much larger foreseeable disturbances in future.

   Foreign policy relates to the management of disturbances to a range of
policy spaces that either originate from sources external to the country, or can
be addressed at sites external to the country. There are three distinct sets of
policy spaces for foreign policy makers. The first is the portfolio of the foreign
policy bureaucracy alone, and is concerned with the interests of the state as a
member of the international system. This relates to the health of the state's
international relationships and representation, to the acceptability of international norms and institutions, and to the general stability of the international
system and the levels of support for it among its member states. These are the
interests of the state as an international actor, rather than the preferences of
particular policy-makers or the contemporary demands of the society, and they
are the enduring responsibility of the state's foreign policy bureaucracy. The
second policy space is defined by the actual needs of the society, where these
are affected by events outside its borders. This refers to a broad range of policy
spaces, often under the primary responsibility of different departments of
government. The demands from these policy spaces are constantly evolving,
and comprise what are most commonly thought of as the subject matter of
foreign policy. While some policy spaces have a permanent external dimension
(immigration, environment, trade) and are thought of as part of the ongoing
brief of foreign policy, other policy spaces (education, health, law and order)
have external dimensions that are more variable in intensity, and comprise the
more changeable subject matter for foreign policy. The third policy space for
foreign policy arises from the political interests of the government in power. In
defining its approach to government, a party elected to power in a democracy
is also setting up a series of measures against which its policy successes and
failures can be judged. While foreign policy used to be thought of as bipartisan
or separate from the inter-party process in Australia,[21] foreign policy makers
are increasingly finding the need to be mindful of the political implications of
foreign policy developments as they monitor the policy space.

Foreign policy issues are defined by whether a certain event introduces significant disturbance into the policy space. The limits of quietude and disturbance are determined by the goals set for foreign policy, or the expectations about how the foreign policy apparatus should promote or protect given social values. It is important to note here that there are two directions from which disturbance can be introduced into the policy space. The vast majority of all disturbances arise from the flow of events through the policy spaces relevant to foreign policy: they impact on the policy space from the bottom up. These include developments in the international system, as well as domestic societal values for which the foreign policy machinery is thought to have at least partial responsibility. Such events become policy issues according to the extent to which they impact on preset policy goals and social values governing the limits of quietude and disturbance in the policy space. However, though rather less common, it is important to recognise that disturbance can also be introduced into the policy space from the top down, through the launch of new policy initiatives, thus changing the limits of quietude and disturbance in the policy space. Policy initiatives can change the goals of foreign policy, requiring the foreign policy process to respond to a different set of demands and aspirations. Such top-down change can occur as a response to events in world politics (such as when the end of the Cold War changed the foreign policy aspirations of most states around the world), or it can occur independently of events, in response to a change in government or an evolution in the thinking of an incumbent minister. Often the relative amounts of top-down and bottom-up disturbance are related, with the ceaseless cascade of events restricting the time and resources policy-makers have to make proactive foreign policy.

Each day, literally hundreds of different developments introduce disturbance into the Australian foreign policy space. Each must be monitored and/or responded to as quickly and as carefully as possible. Each must be assessed not only according to how it impacts on policy goals and social values, but also according to how it might impact on other strands of foreign and domestic policy. This complexity and interdependence introduces one set of constraints on the possible response to each policy event; resource and time constraints supply another set. To become a foreign policy issue, an international event must be serious enough to prompt the state to react and commit resources to its response.[22] Because resources are limited, trade-offs have to be made between the resourcing of foreign policy goals. The urgency of a foreign policy goal can often be measured by the relative amount of resources dedicated to its pursuit. As policy frameworks change over time, relative resourcing of foreign policy goals can evolve as well.

The four levels of foreign policy making

Foreign policy making occurs across four interrelated levels: the strategic, the contextual, the organisational and the operational. Distinguishing between these four levels gives a much clearer picture of the actual dynamics and considerations that inform foreign policy making. Policy-making occurs simultaneously at all of these levels; each level plays a connected and crucial part in the production of actual foreign policy initiatives and responses. Concentrating on any one of these levels yields an ambiguous and partial conception of a state's foreign policy process. The boundaries of the foreign policy making process are constantly in flux, with different actors taking part in the different levels of policy-making at different times. The participants at each level are not mutually exclusive, with some actors able to participate at several levels of the policy process.

The strategic level

At the strategic level, foreign policy making appears at its most proactive and purposeful. Here, foreign policy is made as a series of commitments and attitudes on the relations between a society and the outside world, usually expounded in general policy statements (such as the 1997 foreign and trade policy White Paper)[23] and ministerial speeches. Strategic policy statements self-consciously try to be logically and rhetorically accountable to broad conceptions of the public interest and national values, and general enough to be applied and interpreted variously. They attempt to reconcile past policy, current dispositions and future actions, while allowing some differentiation between successive administrations' policies.

In reality, ministerial policy statements can be at variance with one another. Some administrations and ministers are more attentive to intellectual coherence than others. Sometimes ministers assume office determined to impose a carefully formulated framework for policy on their portfolio area from the outset. This occurred in the case of Australia's two most recent foreign ministers. Within twelve months of assuming office as Foreign Minister, Gareth Evans had produced an integrated plan covering the nature and content of Australian foreign policy, which for the most part was to define the Australian foreign policy approach between 1988 and 1996.[24] On assuming office in 1996, one of Alexander Downer's first initiatives was to commission work by an advisory committee of academics, businesspeople and former policy-makers on Australia's first ever foreign and trade policy White Paper, released in September 1997.[25] Conceived for the same purpose, these two documents are remarkable not so much for their continuities – which are extensive – but for their differences in approach and emphasis. The statements, speeches and decisions of both ministers were strongly influenced by these foundational documents, as were the activities of the foreign policy bureaucracy. The differences in their respective strategic approaches to foreign policy making have in turn translated into remarkably different periods of foreign policy for Australia.

Almost all strategic policy statements appeal to the public interest and national values because this is the level of the policy process that is most accessible to the broader public. Strategic policy-making consciously attempts to reconcile several factors in defining the state's foreign policy stance. One is a vision of Australia in the world: a realistic, if often optimistic, judgement of relative power, key strengths and liabilities, and important relationships. Another is a definition of the national interest, a slippery concept that acts as an anchor to all foreign policy making and foreign policy analysis. The national interest is a subjective understanding of the common good of society – one that is more compelling and enduring than short-term preferences or sectional demands – to which all foreign policy must ultimately be oriented.[26] At another level, the national interest acts as an objective gauge of the appropriateness of a given foreign policy, an "iron necessity which binds governments and governed alike",[27] the loss of sight of which constitutes the utmost failure of foreign policy. For Australia, as for most states, the national interest has invariably been defined as a combination of national security plus national prosperity, with the occasional dash of national values.[28]

A third component of strategic policy is supplied by a government's understanding of, and approach to, foreign policy: is a bilateral or multilateral foreign policy more likely to be effective? On which coalitions of states should Australia concentrate its energies: the regional states of East Asia, or alliances with great powers? Strategic foreign policy making speaks both to "milieu goals" (the most desirable general configuration of regional and global politics) and to concrete goals (the specific policy outcomes required by the interplay of events and societal values).

Strategic foreign policy making involves specific choices, interpretations and definitions of national values, national roles and the international context. These statements help determine the perceived range of the foreign policy space, as well as its criteria of quietude and disturbance, by defining the international issues in which the state has a stake, whether narrowly instrumental and regional, or broadly principled and global. Some strategic policy settings are more or less continuous from government to government: the alliance with the United States; membership of the United Nations; the health of trade relationships with Northeast Asia. Others involve specific interpretations and specific choices, reflecting different understandings of Australia in the world, the nature of foreign policy,[29] and desirable societal values and milieu goals from government to government and between the major parties in Australian politics.[30]

Strategic foreign policy is addressed to several audiences. One is the government itself: to this audience, strategic foreign policy signals how the general approach to foreign policy sits in relation to the broader approach to government. At one level, strategic foreign policy needs to indicate how foreign policy complements other policy commitments and responsibilities of the government. At another level, it draws inspiration from the government's political philosophy and approach to governing. Most important among this audience is the Prime Minister, who, even if only sporadically involved in foreign policy, exercises a decisive influence over the general philosophy and approach to it. Another audience for strategic policy is the electorate. While most of the time the electorate is less attentive to foreign policy than to other policy areas, most governments are concerned that even if foreign policy is not usually electorally decisive, neither should it be electorally costly. Strategic policy statements allow leaders and officials to play a pre-emptive role in shaping public perceptions and debate on foreign policy issues. Strategic policy statements quite often engage rhetorically with vocal domestic critics of foreign policy, while at the same time assuring the broader public that policy is being pursued in the national interest. Foreign policy can be used to electoral advantage, to reinforce images of leadership or legitimacy, but perceptions of too much attention to foreign policy at the expense of other responsibilities can be electorally costly.

Another audience for strategic policy statements is the diplomatic community. Strategic foreign policy can be used to signal a general approach to foreign policy and specific stances on certain issues, whether these are signals of continuity and dependability, or a slight change of emphasis, or a major realignment. Such statements are monitored in the diplomatic world but rarely taken absolutely at face value until matched by corresponding actions. The final audience for strategic policy is the foreign policy apparatus itself. Most foreign policy bureaucrats and diplomats remain closely attuned to statements and directions of strategic policy issued by their own ministers. Strategic policy here plays a crucial role in establishing coordination and direction over the broad range of foreign policy activity, attempting to impart coherence across the policy space. Most policy officers seek "policy hooks" or look for "policy cover" for initiatives, decisions or position papers they make or prepare. If the action is seen to fit with a ministerial policy statement, it is seen as more likely to gain endorsement and reflect well on the officer.

The strategic level is foreign policy making at its most authoritative, gener-alised and abstract, but rarely is it aloof from the actual press of foreign policy issues. Some strategic policy statements set out broad approaches to foreign policy, but even these most abstract pronouncements must address themselves to contemporary trends and configurations of alignment and competition. For the most part, not even strategic policy-making can be absolutely pre-emptive. Often developments occur that require a state to remake broad swathes of its foreign policy approach (the end of the Cold War being a prominent example), or the formulation of an entirely new arena of foreign policy in response to a completely new policy issue (such as the rise of global warming to international prominence).

Strategic policy-making plays several crucial roles in relation to the other levels of the foreign policy making process. Strategic policy statements deter-mine the status and priority of foreign policy issues and establish a guide for their demands on resources, while providing broad guidelines, referents and justifications for lower levels of policy-making. Strategic policy is, at the same time, always responsive to the information and requirements of these other levels of foreign policy making as well. This will become apparent as we survey the nature of contextual, organisational and operational policy-making.

The contextual level

Foreign policy making is profoundly influenced by the context in which each issue occurs, internationally and domestically. Contextual calculations determine what is at stake for the state and its social values, and define what type of prob-lem the issue represents. Considerations of context inform a policy issue with an appraisal of the array of costs, benefits, opportunities and constraints, its rela-tionship to other policy issues and contemporary initiatives, and its relevance to strategic policy goals and values, and assessments of the significance and utility of courses of action. By influencing the basic definition of the issue, policy-making at the level of context determines what action is appropriate in response. The importance of the contextual level reflects how deeply complex and inter-twined any state's foreign policies are across issues and with different aspects of domestic policy. It is the contextual level that demands judgement of foreign policy makers: is this a serious issue? What policy response is required in the light of its impact on social values, national interests and other policy initiatives?

Contextual policy-making must factor in three sets of criteria in making foreign policy judgements. The first is governmental, broadly considering which social values and areas of responsibility are affected by a given event. It also addresses a given response's likely impact on other policy initiatives, either in a positive way through issue linkage, or in a way that detracts from the chances of success of the other policy. It is at the contextual level that policy-makers confront very real and difficult choices between different policy options. After an exhaustive process of gauging the views of foreign policy makers in the course of preparing his 1986 *Review of Australia's Diplomatic Representation*, Stuart Harris arrived at the view that it is at the contextual level of choice that the national interest becomes most manifest: "The national interest does not exist in the abstract. It reflects a judgement made at any time in the light of conflicting sectoral interests".[31] The second set of criteria for contextual judge-ment is political: different responses must be assessed according to how they will resonate with the government's commitments to the electorate and with the political philosophy and approach to government of the party in power. Judge-ments on the political context are most often made by ministers and staff in their offices. The third set of contextual criteria is international. International consid-erations must take into account the identities, dispositions and relative power of the states involved in an issue or potential response; other foreign policy commitments of the state; and coalitions and understandings crucial to the conduct of other strands of foreign policy. Each of these sites is important to most foreign policy decisions; difficult choices and trade-offs often need to be made by foreign policy makers at the contextual level.

Making the task even more difficult is the fact that the policy context is constantly evolving. Each policy-relevant development and policy response changes the policy context to a greater or lesser extent. To avoid policy becom-ing self-contradictory or damaging to other policy interests, the establishment of large and dependable systems for monitoring developments across the foreign policy space is essential to all foreign policy bureaucracies. As we will see in our discussion of organisational policy-making, bureaucratic procedures complement these monitoring systems in ways that ensure that contextualisa-tion is a necessary aspect of the majority of foreign policy making.

A number of situational factors affect the contextualisation of a policy issue. First, an issue's familiarity, or whether the same or analogous issues have occurred in the past, contributes towards the certainty with which the issue can be contextualised. Second, its urgency, or the pressure for a response and the source of this pressure, can affect how the issue is assessed in relation to trade-offs with other policy initiatives. If the issue is pressing enough, it may relegate all other policy considerations to subordinate status. Third, an issue's signifi-cance is determined by the extent to which it is interpreted as impacting on social values, and whether it is thought to have a positive or negative effect on these values. This also affects the nature of trade-offs made against other foreign policy issues. Fourth, the issue's specificity, or the range of issue areas on which it may impact, will have an inevitable effect on the extent of contextualisation and choices that need to be made. Finally, an event's temporality – whether it is a sudden development or a long-term trend – will further affect how it impacts on the remainder of the foreign policy context.

Some foreign policy developments are attended by a range of overlapping and competing definitions of a policy situation; competing contextualisations are often provided by the media, other states, and interest groups. A government that responds to others' definitions of the situation potentially becomes hostage to a different policy agenda. Further difficulties can arise when an issue's international context (and policy imperatives) are at odds with its domestic context (and policy imperatives). Contextualisation is therefore an authoritative process of asserting a particular definition of a foreign policy issue, and mediating between the demands raised by the issue's different contexts.

The organisational level

An integral part of foreign policy making involves, on the one hand, structuring political and bureaucratic resources towards addressing specific challenges and goals, and, on the other, the way in which these political and bureaucratic structures affect the policy responses to given issues. Organisational-level policy-making involves both the process of guiding a policy response through existing organisational structures, and the process of marshalling and apportioning resources to policy issues. The extent to which an issue is dealt with through existing structures, or whether resources are reassigned to deal with the particular issue, depends largely on the seriousness of the issue at hand. If it is an issue of the highest priority, substantial resources will be devoted to it, and organisational processes, structures and assets will be redeployed to deal with it. The less pressing the issue, the more existing resource allocations and organisational structures will determine the response to the issue. For the least pressing issues, the nature of the policy response will be determined by how much attention and how many resources and structures can be spared given the other priorities of the organisation.

Australia's foreign policy bureaucracy is basically hierarchic, and most conventional understandings of foreign policy making centre on conceptions of a hierarchy of reporting, decision and implementation. Foreign policy making that is less pressured by time or other contextual factors normally takes place according to this model, which resembles the working of a central nervous system. First, an issue or disturbance is observed by an embassy, an intelligence agency or a regional desk officer, acting as the "nerve endings" of the organisation. This issue is analysed and reported up through the appropriate levels of the organisation, gaining contextualisation as it rises. The highest levels of the bureaucracy formulate the issue into a concise statement of background, issues, and alternative choices and consequences for the minister. The minister makes a decision on an appropriate response, and the instructions for implementation flow back down the hierarchy to the "nerve endings". However, by no means is all foreign policy made in this way: often policy is initiated at the highest levels of the organisation, in requests by the minister for advice on a certain issue.[32] In situations marked by crisis and the need for a fast response, or for extraordinarily important or delicate matters, most of the layers of hierarchy and formal reporting are dispensed with in favour of flexible consultation between those foreign policy makers most closely involved.

Judgements need to be made about the organisational routines of foreign policy making in order to cope with the day-to-day press of international developments. These judgements are imposed by the two constants of foreign policy work: the volume of issues to be dealt with, and the time constraints faced by all foreign policy bureaucracies. The flow of issues and crises through the policy space is inexorable; these events need to be responded to quickly and with sufficient finality to satisfy diplomatic partners and public expectations, in order to avoid clogging the policy-making machinery and tying up resources. Considerations of time and volume modify given organisational routines. One of the most sacred considerations in foreign policy making is the hierarchy of responsibility, yet time constraints and the volume of information with which the policy machinery must deal requires each level in the policy hierarchy to exercise judgement about whether to exercise initiative or to refer the issue to a higher level. Another crucial procedure is that of informing and consulting all within the foreign policy bureaucracy, and if necessary in the wider government, who have an interest in the issue at hand or may be affected by it. Against this organisational requirement must be assessed the pressures of time and flexibility: consultation takes time, and contextualisation invariably imposes constraints. Finally, each action in response to a policy issue must be carefully documented and brought to the notice of those interested or affected within the bureaucracy, once again adding to the volume of information and taking up time.

The internal structures of bureaucracies are important clues as to a state's foreign policy priorities, both geographically and according to prominent policy issues. More resources will be devoted to areas of the world and issues that are regarded as having higher priority or potential impact on social values or the national interest. The section or department of the foreign policy bureaucracy that is given carriage of an issue can affect the nature of the policy response. Different areas or departments can have slightly different views on policy, different priorities, different interest groups to which they respond, and different experiences of international and multilateral contexts, all of which can affect how they interpret and respond to a policy issue. It is important, however, not to overemphasise the effect of these differences. Graham Allison built an entire model of foreign policy behaviour on the observation that in the United States foreign policy bureaucracy, "where you stand [on a policy issue] depends on where you sit [within the foreign policy machinery]".[33] Pronounced differences in attitudes based on a person's position in the foreign policy bureaucracy may exist dependably in the United States, but cannot exist in Australia, given the rapid rate of circulation of personnel through different parts of the foreign policy bureaucracy.

While the internal structure of the foreign policy bureaucracy has some effect on foreign policy making, at the organisational level the impact of the personalities occupying different positions is easily underestimated. Influential actors within the foreign policy bureaucracy can exercise a profound impact on the shape and direction of policy, while people with vision and drive are most often those who are promoted quickly into positions of authority. Most influential actors in the bureaucracy are able to draw conclusions from their experiences of foreign policy making and knit them into a coherent foreign policy world view. The more structured, detailed and robust a foreign policy professional's world view, the better he or she is able to respond to issues that land on his or her desk, and the more effective and coherent his or her policy proposals appear to be. This, along with so many other aspects of foreign policy making, is impossible to integrate into a general theoretical model of foreign policy making, yet the coincidence of certain influential personalities can have a major effect on the foreign policy machinery.

Focussing on the organisational level of foreign policy making also draws attention to the fact that coordination and internal negotiation are often the goals of foreign policy, as different organisations and interests are drawn into the policy process. While most coordination in the Australian foreign policy making process occurs informally and for the most part collegially,[34] formal mechanisms exist for resolving conflicts over priorities, or over which organisation or branch should have carriage of the issue. Within departments, the organisational hierarchy is expected to resolve conflict, while between departments interdepartmental committees (IDCs) are used. For issues unable to be resolved at IDCs, sometimes the matter is referred to Cabinet for ultimate resolution.

The operational level

Operational-level foreign policy making refers to the activity of those representatives of the state who monitor at the most detailed level developments in the policy space, and who implement the content of foreign policy, whether through diplomatic, bureaucratic, media or other channels. While operational policy can be enacted by leaders and ministers, the bulk is carried out by bureaucrats and diplomats. Policy-making at this level involves minute attention to complex detail, the constant making, monitoring, maintenance and remaking of "micro-level" policy. Operational foreign policy making is more often hostage to developments, reactive to those developments, and oriented towards the "management" of those developments within acceptable policy limits. It is heavily influenced by the policy limits set by the other levels of foreign policy making: relying on strategic statements to orient and justify actions on behalf of the state; problem-solving within the issue definition provided by the contextual level; and relying on resources and structures provided by organisational policy.

At the operational level, a principal motivation is to avoid mistakes, by basing policy as much as possible on certainties rather than risks. This leads to the dominance of certain tendencies and techniques in operational foreign policy making. There is a tendency to rely heavily on the prevailing bureaucratic culture, to be conservative and cautious, and to pay acute attention to detail.[35] Bureaucratic hierarchies and structures of authorisation are all-important and the dangers of unauthorised personal initiative ever-present. Bureaucratic routine exercises a powerful influence, as operational policy-making administers a regular flow of foreign policy activity using pre-programmed ways of dealing with expected and familiar issues. An incremental approach to policy-making is dominant, as policy is altered only when necessary, and then only at the margins, relying on policy comparisons that only differ slightly from current policy.[36] At the operational level, policy objectives often emerge simultaneously with the implementing of policy, rather than being determined prior to implementation. The discipline of time and resource constraints necessitates the technique of "satisficing" by policy officers, who are able to consider alternative strategies only until one is found that meets certain minimum (usually strategically, contextually and organisationally defined) criteria.

The operational level also permits attention to be paid to the functional divisions of labour that exist in foreign policy making. A basic functional division, supplied by the Westminster model of government, is the distinction between administration and politics, whereby bureaucrats tender objective policy advice and impartially administer policy, and it is left to the elected representatives to make final decisions affecting societal values:

> The process ... requires that Ministers make their judgements with as full a knowledge as feasible of competing interests – and accept the community's verdict in due course as to whether they identified the national interest correctly.[37]

In reality, however, it is extremely difficult to keep these activities distinct. In making such decisions, ministers rely on the foreign policy bureaucracy to synthesise and contextualise policy issues into distinctly alternative courses of action, with the consequences of each course of action made as clear as possible also. In practice, it is almost impossible for the bureaucracy to develop such alternative choices without making value choices along the way. The great influence of strategic, contextual and organisational policy-making also brings value frameworks into the realm of bureaucratic work.

Another distinction is that between the collection and monitoring of information and the synthesis and contextualisation of policy issues. In theory, overseas missions and junior policy officers on area desks are intended to play the former role, passing information up through the organisational hierarchy, where more senior officers rely on their experience, judgement and greater breadth of vision across the policy process to value-add to the information. In practice, once again, such a distinction necessarily becomes blurred. Diplomatic posts and junior officers are expected to exercise judgement about information passed on to the organisation, rather than to act as objective information gatherers passing a steady stream of data into an organisation struggling already with information overload. The expectation of judgement and discretion has been impressed on junior policy officers by the foreign policy hierarchy since at least the time of Foreign Minister R.G. Casey:

> I am impressed with the freedom with which our representatives abroad use cables – at immense cost and, in large measure, with material that adds little or nothing to the progress of events. It seems to have become an outlet for impressing us with their energy and effectiveness. I am in the course of discovering the cost of it all – per page of telegram and per month.[38]

A final distinction is that between policy formulation and policy implementation. Once again, however, it is hard to make a clear-cut distinction between foreign policy makers who only do the former and those who only do the latter. Diplomacy has long been attended by greater or lesser levels of latitude to improvise and modify policy in the implementation stage, in order to enhance its effectiveness, as long as such departures are duly reported.[39] Furthermore, the difficulty of distinguishing between ends and means in foreign policy means that even the analytical distinction between formulation and implementation is difficult to make in practice. The fact that various levels of personnel are involved in each type of activity and across the various levels of foreign policy making is yet more evidence of the complex and fluid nature of the foreign policy making process.

These four levels at which foreign policy making occurs – strategic, contextual, organisational and operational – feature different sets of activities. Taken together, they comprise the policy-making process as a whole. Not all levels, however, are equally involved in the responses to all foreign policy issues; neither are they all involved at each stage of the policy process. Many foreign policy issues are relevant to only one or two levels of the policy process: for example, certain minor consular issues are dealt with at the operational level alone. On the other hand, major foreign policy crises are likely to be given sustained attention at all four levels. Part of the process of examining foreign policy making therefore requires an understanding of what tasks are performed by each different level, how these relate to those of the other levels, and which levels are involved in each strand of foreign policy at any given time.

Conclusion

Academic devotees of parsimonious, rational models of foreign policy making are unlikely to be impressed by the account of the foreign policy process developed in this chapter. Our purpose, however, is not to use this as a basis from which to generalise about a theory of the international system. Our aim in this book is to provide an accessible yet realistic account of the Australian foreign policy making process. This chapter is therefore intended as a base on which we can build an account of the functioning and interrelationship of the various different policy-making mechanisms and institutions in Australia and abroad.

It is important in concluding this account of the nature of foreign policy making to re-emphasise the complexity and extreme fluidity (some would say chaotic nature) of the entire process. The order in which the different aspects of policy-making are discussed, and the names given to them, are not intended to imply a particular sequence of activities or a hierarchy of roles, or a demarcation of personnel. Each level of policy-making, each activity discussed here, occurs simultaneously, across policy issues and with respect to the same policy issues. This hardly makes for a neat, easily applicable model; but it is our contention that it makes for a much more realistic account.

Notes

1 For a general account, see Raymond Seidelman, *Disenchanted Realists: Political Science and the American Crisis 1884–1984*, Albany, NY: SUNY Press, 1985; David M. Ricci, *The Tragedy of Political Science*, New Haven, CT: Yale University Press, 1984.

2 Most explicitly and famously in Richard C. Snyder, H.W. Bruck and Burton Sapin, *Foreign Policy Decision Making: An Approach to the Study of International Politics*, New York: Free Press of Glencoe, 1954.

3 The profusion of Rosenau's general schemas alone attests to this drive; see J.N. Rosenau, *Scientific Study of Foreign Policy*, rev. ed., London: Frances Pinter, 1980.

4 See, for example, Michael Brecher, *The Foreign Policy System of Israel*, London: Oxford University Press, 1972; Michael Brecher, *Decisions in Israel's Foreign Policy*, London: Oxford University Press, 1974.

5 For general discussions of the agent–structure problem in international relations, see Martin Hollis and Steve Smith, *Explaining and Understanding International Relations*, Oxford: Clarendon Press, 1990; David Dessler, "What's at Stake in the Agent–Structure Debate?", *International Organization*, Vol. 43, No. 3, 1989; Alexander Wendt, "The Agent–Structure Problem in International Relations Theory", *International Organization*, Vol. 41, No. 3, 1987.

6 Most influential among these was Waltz's *Theory of International Politics*, Massachusetts: Addison-Wesley, 1979, Chapter 4, "Reductionist and Systemic Theories".

7 See Walter Carlsnaes, "The Agency–Structure Problem in Foreign Policy Analysis", *International Studies Quarterly*, Vol. 36, September 1992.

8 David Campbell, *Writing Security: United States Foreign Policy and the Politics of Identity*, Minneapolis: University of Minnesota Press, 1992, p. 43.

9 See James Der Derian and Michael J. Shapiro, *International/Intertextual Relations: Postmodern Readings of World Politics*, Lexington, Mass.: Lexington Books, 1989; and Jim George, *Discourses of Global Politics: A Critical (Re)Introduction to International Relations*, Boulder, CO: Lynne Rienner Publishers, 1994

10 See Roxanne Lynne Doty, *Imperial Encounters: The Politics of Representation in North-South Relations*, Minneapolis: University of Minnesota Press, 1996; Roxanne Lynne Doty, "Foreign Policy as Social Construction: A Post-positivist Analysis of US Counterinsurgency Policy in the Philippines", *International Studies Quarterly*, Vol. 37, No. 3, September 1993.

11 James Der Derian, *On Diplomacy: A Genealogy of Western Estrangement*, Oxford: Basil Blackwell, 1987.

12 See David Campbell, *Writing Security*; David Campbell, "Global Inscription: How Foreign Policy Constitutes the United States", *Alternatives*, Vol. 15, No. 3, Summer 1990. For an application of this type of argument to Australia, see Jim George, "Some Thoughts on 'The Givenness of Everyday Life' in Australian International Relations: Theory and Practice", *Australian Journal of Political Science*, Vol. 27, 1992; and Richard Higgott and Jim George, "Tradition and Change in the Study of International Relations in Australia", *International Political Science Review*, Vol. 11, No. 4, 1990.

13 John Coles, *Making Foreign Policy: A Certain Idea of Britain*, London: John Murray, 2000.

14 See, for example, Henry A. Kissinger, "Domestic Structure and Foreign Policy", *Daedalus*, Vol. 95, No. 2, Spring 1966; Peter Katzenstein, "International Relations and Domestic Structures: Foreign Economic Policies of Advanced Industrial States", *International Organization*, Vol. 30, Winter 1976; Peter Gourevitch, "The Second Image Reversed: The International Sources of Domestic Politics", *International Organization*, Vol. 32, No. 4, Autumn 1978; Andrew Moravcsik, "Taking Preferences Seriously: A Liberal Theory of International Politics", *International Organization*, Vol. 51, No. 4, Autumn 1997.

15 See Steve Smith, "Foreign Policy Analysis and International Relations", *Millennium*, Vol. 16, No. 2, 1987.

16 For example F.A. Mediansky and A.C. Palfreeman (eds), *In Pursuit of National Interests: Australian Foreign Policy in the 1990s*, Sydney: Pergamon Press, 1988; Gary Smith, Dave Cox and Scott Burchill, *Australia in the World: An Introduction to Australian Foreign Policy*, Melbourne: Oxford University Press, 1996.

17 Roy E. Jones, *Analysing Foreign Policy: An Introduction to Some Conceptual Problems*, London: Routledge and Kegan Paul, 1970, p. 1.

18 Rosenau, *Scientific Study of Foreign Policy*, p. 61.

19 See, for example, Michael Clarke and Brian White (eds), *Understanding Foreign Policy: The Foreign Policy Systems Approach*, Aldershot: Edward Elgar, 1989.

20 David Easton, *A Framework for Political Analysis*, Englewood Cliffs, NJ: Prentice-Hall, 1965.

21 T.B. Millar, "Emerging Bipartisanship in Australian Foreign Policy", *Asia–Pacific Community*, Winter 1985, pp. 1–15; Trevor Matthews and John Ravenhill, "Bipartisanship in the Australian Foreign Policy Elite", *Australian Outlook*, Vol. 42, No. 1, April 1988, pp. 9–20.

22 Arnold Wolfers, *Discord and Collaboration: Essays on International Politics*, Baltimore, MD: Johns Hopkins University Press, 1962.

23 Department of Foreign Affairs and Trade, *In the National Interest: Australia's Foreign and Trade Policy*, White Paper, Canberra: Commonwealth of Australia, 1997.

24 See Gareth Evans, *Making Australian Foreign Policy*, Australian Fabian Society Pamphlet No. 50, Sydney: Pluto Press, 1989.

25 See Department of Foreign Affairs and Trade, *In the National Interest*.

26 Friedrich Kratochwil, "On the Notion of 'Interest' in International Relations", *International Organization*, Vol. 36, No. 1, Winter 1982.

27 Charles A. Beard, *The Idea of National Interest: An Analytical Study of American Foreign Policy*, New York: Macmillan, 1934, p. 3.

28 See Michael Wesley, "Setting and Securing Australia's National Interests" in Ian Marsh (ed.), *Australia's Choices: Options for a Prosperous and Fair Society*, Sydney: UNSW Press, 2002.

29 See Michael Wesley and Tony Warren, "Wild Colonial Ploys: Currents of Thought in Australian Foreign Policy Making", *Australian Journal of Political Science*, Vol. 35, No. 1, April 2000, pp. 9–26.

30 See Henry S. Albinski, *Australian External Policy under Labor: Content, Process and the National Debate*, Brisbane: University of Queensland Press, 1977.

31 Stuart Harris, *Review of Australia's Diplomatic Representation*, Canberra: AGPS, 1986, pp. 186–7.

32 Coles, *Making Foreign Policy*, p. 85.
33 The model is, of course, his famous bureaucratic politics paradigm; see Graham T. Allison, *Essence of Decision: Explaining the Cuban Missile Crisis*, Boston: Little, Brown, 1971, p. 176.
34 Once again, the levels of conflict that Allison relies on to construct his "pulling and hauling" model of foreign policy outcomes do not appear to exist in the Australian foreign policy bureaucracy; see Allison, *Essence of Decision*, p. 158.
35 Jones, *Analysing Foreign Policy*, pp. 14–16.
36 Charles E. Lindblom, "The Science of 'Muddling Through'", *Public Administration Review*, Vol. 19, Spring 1959.
37 Harris, *Review of Australia's Diplomatic Representation*, p. 187.
38 R.G. Casey, *Australian Foreign Minister: The Diaries of R.G. Casey 1951–1960* (ed. T.B. Millar), London: Collins, 1972, p. 23 (diary entry, 27 June 1951).
39 Keith Hamilton and Richard Langhorne, *The Practice of Diplomacy: Its Evolution, Theory and Administration*, London: Routledge, 1995, pp. 240–1.

CHAPTER 3

The Policy Process

Foreign policy – the anticipation of and response to disturbances flowing through a predetermined set of policy spaces – is by its nature a highly varied, unpredictable process. For this reason, we have departed from the usual way of depicting the foreign policy making process as a relatively fixed template of routines undertaken by regular participants resulting in identifiable outcomes. Rather, we characterised foreign policy as a set of activities that takes place across four distinct levels: the strategic, the contextual, the organisational and the operational. What remains to be done in setting the scene for discussing the institutions of policy-making and their policy environments is to characterise the policy process: how the different institutions and actors relate to each other; the "flow" of policy work through the components of the process; and the crucial institutional (as opposed to environmental) determinants of policy. We are particularly concerned with two questions that take centre stage in most discussions of policy-making: how are the various foreign policy institutions and actors involved in the policy process, and what is the extent of their influence?

To these questions, most models of foreign policy making have developed answers that cluster around a particular set of conventions about the foreign policy process. In this, they have been heavily influenced both by the US behaviouralist approach to assessing political power and influence, and by Graham Allison's highly influential study of foreign policy decision-making during the Cuban missile crisis, *Essence of Decision*.[1] Three features are common to many foreign policy making models: a regular cast of characters, each pursuing divergent foreign policy goals, with the interplay of their competing influence determining the policy outcome. In other words, policy results from a mixture of the interests of those involved in the process, and the varying levels of their capacity to prevail in advancing those interests.

These models are of limited use for understanding the Australian foreign policy making process because they impose certain "requirements" on the policy process before they can yield any information. They need to be able to isolate individual policy decisions and initiatives; they need to concentrate on policy issues that involve distinct actors and institutions; and they need to work with issues on which those involved have competing interests or opinions. The classic behaviouralist method for ascertaining involvement and influence over decisions was outlined by Robert Dahl in his highly influential *Who Governs?* Dahl argued that to identify "what really happened in the course of each decision", the researcher must determine:

> What the participants saw as the alternatives, who proposed the alternatives, how the participants responded, which alternatives were approved, modified or rejected ... [in order to gauge] ... for each decision which participants had initiated alternatives that were finally adopted, had vetoed alternatives initiated by others, or had proposed alternatives that were turned down. These actions [can] then [be] tabulated as individual "successes" or "defeats". The participants with the greatest proportion of successes out of the total number of successes [can] then [be] considered to be the most influential.[2]

The problem with this type of behaviouralist approach is that involvement can only be gauged when different actors have diverging self-interested "stakes" in the policy issue at hand,[3] while influence can only be measured when cases of conflict can be isolated within the policy process. (Even Stephen Lukes's "radical" view of power, which criticises the "one-dimensional" and "two-dimensional" conflictual power conceptions, presupposes diverging interests; that is, those that the object of power is not aware of at the time of the exercise of power.) Furthermore, the pluralist assumptions of such models presuppose high degrees of independence and equality of influence between the various actors.

Such assumptions may be justifiable for the foreign policy making system of the United States, where the strict separation of powers, institutional rivalries, and culture of competing interests generate greater controversy over more issues. They are highly problematic for Australia, where foreign policy making is heavily concentrated in the executive, is institutionally relatively hierarchic, and for the most part has a pervasive culture of collegiality, especially among the senior officials of the various foreign policy institutions. Quite simply, an Allison-type model would be silent about all but a small sector of Australian foreign policy. We must therefore look elsewhere for guidance in characterising the various types of involvement and influence in the Australian foreign policy process.

Gauging involvement and influence

Foreign policy making in Australia is invariably characterised by three properties: it is consensual more often than conflictual; its various actors play complementary rather than competing roles; and the vast bulk of policy work involves ongoing policy issues or "flows" rather than sequential and distinct decisions and initiatives. Our conception of involvement and influence is therefore drawn more to consensual notions of power, such as that of Hannah Arendt, who defines power as a property allowing people to act in concert;[4] and Bertrand de Jouvenal, who identifies common action towards a broadly shared conception of the common good as evidence of the operation of power.[5] By far the most useful conception, however, is that of Michel Foucault, for whom the operation of power is situational, relational and highly varied. For Foucault, power is not a fungible entity – an attribute that is possessed and cashed in to obtain certain objectives – but an attribute of social relationships: "power is exercised rather than possessed".[6] Nor is power a fixed quantity that is permanently held by some and exercised against others: power relationships are highly differentiated, often mutual, and are never fully controlled by any of the parties to them.[7] And rather than being a force that operates directly on people or institutions, power, according to Foucault's notion, is as a series of "techniques" that structures the possibilities and options for action of the actors within a power relationship:

> The exercise of power is a "conduct of conducts" and a management of
> possibilities. Basically, power is less a confrontation between two adversaries or
> their mutual engagement than a question of "government" ... To govern, in this
> sense, is to structure the possible field of action of others.[8]

Power, as the capacity to shape possibilities for action within specific relationships is, for Foucault, heavily dependent on surrounding institutional structures: "Power exists only as exercised by some on others, only when it is put into action ... it is inscribed on a field of sparse possibilities underpinned by permanent structures".[9] It is Foucault's concentration on institutional structures that makes his conceptualisation of power so relevant to characterising the Australian foreign policy process. Specifically, for Foucault, power relations are structured by several aspects of institutional environments. The first is

> *The system of differentiations* ... that permits one to act upon the actions of others
> ... Every relationship of power puts into place differences that are, at the same
> time, its conditions and its results.[10]

Second, the *types of objectives* pursued by participants as a function of their institutional position – whether role-defined, shared or competing – can affect the nature and operation of influence. Third, Foucault draws attention to the *instrumental modes* through which influence is exercised, as determined by the institutional environment: through rules, procedures, communication patterns. For Foucault, importantly, power can be exercised coercively or consensually: obviously it is the latter sense, which works through rules, norms, communication patterns and procedures, in which we are more interested. Fourth, *forms of institutionalisation*, "with … specific loci, [their] own regulations, [their] hierarchical structures that are carefully defined …" can structure techniques of influence. Finally, there are *degrees of rationalisation* that allow power and influence to be exercised over a range of different situations:

> The exercise of power is not a naked fact, an institutional given … it is something that is elaborated, transformed, organised; it endows itself with processes that are more or less adjusted to the situation.[11]

It should be apparent by now that "power" in Foucault translations is much closer to a conception of influence than to the traditional coercive connotations of the word in anglophone political science. (Indeed, Foucault repeatedly stated that he was uncomfortable with the word "power".)[12] This conceptualisation is a useful guide for thinking about the different levels of involvement of institutions and people in the policy process, and their levels of influence as determined by institutional structures. In the two sections that follow, we take the lead from Foucault's direction of our attention towards the system of differentiations, forms of institutionalisation and types of objectives to explore, respectively, how Australia's foreign policy institutions are separated into distinct functional roles, and how they are differentiated according to their responsibilities and their authority. In the final section, we explore Foucault's categories of instrumental modes and degrees of rationalisation through a characterisation of the modes of communication that operate within the policy-making process. It is by understanding these principles that we can fit our discussion of the institutions of foreign policy making in the four chapters following this one into a single coherent conception of a policy process featuring varying levels of involvement and influence by these institutions.

Institutional roles

Basic to the effective management of any complex field of human activity is modern, rational organisation. Max Weber compared such "bureaucratic" organisation to earlier forms with a striking analogy:

> The decisive reason for the advance of bureaucratic organisation has always been its purely technical superiority over any other form of organisation. The fully

developed bureaucratic mechanism compares with other organisations exactly as does the machine with non-mechanical modes of production.[13]

Since at least Adam Smith, the foundational principle of rational organisation has been the functional division of labour: "Each individual becomes more expert in his own peculiar branch, more work is done upon the whole, and the quantity of science is considerably increased by it".[14] For Charles Lindblom, specialisation is the basic defining aspect of modern government: in a reciprocal way, specialisation decisively affects how policy is made; and policy-making in turn reinforces functional division and specialisation of the policy machinery.[15] The functional division of tasks within policy administration permits a number of desirable qualities: the development of specialist expertise through constant contact with a certain task; the most complete and detailed knowledge of a particular policy area; and the covering of each aspect of the policy space deemed to be important by officials with continuing responsibility for monitoring them. Such functional divisions are meant to be complementary: dividing power and responsibility in such a way as to ensure that all of the important functions of government are managed effectively by the apparatus as a whole.

There are three principles of role differentiation within the foreign policy making machinery. Two of them – geographic division and functional division – are used to apportion the basic monitoring tasks of the policy space, and also to cover the various important aspects of the policy process. Internally, the foreign policy institutions are divided into geographic regions and specific aspects of foreign policy. Functional division also operates between the foreign policy institutions: separating everyday management of the policy space from oversight of its whole-of-government implications; policy management from political judgement; implementation from analysis; public presentation from careful drafting; defence from foreign affairs. Obviously at a practical level these distinctions are often blurred, but they remain basic to the overall way in which the policy institutions are differentiated. At a basic level these geographically and functionally defined roles are crucial determinants of the level of involvement, and the amount of influence, these individuals and institutions have on the ongoing policy process.

The third principle of role differentiation is hierarchic: the machinery as a whole, as well as each institution, has "a firmly-ordered system of super- and sub-ordination in which there is a supervision of lower offices by higher ones".[16] The hierarchic differentiation of roles establishes a distribution of responsibility and accountability, which we will discuss in the next section; what interests us here is its effect on the distribution of authority and the spread of oversight and specialisation. The "supervision of lower offices by higher ones" is the most obvious effect of hierarchic role differentiation on the distribution of authority. Higher-level roles are able to determine the priorities and policy work of lower roles, while lower roles are required to report significant policy issues to higher roles for resolution, decision and direction.

Yet a different type of authority also works in the opposite direction: an "authority of expertise", as opposed to formal, hierarchic authority. Through the information they hold because of their ability to monitor a certain aspect of the policy space on a continuous basis and at a relatively detailed level, lower offices possess an authority that higher-level roles, which monitor lower offices rather than aspects of the policy space, find it difficult to challenge.[17] In the fourth section we will discuss the effects of the "information funnel", where more senior offices in the hierarchy are provided information about the policy space of decreasing levels of detail and specificity. It is precisely this imbalance in information richness that provides lower roles with a certain authority. Of course, this is offset by the capacity of higher offices to contextualise the information they receive, and their access to a broader range of information from the offices under their supervision. The hierarchic differentiation of roles, therefore, also affects the involvement and influence of different parts of institutions on the policy process in complex ways. While the distribution of authority and oversight sees involvement and influence determined largely from the top down, the distribution of specialist knowledge determines involvement and influence largely from the bottom up.

We can begin to construct a portrait of the influence and involvement of various geographically, functionally and hierarchically distinguished roles on the policy process as a whole. The differentiation of roles emerges as a major determinant of the involvement of institutions, their parts, and individual actors in any given part of the policy process. Role distinctions partly determine contributors to a particular strand of policy by selecting those players with the required geographic expertise, functional specialisation and levels of authority adequate for the making of policy on a particular issue. But roles can be self-selecting also: often those who become involved in a policy issue are those who believe it will have a significant impact on their role-defined interests and responsibilities. Role differentiations also affect extents of influence on policy-making. Our Foucauldian conception of power suggests that influence is exerted on policy-making through functionally defined, role-specific relationships between the policy actors involved. Different types of role exercise different types of influence based on role-defined levels of authority, expertise and oversight. Functional differentiation and definition determine the "possible fields of action" for each actor in relation to the policy process, especially when these functionally distinct roles are also complementary. Influence, then, is exerted when actors affect each other's "possible fields of action" in relation to the policy. This conception of influence serves particularly well in a policy process that is largely consensual, non-competitive, and concerned with ongoing or regularly revisited policy initiatives.

Responsibility and authority

Basic to the structures of policy-making is a distribution of authority and responsibility within individual institutions, as well as between institutions. The two main principles of this distribution are the separation of powers between different parts of government, and the hierarchic organisation of policy-making institutions. Understanding these complex systems of authority, responsibility and accountability is necessary for grasping the involvement and influence of various actors in the foreign policy process.

Hierarchy

A hierarchic, pyramidal grading of authority is characteristic of individual foreign policy institutions and the Australian government as a whole. Such a clearly articulated system of supervision of lower by higher offices is what makes structures of government that have been functionally differentiated able to operate for the most part in a coherent, unidirectional manner. As we discussed in the previous section, higher levels of the organisation determine the priorities, work program and policy directions of the lower levels. In most cases, such authoritative policy direction is exercised in a strictly graded way: each higher office gives direction to the offices directly below in the hierarchy, which in turn give direction to those offices directly below them, and so on to the lowest offices in the organisation.

The counterpart of authority is responsibility. The grading of authority also ensures that the functional division of labour leaves no doubts as to the flow of accountability for specific issues, parts of the policy space, and policies. Again, in a clearly articulated way, each higher office is responsible for the adequate functioning and performance of certain subordinate roles, as well as for ensuring that directives issued by higher offices are implemented faithfully at lower levels. As we rise through the hierarchy, responsibility becomes cumulative; for example, in the Department of Foreign Affairs and Trade the lower levels of staff are organised into functional or geographic sections, clustered in branches, which report to their respective branch heads; the branch heads report to a division head; the division heads report to one of four deputy secretaries; each of whom in turn reports to the departmental secretary. Each level relies to some extent on the adequate management and oversight of the levels immediately below. Ultimately the Secretary is responsible for the performance of the most junior desk officer, but in a way mediated through the other hierarchic levels of the organisation.

The hierarchic structure of authority and responsibility supplies within the foreign policy making institutions a clear division of roles that determines the involvement and influence of the various levels in the policy-making process. Hierarchic roles are crucial in apportioning different levels of policy initiative and accountability throughout the organisation. Higher levels are granted greater amounts of initiative and creativity in formulating and interpreting policy directions; however, they also carry a greater burden of accountability for the policies that issue from the organisation. While lower levels may have a much closer appreciation of developments in sections of the policy space, they are required to report significant policy issues to superior levels for resolution, decisions and direction. To return to our Foucauldian conception of influence, while the lower offices can determine much of the content of the policy program by reporting significant events, the progress of initiatives, and emerging problems to higher levels, the higher offices exercise influence by "structuring the possible field[s] of action" of policy responses for lower levels. Hierarchy means that the structure of policy choices is successively defined through the lower levels of the organisation.

Elected and appointed officials

The Australian version of the Westminster system of government – where Cabinet and ministers are responsible and accountable to the House of Representatives, which in turn is accountable to the electorate – formally establishes a clear demarcation of responsibilities between elected politicians and appointed policy officials. In theory, elected ministers derive their power from the endorsement of the electorate, to which they are accountable and which may vote them from office if they are seen to have performed poorly or venally. The ministers derive policy from political values that, in theory, they clearly articulate and distinguish from those of their political competitors. Their tenure as policy-makers depends on the ongoing endorsement of the electorate. Appointed officials, in the traditional conception, are the apolitical servants of the state, accepting the responsibility for the faithful management of a set of clearly defined responsibilities in exchange for a secure existence and an ongo-

ing career structure. The bureaucracy continues through changes in government and ministers, providing successive incumbents with an institutional
memory and an ongoing set of policy skills and personal networks, and policy
with a certain consistency of direction and commitments. For this reason,
bureaucrats are supposed to remain beyond partisan political loyalties, competition and suspicion. Appointed officials are responsible to elected officials
(who are then periodically accountable to the electorate) for the adequate
management of policy and the faithful implementation of policy directions,
while elected officials rely on competent appointed officials to manage the
details of the policy space efficiently.

Underlying the politics–administration divide are widely held beliefs about
the separation between two qualitatively different tasks in policy-making. As
Hawkesworth explains in relation to a slightly different context, these beliefs
rest on a distinction that is often made between the hard, objective "facts" of a
policy issue, and a more subjective realm of "values", in which political judgements need to be made in response to these "facts":

> Restricted to the activities of description, explanation, and prediction, empirical
> policy analysis is committed to the development of objective knowledge about the
> policy making process, the key determinants of policy decisions, the necessary
> means for achieving policy objectives, and the predictable consequences of
> various strategies of policy implementation.[18]

The political process, however, is heavily subjective, value-laden and incapable
of empirical appraisal:

> Undiscernible by the senses, unresolvable by scientific techniques, and dependent
> on subjective assessments, questions of value constitute the agenda of the political
> process. The realm of values, of questions of right and wrong, good and bad, of
> what ought and what ought not to be done, fall beyond the sphere of scientific
> policy investigation.[19]

Intriguingly, Hawkesworth's observations about the separation of the
domain of behaviouralist policy analysis from what are taken to be the value-
laden concerns of political philosophy are mirrored in traditional distinctions
made between the legitimate work of elected officials and that of appointed
officials. The appointed official, unelected and with ongoing tenure, should
provide only frank and objective policy advice about knowable "facts" in the
policy space; the elected official is the only official who may legitimately make

value-laden "political" decisions on behalf of the community, because he or she is ultimately subject to the appraisal of the electorate. For Weber, politics is a vocation for both types, but in different senses. An elected official lives "for" and "off" politics in his or her commitment to securing power and prestige, and in the service of an ideological calling, while the appointed official is committed functionally and impersonally to a given set of role-defined responsibilities.[20] The bureaucrat is a "specialist", bringing ongoing expertise, knowledge of the historical context, and information about available resources to the policy process; the minister is a "dilettante", without specialist knowledge but expected to make specific decisions about general policy directions.[21]

It is important here to distinguish between the formal conceptual roles in constitutional theory and actual practice in Australia. Even more so than in the case of functional role divisions, the distinction between elected and appointed officials is blurred in important ways. There are a number of reasons for this blurring. One is simply the amount of policy work that arises on a daily basis: invariably the minister is unable to make all value-laden policy decisions that arise, meaning that some inevitably must be taken by appointed officials of one type or another. Officials make these decisions according to the anticipated values of the minister; no official would last long who made a decision contrary to the strong beliefs of the minister. Second, as Hawkesworth argues convincingly, it is almost impossible to make "fact–value" distinctions of the sort that predicate the politics–administration divide: even those "facts" that look completely objective will have been selected as important by some underlying values system on the part of the administrator.

A major cause of blurring has been the managerialism revolution in the Australian public service. Managerialism has, among other things, seen the creation of a defined rank of senior managers subject to forms of contract employment that temporarily define tenure while increasing management authority over and responsibility for programs. This has lifted senior bureaucrats out of the traditional bureaucracy model and brought them close to the logic of the political process in terms of tenure, performance appraisal and levels of political accountability.[22]

Finally, there is the role of ministerial advisers, appointed officials who have a major role in making and influencing policy judgements. This is a new category, made up partly of people seconded under legislation from within the foreign policy bureaucracy to political jobs, and partly made up of people recruited directly from within the respective political parties in government at the time. With ministers as busy as they are, advisers often make important judgements on their behalf; and even on judgements made by the ministers, advisers usually are able to inject comments and opinions on all submissions before they reach the ministers' desks. As a number of parliamentary inquiries discovered early in 2002, these advisers are uniquely able to escape parliamentary scrutiny, unlike ministers and traditional bureaucrats.

Despite such blurring, demarcations of authority and responsibility are important determinants of the involvement and influence of various actors in the policy process. Even if they are sometimes departed from by necessity or design, these demarcations carry with them a strong resonance of legitimacy: when they are transgressed, it is usually done in a non-public way, with a conscious sense that lines are being crossed. This accords with what March and Olsen called a "logic of appropriateness", which operates when actors' awareness of their respective roles is a strong determinant of the part they are prepared to play in the policy process, as opposed to the more frequently acknowledged "logic of consequences", in which actors become involved from convictions that they need to act in certain ways in order to achieve a certain outcome.[23] Understandings of administrative hierarchy, and of the distinction between appointed and elected officials, then, determine the level and type of involvement of various actors in the policy process. They also dictate the extent of involvement that is possible for various actors: since more senior administrators and ministers are responsible for larger and larger portions of the policy space, they are only physically capable of being involved usually at the most abstract levels and for much shorter periods in any given policy issue. Lower-level officials, on the other hand, responsible for smaller sections of the policy space, are able to be involved in policy relevant to that area in a much more sustained and detailed way. Here we can see that involvement and influence are related in a complex way: the most authoritative players – the ministers, the Prime Minister, perhaps ministerial advisers and departmental secretaries – are able to exercise decisive influence, but are able to attend to only a portion of the policy issues that arise, while lower-level bureaucrats are unable to exercise decisive influence but can subtly impact on policy in an ongoing way.

Distinctions in administrative hierarchy, and between appointed and elected officials, also determine the types of influence exerted on the policy process. The clear structures of authority – hierarchic within bureaucratic institutions, and elected over appointed officials more generally – define gradings of influence in a conventional sense. As the responsibility for policy accrues to higher levels in the bureaucracy, and ultimately from the bureaucracy to ministers, so ultimate policy influence, in the sense of setting overall policy directions and making authoritative decisions, flows back from politics to administration and down the bureaucratic hierarchy. However, policy influence of a different sort operates the other way. As discussed in the previous section, the expertise and knowledge of an issue area wielded by lower levels carry much authority. In another sense, as lower levels of the bureaucracy monitor the policy space and do the detailed work on preparing briefing notes and policy submissions for higher levels and ultimately the minister, they are able to exercise significant influence through their selection of information and the various alternatives they present for decisions. However, in a highly Foucauldian way, the bottom-up options are constrained by the top-down values. By the time most policy submissions reach the minister, they have been structured into a strict format of concisely stated policy options and likely outcomes that the minister is required to choose between. Often one of the options is implicitly or explicitly recommended. Both from the top down and from the bottom up, therefore, influence in the form of the structuring of choices occurs between roles differentiated by authority and responsibility.

Modes of communication

All involvement, influence, coordination and conflict within the policy-making process take place by virtue of certain established modes of communication. At a basic level, all politics and policy are about communication, and consequently, as Michael Oakeshott observed, it has developed its own discourse and vocabulary:

> The vocabulary of political discourse is composed of words and expressions used to diagnose situations alleged to call for redress in an official response, to identify the shapes of the features and characteristics of a state or alternative, more desirable shapes, to express and to recommend beliefs, doctrines, or dispositions alleged to be important in formulating political proposals, or to denote allegiances to considerations of desirability in respect to arrangements of state.[24]

In other words, policy-making – like any other realm of life – has crafted language in ways that fit its own particular needs. It appears similar to the language used in other realms of life because, as Wittgenstein observed, "the clothing of our language makes everything [appear] alike".[25] Participants in the policy process communicate within a shared context of meanings: what they say and write and do all acquires meaning for themselves and other participants within an overall shared structure of meanings specific to the foreign policy process. The policy space itself is monitored by actors with shared expectations: certain situations trigger particular judgements of significance, value-informed beliefs, and reactions. The exercise of authority and responsibility, and the work-ability of role differentiation are contingent on these shared structures of meaning and modes of communication. To properly understand the policy process, one must understand the distinctive modes of communication its participants use to describe, to order, to direct, to classify its contents to each other.

The language of the policy process presupposes between its users a certain set of common understandings about the nature and subject matter of the policy process. This does not mean that all policy-makers think exactly the same things about foreign policy. Their shared understandings occur at a level below their specific opinions about policy. When policy-makers communicate, their words carry a substructure of knowledge specific to participants in the policy process, providing vital information and context to what they actually say; they are thus an essential part of the message, and may be lost to someone listening from outside of the policy-making world. These common understandings are institutional: about the relationship between those communicating; about the nature and dynamics of the overall policy process; about reciprocal responsibilities and authority. They also relate to the policy realm: which events are significant or trivial; the way in which some issues will impact on others; the delicacy, complexity and diversity of the policy environment. They also reflect conventions of behaviour: how things are said and done; the required professional standards of conduct relevant to various policy-making roles; the appropriate personal and institutional responses to various types of situation.

Communication and policy action are also intimately related. Certain words, phrases and terms trigger common policy understandings among those listening, which have immediate implications for subsequent policy responses. At the strategic level of policy, for example, phrases such as "constructive engagement" or "practical regionalism" trigger specific policy actions in a range of issue areas. Words and phrases carry a distinctive power at other levels of policy-making as well. Phrases including words or combinations like "confrontation", or "escalation" or "defaulted on commitments" themselves trigger subsequent words and phrases – "mediation", "stabilisation", "enforcement", "quarantining the issue from the broader relationship" – which also signify certain templates for policy action in response. Such communication–policy combinations can cascade through the policy-making machinery, affecting policy-making on all levels. Certain words and phrases can also stop such policy cascades; for instance, "appeasement", "backsliding" or "we're the only ones complying". It is important to keep in mind that, rather than functioning as a passive, objective set of signifiers referring to a separate realm of policy action, the language of policy-making is itself a foundational part of the policy process.

Partly the distinct modes of communication are determined by the subject matter of foreign policy making. Recalling Foucault's conception of "instrumental modes", however, we can see that policy-making discourses are also heavily influenced by institutional structures. Not only do these structures of role distinction, hierarchy and accountability determine which parts of the policy-making machine relate to which other parts, but they also imbue political-bureaucratic communications with certain patterns of significance based on the identities of the senders and receivers of the message. It is also significant that most communications in the policy process occur either vertically, along the hierarchic structures within each bureaucratic department and up to its portfolio minister, or horizontally, between similar levels of the separate departments: ministerial office to ministerial office, secretary to secretary, division to division, branch to branch, and so on. Rarely does significant communication occur diagonally; for example, from Defence ministerial office to DFAT branch head. When it does, it usually involves a significant crisis or out-of-the-ordinary issue.

The other important structural influence on communication is the "information funnel" that operates as part of any bureaucratic organisation. The inverted funnel of information works in two ways. The process of reporting means that information is sifted so that only that judged to be "significant" is passed to higher levels. Such sifting occurs at all points of ascent up the hierarchy. This means that those at the top of the organisation have a broader but much more general conception of the policy space. The information funnel operates the other way as well. Both general and more specific policy directives from the minister and senior levels of a department are divided up to reflect their relevant functional and geographic specialisations as they pass down the hierarchy for implementation. This means that the lower levels of policy-making get to see a smaller portion of the overall policy picture, a tendency that is only partly rectified by consultation procedures. These structural attributes of communication flows have a significant effect on the modes and structures of involvement and influence within the foreign policy process. All of these influences allow us to characterise certain predominant patterns of communication.

An important pattern of communication capable of having great effect is that of loose coalitions of bureaucrats and advisers. Given the small number of people in the Australian foreign policy machinery, specific agreement on policy positions or directions can create clusters of people that communicate with more regularity and mutually inform each other's opinions on a range of issues. Policy-makers with strong beliefs about the policy world can tend to identify and behave more collegially towards like-minded colleagues. These "bands of brothers", while difficult to conceptualise formally in relation to the structures of the foreign policy machinery, can be extraordinarily influential in the moulding of foreign policy. If argued for with enough force, by like-minded officials throughout the policy structures, certain opinions and policy positions can gain significant support.

In terms of actual communications patterns, the first distinction that can be made is between authoritatively structured and functionally structured communication. Authoritative communication sees the content of a message or direction or request take on an imperative structure by virtue of the position of the sender of the message. Such communication is much more clearly identifiable as what Austin classified as "perlocutionary speech acts", or communications that are designed to bring about an immediate, clearly specified response on the part of others.[26] Authoritative communication occurs between the political and administrative realms and from the top down through the bureaucratic hierarchy. Functional communication takes place either horizontally between similar levels of different organisations, or from the bottom up in the organisational hierarchy. It involves the communication of policy-relevant information that has been gleaned and passed on according to shared structures of significance and meaning. This latter form of communication is closer to Austin's concept of "illocutionary speech acts", where communications have a "certain conventional force" but through informing others about a certain state of affairs that may or may not impact on their own structures of significance and policy calculations.[27] Authoritative communications require corresponding responses by virtue of surrounding institutional structures, understandings and sanctions, rather than by virtue of the content of the message, while functional communication seeks a response by relying on the anticipated inherent significance of the content of the message. Both rely on shared structures of meaning and significance, but in different ways: perlocutionary statements rely on shared understandings of authority, while illocutionary statements rely on shared understandings of what is important and significant.

Beyond this basic distinction another set of classifications needs to be made. Aided by Habermas's theory of communicative action,[28] we can identify four basic types of communication that flow regularly through the policy process; they are used variously by different participants at different times. Some are restricted by hierarchic structures, others are not. First, there are *imperatives*, where the speaker enunciates a desired state of affairs to be achieved by others, which derive their force from surrounding hierarchic institutional structures.

These most often take the form of policy directives from a ministerial office or the senior levels of a department. Closely related are *regulatives*, which refer to desired states of affairs in the common social world of those communicating. These are less authoritative, and need not rely on hierarchic structures: they are shared understandings of policy positions on certain issues. They often take the form of strategic policy statements as discussed in Chapter 2. *Constantives* are used to report on states of affairs in the policy space or the policy-making machinery; they are designed to influence the policy process by altering in some way the knowledge or dispositions of the hearer. Falling almost wholly within the functionally structured modes of communication, they rely for their influence on the content of the message rather than on surrounding institutional hierarchic structures. Finally, and less relevant to actual policy influence than in affecting the overall institutional culture, are *expressives*, which refer to the subjective dispositions or perceptions of the speaker in relation either to specific issues or to the policy process in general.

Modes of communication are crucial determinants of involvement and influence in the policy process. The various structured communications channels – vertical–horizontal, the information funnel – determine patterns of involvement in policy issues, where the communications flow demarcates those actors and institutions involved from those which are not; they also determine the breadth of involvement of different parts of the policy machinery. Furthermore, by using different types of communication, participants justify their own involvement (or non-involvement) in specific policy issues. By triggering different linguistic-policy responses, they also try to determine the involvement or non-involvement of other actors.

Communications patterns are also the carriers of influence on the policy process. They determine the forms of influence open to each of the different participants by allowing each to structure the choices and information of others in certain ways. Words and statements, whether authoritative or functional, can have immediate effects on the "possible field of action" of other actors or institutions. Influence can also be exerted by anticipating others' dispositions, seeking to make some of their possible choices more viable than others in the light of the content of the message or the position of the speaker. Whether authoritative, in the form of imperatives or regulatives, or functional, in the form of constantives and expressives, policy-specific communication flows constantly through the foreign policy institutions. Authoritative forms rely on hierarchic structures to direct the actions of those closer to the policy environments, while functional forms are able to affect the range of choices of higher levels of the organisation, or of the same level but in different institutions, by feeding in information that is designed to push certain policy buttons.

Conclusion

By discussing these aspects of the foreign policy making machinery, we have attempted to provide a dynamic portrait of the policy process, in its various forms. We have also developed a framework for assessing the involvement and influence of various actors and institutions in the policy process. While the process itself is highly variable, according to different issues, settings and policy environments, similar patterns of role differentiation and coordination, authority–responsibility structures and communications patterns recur in various iterations. The particular combinations may differ, but the pieces behave according to a fairly constant logic across the various permutations.

Taken together, this chapter and the one before it provide a characterisation of the different manifestations of the foreign policy making process in Australia. Chapter 2 used four levels – the strategic, the contextual, the organisational and the operational – to describe the forms of policy that are made on a constant basis. This chapter examined how the various parts of the policy machinery are differentiated and relate to each other, and how this affects patterns of involvement and influence. When combined, these two frameworks are intended to provide a conceptual portrait of the nature of foreign policy making in Australia. At the strategic level of policy, role differentiation dictates the greater involvement of ministers and their offices than institutions; influence is wielded through the authoritative enunciation of imperative and expressive statements indicating overall policy directions and parameters. The contextual level acquires its importance through its relevance to the merging of oversight and specialisation roles: it is here that various aspects of specialised monitoring of the policy space are merged in a coherent policy vision. This level of policy sees influence wielded hierarchically as those higher levels of the administration gain authority through their ability to contextualise issues and decisions; they make use of all of the modes of policy communication to do this. At the organisational level, the involvement and non-involvement of participants is determined authoritatively; resources and roles essential to policy-making on a particular issue are brought into play, and complementary and sometimes competitive relationships are established. The operational level is divided into geographic and functional specialisations directly monitoring the policy space. The specialist knowledge and sustained responsibility for the monitoring of the operational level give it a certain authority and influence in the process through constantive and regulative communication, and through a certain capacity to select information.

In the four chapters that follow, we will take a closer look at the major institutions of foreign policy making: the bureaucracy, the executive, the overseas network and the intelligence community. In the course of our discussion it will become clear how each institution fits into the overall policy process, how the various parts of each relates to those of the others, and what contributions on which levels of policy-making are made by each.

Notes

1 Graham T. Allison, *Essence of Decision: Explaining the Cuban Missile Crisis*, Boston: Little, Brown, 1971.
2 Robert A. Dahl, *Who Governs? Democracy and Power in an American City*, New Haven, CT: Yale University Press, 1961, p. 336.
3 See Steven Lukes, *Power: A Radical View*, London: Macmillan, 1974.
4 Hannah Arendt, *On Violence*, London: Penguin, 1970.
5 Bertrand de Jouvenal, *On Power: The Natural History of Its Growth*, Indianapolis: Liberty Fund, 1993.
6 Michel Foucault, *Discipline and Punish: The Birth of the Prison*, trans. Alan Sheridan, London: Penguin Books, 1991, p. 26.
7 Michel Foucault, "'Omnes et Singulatim': Toward a Critique of Political Reason" in *The Essential Works of Foucault, 1954–1984, Volume III: Power*, ed. James D. Faubion, trans. Robert Hurley, London: Penguin Press, 1994.
8 Michel Foucault, "The Subject and Power" in *The Essential Works of Foucault, 1954–1984, Volume III: Power*, ed. James D. Faubion, trans. Robert Hurley, London: Penguin Press, 1994, p. 341.
9 ibid., p. 340. The following classification comes from the same lecture.
10 ibid.
11 ibid., p. 345.
12 See the discussion in Bent Flyvbjerg, *Making Social Science Matter: Why Social Inquiry Fails and How It Can Succeed Again*, trans. Steven Sampson, Cambridge: Cambridge University Press, 2001, p. 117.
13 Max Weber, "Bureaucracy" in H.H. Gerth and C. Wright Mills (eds), *From Max Weber: Essays in Sociology*, trans. H.H. Gerth and C. Wright Mills, London: Routledge and Kegan Paul, 1977, p. 214.
14 Adam Smith, *An Inquiry into the Nature and Causes of the Wealth of Nations*, London: J.M. Dent and Sons, 1981, p. 10.
15 Charles E. Lindblom, *Politics and Markets: The World's Political–Economic Systems*, New York: Basic Books, 1977, p. 27.
16 Weber, "Bureaucracy", p. 197.
17 John Wanna, Ciaran O'Faircheallaigh and Patrick Weller, *Public Sector Management in Australia*, Melbourne: Macmillan, 1992, p. 29.

18 M.E. Hawkesworth, *Theoretical Issues in Policy Analysis*, New York: State University of New York Press, 1988, p. 4.
19 ibid.
20 Max Weber, "Politics as a Vocation" in H.H. Gerth and C. Wright Mills (eds), *From Max Weber: Essays in Sociology*, trans. H.H. Gerth and C. Wright Mills, London: Routledge and Kegan Paul, 1977.
21 ibid.
22 Mark Considine and Martin Painter, *Managerialism: The Great Debate*, Melbourne: Melbourne University Press, 1997, p. 3.
23 James G. March and Johan P. Olsen, *Rediscovering Institutions: The Organisational Basis of Politics*, New York: Free Press, 1989, pp. 160–2.
24 Michael Oakeshott, "Political Discourse" in *Rationalism in Politics and Other Essays*, Indianapolis: Liberty Press, 1962, p. 438.
25 Ludwig Wittgenstein, *Philosophical Investigations*, trans. G.E.M. Anscombe, Oxford: Blackwell, 1999, II, XI, 224.
26 J.L. Austin, *How To Do Things with Words*, Oxford: Clarendon Press, 1955, pp. 103–10.
27 ibid.
28 Jürgen Habermas, *The Theory of Communicative Action, Volume 1: Reason and the Rationalisation of Society*, trans. Thomas McCarthy, Boston: Beacon Press, 1984, pp. 273–337.

CHAPTER 4

The Foreign Policy Bureaucracy

World politics is at times a dangerous, and always a complex and resistant realm within which states seek to protect themselves and advance the interests of their societies. By virtue of size, wealth or membership in a regional grouping, some states have a head start in remaining safe and getting their way. Australia, pre-eminent in none of these characteristics, must rely on a different, more difficult-to-define quality – foreign policy capacity – to secure its foreign policy objectives. Foreign policy capacity can be measured by the extent to which a state's foreign policy making provides for flexible and quick responses to international developments, but at the same time provides dependability and a sureness of touch in a rapidly evolving policy realm. Policy capacity also combines discernment – the ability to determine what is significant, and when and where to devote foreign policy resources – with analytical skills and the capacity for creative thought and strategic judgement. Various institutions contribute to a state's foreign policy capacity; these are the subject of this and the next three chapters. In this chapter, we examine the foreign policy bureaucracy, the essential backbone of the foreign policy process.

Whether or not conceived in terms of policy capacity, effective bureaucratic organisation of foreign policy has historically played an indispensable role in the rise of the modern state form, and in the sequential predominance of various great powers. Observing that modern bureaucratic structures bring "[p]recision, speed, unambiguity, knowledge of the files, continuity, discretion, unity, strict subordination, reduction of friction and of material and personal costs" to states, Max Weber linked the international context of early modern states – particularly in terms of their "zones of friction with the outside" – to their development of modern, rational forms of bureaucracy.[1] This observation seems to be borne out by a glance at the history of foreign policy administration in post-Reformation European states. As the sovereign state emerged from the feudal structures of Christendom and empire, the development of permanent diplomatic relations began to place greater demands on the direction and administration of foreign policies.[2] The inadequacies began to become manifest in systems of foreign policy administration that were often haphazardly divided between royal favourites, in which ambassadors often had to rely on personal relationships to communicate their observations with the monarch, and where methods of information storage were mostly chaotic. While the Spanish made early moves towards a proper bureaucracy, it was Cardinal Richelieu who formed the first distinct foreign ministry in 1626, combining the work of several secretaries of state. As Hamilton and Langhorne point out, this was only possible after foreign policy was able to be conceptualised as a separate branch of government, in need of constant monitoring and attention by a permanent member of the *Conseil d'État*.[3] Because France dominated European power politics in the century after Richelieu's death, its methods of foreign policy organisation were gradually emulated by other states.

The bureaucracy is the essential core of the foreign policy making process in Australia. While in Australia's robust democracy foreign policy direction is determined by the elected government, such authoritative policy direction could not be conceived, let alone enacted, without the bureaucratic structures underpinning government. Changes in foreign policy direction are rare but important. The most significant postwar changes in the focus of Australian foreign policy came with the election in 1972 of the Whitlam Government, which introduced a more independent and internationalist foreign policy with a clearer focus on Asia, and the 1996 election of the Howard Government, which abandoned the post-Whitlam bipartisan consensus to focus foreign policy more openly on the national interest and link it more directly to the domestic political agenda. However, the shifts in both 1972 and 1996 took place despite a high degree of continuity among senior officials.

If the direction of foreign policy and the key decisions are firmly in the hands of ministers, the policy is nevertheless shaped, tweaked, interpreted and implemented by a supporting bureaucracy whose world outlook and culture continue to have a significant impact on Australian foreign policy. It may be a bold foreign ministry official who will give the government advice that is known to be unpalatable. But it is also a bold government that will act in direct opposition to the written advice of its professional advisers. We examine the various bureaucratic departments and parts of departments that are involved in the formulation and management of foreign policy in what follows. A number of departments and agencies play a part in the foreign policy process, but the dominant bureaucratic institution is the Department of Foreign Affairs and Trade (DFAT). Much of the first half of the chapter is devoted to this institution: its history and evolution; its role in the policy process; its bureaucratic structures and routines. Our examination of DFAT concludes with an examination of two of the more intangible factors influencing its approach to foreign policy making: departmental culture, and how this has changed over time; and the characteristics of the dominant "world view" of people who work in that institution, an interpretation of the nature of international relations that is to varying extents shared with other aspects of the foreign policy bureaucracy. The two final sections of the chapter survey the involvement and influence of other Federal Government departments in foreign policy making; and how their involvement is coordinated through the Department of Prime Minister and Cabinet (PM&C) and various other mechanisms.

The Department of Foreign Affairs and Trade

Just across State Circle from Parliament House in Canberra, the Department of Foreign Affairs and Trade occupies the large, assertive and self-confident R.G. Casey Building. Planned by a Labor Government, it was finished in 1996, late enough to ensure that the Coalition Government had naming rights after one of its own. On the five floors of this building, around a large central atrium, more than 1,200 people work (including the Australian Secret Intelligence Service, which is housed, for reasons of cover, within the same building). Hanging in the foyer, John Olsen's tapestry *Rising Suns over Australia Felix* mirrors the building's confident nationalism.

It is this department, along with its staff in overseas posts, that is responsible for the day-to-day management of Australia's international relations. The operational centre of the foreign policy making process in Australia, it provides advice to government about what is happening in the outside world and what might be done to shape developments. Through its overseas posts (see Chapter 6) it is responsible for implementing policy – that is, persuading another government to follow a certain course: to accept an Australian proposal for a refugee settlement centre; to permit further imports of Australian lamb; to sign the Chemical Weapons Convention. Its involvement in the majority of foreign policy making is constant, in one form or another, and its influence is pervasive. If the bureaucracy is the core of the foreign policy making process, DFAT is the core of the foreign policy bureaucracy. Understanding the various aspects of this organisation is basic to understanding the process as a whole.

History and evolution

In 1941, little more than fifty years before the opening of the R.G. Casey Building, another future minister, Paul Hasluck, was entering a department that occupied "about ten rooms on the first floor of one wing of the administrative building in Canberra known as West block".[4] Although Australia had had departments of external affairs in various permutations ever since 1901, they were tiny and operated principally under the Prime Minister and his department. It was not until November 1935 that External Affairs gained full administrative autonomy with the appointment of its own Secretary, Lieutenant Colonel W.R. Hodgson (1935–1945). According to one of the best historians of Australian foreign policy, Peter Edwards:

> This, more than any other single event in the confused history of Australian external policy administration may be taken as the birth of the present day Department of Foreign Affairs. By the end of 1935 the growth in Australia's international commitments, the deterioration in the international situation and the increasing interest by Australians in world affairs combined to force a reluctant government to accept that its tiny foreign office at least had to be regarded as a department in its own right.[5]

One year later, the department's total establishment was ten officers and four typists in Canberra, and three officers and two typists in London.[6]

The first great period of growth for the External Affairs Department came at the end of the Second World War, under H.V. Evatt. For the first time the department began to recruit and train its own people. In the three years from 30 June 1946 the total staff more than trebled from 210 to 642.[7] Through the 1950s and 1960s the department's growth continued as Australia's neighbourhood was transformed by decolonisation into a region of newly independent states and the country developed for the first time a distinct national foreign policy. By 1962 the department employed 1,100 staff. This number had doubled by 1969. In 1972 (the year after the McMahon Government changed the department's name from External Affairs to Foreign Affairs) it had 3,000 staff, and it reached 4,700 in late 1974.[8] It would never reach that number again. After the Whitlam Government's expansion, a decade of public-service-wide 'razor gangs' and efficiency dividends cut into departmental numbers.

In 1987 came the most significant structural change since the department's foundation, with the amalgamation of the Department of Foreign Affairs, the Department of Trade and the Australian Information Service. This was part of a wider reorganisation of the public service and amalgamation of departments by the Hawke Government. In the view of Stuart Harris, the first Secretary of the integrated department, however, the amalgamation reflected broader trends in international relations, as well as changing approaches to public administration: the greater integration of political and economic events internationally, the growing priority of economic as against political issues with the passing of the intensity of the Cold War, and "interdependence and more generally, the continued growth in the linkages of domestic and foreign policies".[9] Like External Affairs, Trade and Customs had been one of the original federal departments. Trade was separated from Customs in 1956, and had at various times been merged with Industry and Resources. It had been at its most dominant politically and bureaucratically during John McEwen's twenty-two-year tenure, ending in 1971, when it had been a political and policy fiefdom of the Country Party (later the National Party) and the principal instrument of McEwen's protectionist policy push. Genuine policy differences lay behind some of the interdepartmental disputes between Foreign Affairs and Trade during those years, but more of them had their origins in battles for turf. The 1987 amalgamation removed at a single stroke a great deal of the bureaucratic conflict in Canberra, or at least shifted it from an interdepartmental to an intradepartmental level, where compromise and resolution came more easily.

The amalgamated department now employs more than 3,300 people[10] in Australia and in eighty-nine countries around the world. An estimated 800 of them are involved in one way or another in the foreign policy making process.[11] To a significant extent, DFAT's current structures and policy processes reflect the evolution of an organisation that developed largely in response to momentous changes in its policy environment. The structures in turn influence the foreign policy making process that occurs therein.

Departmental structures

The internal structures of DFAT combine geographic and functional divisions that reflect how Australia views international relations in terms of the importance of regions and issues, along with a hierarchic structure of authority and responsibility ensuring as much as possible a coherent and coordinated foreign policy (see Chapter 3). These structures – the organisational level of foreign policy – have a major influence on how particular foreign policy issues are dealt with by the department.

The Foreign Affairs and Trade portfolio operates under the direction of two ministers, with separate but related responsibilities for foreign affairs and trade, and one parliamentary secretary. The Foreign Minister has always been the portfolio minister, holding overall responsibility for the management of the department. In response to new priorities and pressures, the department's internal administrative organisation changes, sometimes from year to year. For fifty years, however, the department has remained structured around a mix of

Figure 4.1   Divisional structure of the Department of Foreign Affairs and Trade, 2003

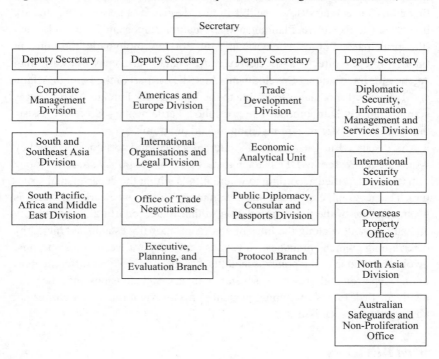

geographical divisions (Asia, Europe, the South Pacific, dealing predominantly with bilateral relations with individual overseas countries) and specialist functional areas (legal, security, multilateral, dealing predominantly with transnational or multinational issues).

In 2003 the department's senior management comprised the Secretary and four deputy secretaries, who had broad oversight of fourteen divisions and offices: North Asia; Americas and Europe; South and Southeast Asia; South Pacific, Africa and the Middle East; Trade Development; the Office of Trade Negotiations; International Security; International Organisations and Legal; Diplomatic Security, Information Management and Services; Public Diplomacy, Consular and Passports; and Corporate Management. The Overseas Property Office, the Economic Analytical Unit and the Australian Safeguards and Non-Proliferation Office also fall within this divisional structure (see Figure 4.1). Not all divisions are equally well-staffed: as discussed in Chapter 9, the weight of staff and resources in some divisions rather than others says a great deal about those regions of the world that are important to Australian foreign policy, and those that are less important. Each division is headed by a first assistant secretary (FAS), and is in turn divided into between two and six branches. The Executive, Planning and Evaluation Branch and Protocol Branch (the principal point of contact with the foreign diplomatic missions in Canberra) report directly to the Secretary. Australia's aid agency, the Australian Agency for International Development (AusAID), is part of the Foreign Affairs and Trade portfolio, and responsible to the Minister for Foreign Affairs, but is administratively autonomous. The portfolio's Parliamentary Secretary assists the Foreign Minister in administering the aid program.

As discussed in Chapter 3, this internal structure determines how policy issues are addressed by DFAT. Each disturbance in the policy space or policy initiative is classified according to where it falls within the departmental structure. The geographic or functional area into which it most clearly falls then is given carriage of the policy in relation to that issue; reporting, responsibility and authority flow along the lines of an organisationally established hierarchy determining which branches, divisions and deputy secretaries become involved. Of course, if a policy issue falls – as most do – across different areas of the departmental structure, several branches and divisions may become involved. Task forces combining personnel from several sections are often set up to deal with such issues.

What DFAT does

In Chapter 2 we described foreign policy as comprising a range of functions across four levels – the strategic, the contextual, the organisational and the operational. For the most part DFAT's work consists of responding to developments within the policy space or pursuing initiatives anticipating developments in that space. Events can impact on the policy space from a range of different directions: a coup in Fiji; the arrest of Australians in Laos; a proposal by the Department of Immigration and Multicultural and Indigenous Affairs to build asylum-seeker processing centres in South Pacific countries; a question without notice asked of the Trade Minister in Parliament. Most of the work of all members of DFAT – from the Secretary down to desk officers – is in some way related to responding to the never-ending flow of developments through the policy space.

Of course, this does not mean that DFAT is a passive organisation that sits around waiting for events to which it should respond. Much of its work consists of anticipating policy developments, advancing initiatives judged to be in Australia's interests, and sustaining those processes that ensure that policy developments are detected early and responded to competently, and that action in response to such developments does not contradict the other strands of foreign policy that the government is pursuing.

At the strategic level, DFAT makes use of overall frameworks and statements of purpose to determine and prioritise the issues to which it responds. In its corporate plan for the period from 2000 to 2002, DFAT described its aim as being "To advance the interests of Australia and Australians". It then set out a series of subsidiary goals: to enhance Australia's security; to contribute to growth in Australia's economy, employment and standard of living; to assist Australian travellers and Australians overseas; to strengthen global cooperation in ways that advance Australia's interests; to foster public understanding of Australia's foreign and trade policy; and to project a positive image of Australia internationally.[12] These categories are not natural or obvious. By way of contrast, less than a decade earlier, in its 1993–94 corporate plan, the department's aim was "To win a future for Australia in the world", and its goals were: to increase Australia's economic prosperity through trade and investment flows; to ensure a favourable security environment for Australia; to advance Australia's standing as a good international citizen; to promote global cooperation based on fair rules; and to help Australians overseas.[13] The two documents show obvious similarities, but they differ in interesting ways as well. The 2000 goals ("To advance the interests of Australia and Australians") reflect the Howard Government's more overtly interests-oriented approach to foreign policy. They also place foreign policy in a more obviously domestic context. The aim of contributing "to growth in Australia's economy, employment and standard of living" replaces the narrower reference to "trade and investment flows", and consular aims have leapt up the chart. Meanwhile, the traditional liberal internationalist goal of "good international citizenship" has disappeared, to be replaced by the more nationally focussed phrase "to strengthen global cooperation in ways that advance Australia's interests".

To some extent, of course, the differences between the two documents are more rhetorical than real, but they show usefully that even the way foreign ministries think about what they do, and the priorities they attach to very broad goals, change with time and with different governments. To a significant extent, the government's strategic framework for foreign policy priorities is accepted and endorsed through the various levels of DFAT. In response to our survey in 2001, we found DFAT policy officers nominating priorities and outlooks very similar to those of the current government. These views were prominent also among staff who had served under the previous government. Seventy-five percent of respondents nominated security as the first, second or third most important foreign policy goal; 69.6 per cent nominated economic prosperity in the top three (36.6 per cent listed free trade and investment in the top three); and 19.2 per cent placed the safety of Australians overseas in their top three. The previous government's objectives "to strengthen global cooperation" scored in the top three of just 10.7 per cent of respondents, while the current government's emphasis on bilateralism was nominated by 42.2 per cent of respondents in their top three. Regional engagement, another area of different emphasis between the previous and current governments, was listed by 25.9 per cent of respondents as first, second or third in importance.

Some idea of the day-to-day work of the department at the other levels of policy-making can be gathered from the statistical commentaries at the back of its annual reports. In 2000–01 the department made 20,760 representations to other governments and international organisations in support of Australia's international interests, and attended 13,844 international meetings or negotiations, its 84 overseas posts produced 72,770 reporting cables, it presented 1,561 ministerial submissions and 20 Cabinet submissions, and it wrote 195 speeches and produced 4,069 briefings for its ministers. It is not necessary to accept the doubtful precision of the statistics (which have about them the whiff of a Soviet automobile factory's report on the Five-Year Plan) to accept that they show an authentic pattern of departmental activity. Importantly, the statistics show immediately that the department writes a lot. It deals with words.

When Cardinal Richelieu invented the idea of the modern foreign ministry in 1626, he was responding to a need to coordinate and centralise information that had previously been spread among different secretaries of state. That basic job of coordinating information has been at the centre of what foreign ministries do ever since. Like all foreign ministries, DFAT's Canberra headquarters is at base a storage and retrieval device for information.

Record-keeping is the core of any bureaucratic system, of course. But it is especially important in foreign affairs because policy often has to be implemented in several different countries at different times. It needs to be filtered through several different languages and cultures, and to be expressed by different officials. Once ministers have conveyed their views to overseas counterparts, to domestic colleagues and to the media, and DFAT officials have talked to local diplomatic missions, and ambassadors in several different countries have spoken on instruction to foreign governments, the dangers are high that unless the policy is clearly expressed through all these processes, what results will be a game of Chinese whispers. "The high-roads of history", wrote Sir Harold Nicolson, "are strewn with little shrines of peace which have either been left unfinished, or have collapsed when completed, for the sole reason that their foundations were built on the sands of some verbal misconception".[14]

Words shape DFAT's daily agenda in the way figures do Treasury's. On the one hand are the words in the 72,000 reporting cables from its overseas posts, piling up relentlessly in the computers of its staff, describing the outside world and prescribing and requesting actions to deal with it. (In responses to our 2001 questionnaire, 61 per cent of DFAT policy officers nominated cables from overseas posts as the main source of their information on foreign policy.) On the other hand are the words of the Australian media, shaping the government's priorities in Canberra. As discussed in Chapter 3, the department's routines and policy formulation take place largely through the currency of foreign policy specific language, complete with its substructures of shared understandings between participants. Words form a predominant part of DFAT's policy responses as well: in the form of instructions to missions; messages or negotiations with other governments; speeches delivered by the ministers; responses to media inquiries; or memos to other departments of government.

At times, DFAT's relationship to words has contributed to criticism and stereotyping. Writing of the early years of the department, Paul Hasluck reflected that:

> It pondered long to produce little. It had little administrative capacity or experience in handling a subject in the full manner of the public service but seemed to concentrate on forming and expressing an opinion rather than considering ways in which the desired end could be achieved. It tended to leave administrative action to other departments and devote itself to preparing well-considered appreciations of diplomatic situations.[15]

It is no longer a fair comment. Like the Australian public service as a whole, DFAT has become much more conscious of its accountability and responsiveness to government, and of the need for its work to focus on outcomes rather than analysis. Increasingly, DFAT is expected by its ministers to be able to tender almost immediate contextualisation and advice about breaking developments, and to respond rapidly to the policy initiatives of other states.

Another aspect of organisational policy-making involves the marshalling of resources to meet the demands of ongoing policy work. Here the Secretary of DFAT, like his counterparts in the domestic departments of the Australian public service, has great autonomy in how to spend the department's running-costs budget (around $766 million in 2001–02).[16] The Secretary can determine staff numbers, recruit people, and decide how much to pay them, where they should work and under what conditions, so long as the relevant provisions of the Public Service Act are met. This flexibility sets DFAT apart from most comparable foreign ministries according to a 2000 Best Practice Review, which compared the department with counterpart organisations in Canada, Germany, Japan, the Netherlands, New Zealand, Sweden and the United Kingdom.[17]

Because there is no central public-service board or finance department second-guessing or resisting the deployment of resources where the Secretary wants to send them, the Australian foreign ministry is able to respond reasonably quickly and fluidly to changing priorities. The opening and closing of specific diplomatic posts remains a decision for the government, however, not least because of the potential domestic political implications. This is seen most clearly in the history of a number of Australia's smaller Mediterranean posts like Malta and Cyprus, whose continued existence owes more to pressure from migrant communities in Australia than to the needs of Australian foreign policy.

DFAT has important tasks beyond foreign policy. It takes care of the consular needs of the 3.6 million Australians who travel overseas each year, and especially the 24,000 or so who find themselves in trouble of some sort. It issues passports (almost 1 million in 2001–02). In addition, it has to manage the financial and physical resources (property, communications infrastructure and money) necessary to perform these tasks.

Organisational routines

Like most other bureaucratic institutions, DFAT also operates according to a system of annual, weekly, daily and other periodic routines that ensure effective coordination of policy work, coverage of the policy space, and accountability. Internal coordination takes place through a regular and formalised series of meetings between the Secretary and senior staff and down through the divisional structure.

A major aspect of DFAT's annual cycle is its review process (discussed further in Chapter 10). Posts, divisions and individuals within the department are subject to formal and elaborate performance and resource-allocation reviews. All staff are on performance pay. While the work of monitoring and responding to significant developments in the everyday foreign policy space is constant and largely unrelenting, each year brings with it a prearranged, and increasingly full, diary of international and regional meetings, consultations, dialogues, and ministerial and prime ministerial visits. Each of these events generates substantial work during its lead-up, during the course of the event, and in its aftermath as agreements and resolutions are "actioned" in one way or another. Periods during which Parliament is sitting also generate additional work in preparing responses to parliamentary questions asked on notice, and trying to anticipate and brief the ministers for questions asked without notice.

Each week begins with a meeting on Monday morning between the Secretary and the deputy secretaries to set the week's work agenda. This agenda is determined by pressing foreign policy developments, upcoming meetings and other developments in the policy space, by the particular interests of the government and by the constant management demands of running a complex organisation. Meetings are also held weekly with division heads, and Strategic Planning meetings, at which major corporate and policy questions are addressed, are held regularly.[18] These various meetings are the principal means by which political and corporate priorities are determined and disseminated through the department.

In 2002, the Secretary and the four deputy secretaries met once a week with the Minister for Foreign Affairs and separately with the Minister for Trade if they were in Canberra. The relationship between Secretary and ministers is critical to effective foreign policy making.[19] The department works best when the relationship between the minister and the Secretary is sound without being subservient. The Secretary has to have the minister's trust, but to be confident enough to argue forcefully against bad policy. When the relationship is unhealthy – and that can mean too close as well as too distant – the consequences for policy can be serious.

At senior levels in DFAT, the daily cycle begins at 9 a.m. with a short meeting of the senior executive and the departmental spokesman to run through what the newspapers and early electronic media are saying, and to foreshadow what questions or requests from the ministers are likely to follow. Recently, technology has improved the access of most officers to the news clippings by making them electronically available. Depending on the day in question, the content of the newspapers can determine the work of parts of the organisation (as well generating requests to overseas posts for clarification or contextualisation of an issue) for the rest of the day.

At lower levels of the organisation, the daily routine develops usually in response to instructions flowing from the senior planning and media meetings, ongoing policy work, and the flow of incoming cables. For departmental desk officers, much of the day-to-day work of foreign policy can be routine: preparing briefings for the minister before a call by a visitor, replies to inquiries by Australian businesspeople, answers to possible parliamentary questions, comments on briefing notes written by others, cables of instruction to posts, responses to letters from irritated citizens, formal or informal consultation with other departments – all the inevitable and interminable cycle of bureaucracy. Just as importantly as the less-frequent major Cabinet submissions or policy papers for ministers, this accretion of day-to-day activity helps to shape foreign policy. The department is the filter through which much information reaches its ministers, and it prepares the drafts of the speeches and statements that articulate government policy.

A significant part of the day of a large proportion of policy officers involves reading and responding to the cables that come in from the posts. Whereas once they were laboriously drafted, typed, encoded and telexed, cables now come in via an enclosed and encrypted email system known by the acronym of SATIN, which recently replaced its predecessor, ADCNet, which pioneered the new form of communication with the posts. We discuss the implications of ADCNet and SATIN for the work of foreign policy makers in Chapter 10.

DFAT's staff

Who are the people who are advising on and implementing Australian foreign policy? In 2001–02, DFAT's Australian-recruited staff numbered 1,959. Seventeen per cent of them (332) were overseas. Nearly 1,500 additional staff were designated "staff recruited overseas"; that is, mainly support staff for overseas missions.[20]

The first thing to say about the advisers on whose judgement so much foreign policy rests is that they are clever, competent and lucky enough to have made their way through a demanding and highly competitive selection process. Foreign and trade policy work is complex, demanding and engrossing. It carries with it an aura (fading but pervasive) of glamour and adventure that can not be matched by, say, the Australian Bureau of Statistics or the Department of Industry. As a result, DFAT is able to recruit from a very large pool of highly qualified applicants. Around 25,000 Australian university graduates applied for 25 positions in the department's 2003 intake.[21]

Although efforts are made to encourage applications from a wide variety of backgrounds, 60 per cent of departmental officers surveyed in 2001 reported that their principal area of academic study had been the humanities or social sciences (24 per cent studied political science or international relations, 17 per cent history or classics). Seventeen per cent had economics backgrounds, 12.5 per cent had studied law and fewer than 5 per cent had studied sciences. Of the 2002 intake of twenty-five graduates, three held PhDs, four had masters degrees and fourteen a combined or double degree. The bulk of the 2002 recruits had arts degrees (sometimes combined with others). Eight were lawyers, eight had economics, business or commerce backgrounds, and one had training in nursing. They were mostly aged in their mid-twenties. Asian-language skills were marked (four were Japanese speakers, three spoke Mandarin, two Korean, three

Indonesian and one Vietnamese). French (seven speakers) was still the most widely spoken language, however.

The department has traditionally been one of the great seedbeds of recruitment for the Australian public service. Many departmental officers have gone on to occupy high positions in other departments or in politics. Four of its ministers (Casey, Hasluck, Gordon Bilney and Alexander Downer) have previously worked in the department. In 2003, the department was in the unique position of having former officers as both minister and shadow minister. This is a valuable bureaucratic asset, not because ministers who have served in the department are likely to be a mouthpiece for its interests, but because there is less distance to go in establishing the trust that makes the policy-making process easier and, at least arguably, more productive.

Departmental culture

An often-commented-upon attribute of DFAT's staff is the extent to which they share a common departmental culture: a set of understandings, behaviours and norms that affect the ways in which they do their work. It has long been known that any recruit joining a large organisation is subject to some level of acculturation into the environment of his or her new workplace. There are a number of attributes that contribute to a powerful departmental culture in DFAT. One is the awareness of its recruits that they have been selected from among thousands of applicants for one of a handful of highly sought-after jobs. Another is the knowledge that they are (actually or potentially) dealing with highly sensitive policy issues that could affect the fortunes of the country. Yet another factor is that DFAT staff cycle between overseas postings and Canberra, a process that tends to isolate them from much of the rest of the bureaucracy.

The DFAT culture has changed over time. It is less intense and exclusive than it once was, but it remains powerful. In its force, if not its form, it is as strong as military culture. And like military culture it is shaped by the shared, distinctive experiences of departmental officers who work in more intense relationships with each other than do most Australians, sometimes in hard conditions in small overseas posts, whose jobs involve all members of their family, who are used to frequent changes of assignment and who share a sense of distinctiveness from the rest of the workforce.

The earliest model for the culture of the new Australian diplomatic service was British. Writing about the diplomat and minister after whom the DFAT building is named, an early External Affairs officer, Harold Marshall, recalls that:

> Casey's own beginnings in External Affairs ... gave him an abiding concern for
> the expansion of its staff to cope with ever-growing interests and commitments.
> In particular he was on the lookout for 'good men', which for him meant that
> they should be well-educated with appropriate background, namely private school
> or senior military and well-connected socially. He was attracted not just to
> Australians but also (and to some extent more so) qualified Britishers whose
> vision and experiences were usually so much wider than our own.[22]

Some felt, however, that not enough of a service culture was developing. After
his retirement, Sir Walter Crocker, a senior diplomat who served for eighteen
straight years as a head of mission, regretted that, "The terms of service and the
appeal of the diplomatic life are such that we could have got a *corps d'élite*
rather in the way the British did in the old Sudan Service". But Australia had
failed because "a *corps d'élite* is too uncongenial to Australian prejudices".[23]

Through the 1970s and 1980s, social changes in Australia and the world
further altered the character and culture of the department. First, women, who
under Australian public-service regulations had to resign on marriage until
1966,[24] came to form a much larger percentage of the department's staff. By
2002, 46 per cent of total Australia-based staff and 20 per cent of the members
of the Senior Executive Service (SES) were women, compared with 43 per cent
of total staff and 13 per cent of the SES in 1996. (As late as 1991 just 2 per cent
of the senior ranks of the department were women.) Of the seventy-nine grad-
uate trainees recruited from 2000 to 2002 (around twenty-five each year), more
than half were women (forty-three, compared with thirty-six men). By 2002,
however, women were still leaving the department in disproportionate numbers
at middle ranks for family reasons.

A second important change was that the "closed shop", which preserved
almost all jobs in the department for its own cadre of specially recruited officers, crumbled before legislative and social pressures. Legal and administrative
reforms made it mandatory for all jobs in all Australian Government departments to be open to all Australian citizens. In 2001, around 20 per cent of bulk
round promotions (that is, promotions to generic foreign service officer positions) were filled by external applicants, and 70 per cent of specialist positions
went to outsiders. Although the rates at which DFAT staff have left the department have remained relatively consistent over thirty years, the most recent
trends in the development of a departmental culture further weaken the idea of
diplomacy as a lifelong commitment. Reflecting a more mobile Australian
workforce, the tendency of some new entrants to "get a language, do a posting
and piss off", as one of them put it, is growing.

A third cultural change has been driven in particular by the revolution in information technology and the subsequent blurring of "policy" and "support" jobs as electronic communications transformed the workplace. This saw the formal end of "streaming", under which an elite of specially recruited foreign affairs officers, with a career path likely to take them to jobs as ambassadors, were assisted by separate groups of clerical and administrative officers, keyboard staff and communications specialists. Multiskilling and de-streaming became the watchwords of departmental administration in the early 1990s.[25] Formal barriers for advancement from bottom to top were dismantled. The results were mixed. Some very able officers recruited outside the DFAT main-stream were given opportunities they would otherwise have missed. Others found it a struggle to adjust to policy work.

The most important change in the culture of the department, however, came in 1987, with the amalgamation of Foreign Affairs with the Trade Department, a department with its own strong cultural sense. Trade officers saw themselves as can-do, practical, tough-minded, and focussed on Australian interests, espe-cially in contrast with the wimpy foreign affairs types with whom they were now forced to cohabit. The shock was great on the other side as well. ("They wore shorts and long socks. They knew about peas and beans and loved knowing about them", one observer recalled.) But although the transition was difficult, it was handled effectively by successive departmental secretaries and senior staff, and by as early as 1992 a new synthesised departmental culture – stronger than either of its two component parts – was evident to people inside the department. The trade policy role strengthened the department by helping it to build a domestic constituency and to articulate its role much more easily to the general public. The environment, especially at overseas posts, became more practical and more commercially aware. Few within the department would argue in favour of a return to a separate trade ministry. Strong debate takes place about ways of preserving and developing technical expertise on trade, and old trade hands complain that the "political" types have taken over, but for most of the department's younger officers the debate has an increasingly artificial feel.

The world view of DFAT officers

There is nothing natural or obvious about how people approach foreign policy work. Making foreign policy is as heavily influenced by the world view of the people involved in the process as it is by a range of other more obvious factors: the ideology of the government; the stance of allies; the issues at stake. Because of its great complexity, anyone contemplating international politics has to adopt a mental framework that selects some events as important while disregarding others. Such frameworks comprise a range of concepts and beliefs about the nature of world politics that are knitted together into a more or less coherent pattern. They also are shaped by value judgements about conditions in the outside world: trade barriers, authoritarian regimes, terrorism, anti-globalisation protests, the poverty of some states. These world views strongly affect how their holders react to various events in world politics: which are important; whether they are good or bad for the country or more generally; what is the appropriate type of response.

In 2001 we sent a lengthy questionnaire survey to the department's policy officers (that is, those who described themselves as being involved, either in Canberra or at overseas posts, in policy work). One of our aims was to examine how Australia's diplomats understand the world in which they are working (the results of the survey can be found in the Appendix). Interestingly, it seemed to be experience rather than inclination that shaped the world views of DFAT officers. Asked whether their views on the way the world operates had changed as a result of their experience in working in DFAT, 48 per cent said they had changed "a great deal" and a further 49 per cent said they had changed "somewhat".

Our questionnaire was partly designed to gauge which of three different conceptions of the nature of world politics foreign policy makers fell into. At the risk of simplifying a broad range of impressions about the outside world, we coded the responses according to whether they fell into one of three basic orientations to world politics, loosely based on the three-part framework developed by Martin Wight and later Hedley Bull.[26] Based on conceptions of the "logic" of world politics, the relative importance of interests and ideals in state action, the nature and status of the state, and the possibilities of complementary interests in world politics, we classified responses in terms of the categories of realist, liberal and idealist.[27] These are broad, approximate characterisations. They differ from Wight's and Bull's "Hobbesian, rationalist/Grotian and Kantian" simply because we are uncomfortable with their application of the philosophy of these thinkers to contemporary international relations. On the other hand, realist, liberal and idealist are readily identifiable tags in twentieth-century international relations, and thus not as vulnerable to the danger of anachronism.

A realist world view tends to see world politics as invariably conflictual and driven by power calculi; states as best-served by attending to their interests rather than general ideals; and the state as the predominant actor in world politics for a long time to come. Liberals tend to see world politics as sometimes conflictual but often cooperative as states are motivated to maximise their own welfare; they believe that states should look to their own interests but should seek to advance certain ideals where this is consistent with their interests, and that states operate – whether conflictually or cooperatively – within norms of acceptable behaviour identified as being to the common good of all. Idealists abjure much of the status quo: they see world politics as potentially evolutionary towards a more just structure; ideals as the most important motivator in world politics; the old, interest-based state as inevitably on the decline; and the growing importance of ideals as bringing about a more cooperative, just international system.

Our survey revealed strongly that with a few deviations on specific issues, the "default" world view of most of those surveyed is traditionally realist; that is, power-based and interest-based, and centred still on the nation-state. Sixty-eight per cent of respondents agreed that

> as a result of your experience in working in DFAT you believe that traditional considerations of power relativities – in other words "realist" approaches to foreign policy – offer the best understanding of the way the world works.

In other questions on the nature of the "logic" of world politics, a more liberal conception is dominant over the relentlessly conflictual view of realism. Eighty-seven per cent of policy officers responding defined the international system in competitive terms; but of these, 50 per cent thought world politics was "basically competitive, but usually within the limits of acceptable behaviour". Just 13 per cent of them thought it was "potentially dangerously competitive at all times" (the hardline realist position). And the idealist position – seeing the world as basically or increasingly cooperative – gained just 12 per cent of responses.

Similarly, respondents clustered mostly around liberal conceptions of the place of values *vis-à-vis* interests in the conduct of foreign policy. While realists often see values in foreign policy as either dangerous or hypocritical, and idealists see values as crucial in moving foreign policy away from interest-based conceptions, liberals see values as important – particularly where they uphold order and have a stabilising influence on world politics – but never to the extent that they can damage a state's interests. This view of the world was reflected in judgements about the values officers thought should be injected into policy-making. When it was put to them that, "The only time that principles demonstrating concern for human well-being in other societies should be a determining factor in foreign policy is when it enhances the effectiveness of that policy", 77.2 per cent answered that it "depends on the stakes involved" (only 4.5 per cent agreed in all situations, and a significant 17 per cent argued that concern for human well-being should never be subordinated to other policy goals). Sixty-two per cent approved of the statement "the policy is intended to benefit Australia, even if disadvantageous to other states", while 87.1 per cent disagreed that policy should be determined by considerations that it would not hurt anyone.

Importantly, these realist–liberal conceptions – more inclined to see the "logics" underlying world politics as fairly constant – endured, despite a majority of those surveyed reporting a belief that world politics had changed in important ways on the surface in recent years. A huge majority (91 per cent) believed that the subject matter of world politics had changed since they joined the department. The changes with the greatest effect on foreign policy making were seen as globalisation, the end of the Cold War, "new security issues", a rise in ethnic conflict, and a shift from strategic to economic competition between states. Significantly, 59 per cent of respondents described these changes as profound and enduring. Just 13 per cent thought they were surface changes and that the underlying logic of world politics was unchanged. Asked whether and how globalisation was changing foreign policy making, 92 per cent saw the realm of foreign policy as becoming more diffuse, with more issues and more complexity. The same percentage saw a greater need to interact with actors other than the foreign ministries of states. This recognition of globalisation's changes does not seem to translate into any fundamental change of view about the role of the nation-state, however: 55 per cent of respondents disagreed that states were becoming less influential in world politics (33 per cent agreed).

Respondents to the questionnaire had a complex range of views about Australia's influence in international relations and their own influence on Australian foreign policy making. Although 67 per cent disagreed that Australia was a marginal player in the world, 28 per cent agreed. And while 51 per cent agreed that Australia was important in the East Asian region, only slightly fewer (46 per cent) disagreed. Asked how much freedom of choice and initiative Australian foreign policy makers have in world politics, 59 per cent believed that Australia had some freedom of choice and initiative "on issues other than those of interest to great powers", and 30 per cent believed that "Australia is able to influence major issues in ways important to Australia". Eight per cent said Australia had "almost no" freedom of choice, except in less-compelling issues. Just 0.4 per cent believed that Australia had a "great deal" of choice and initiative. Interestingly, for most respondents Australia is losing ground in its international influence. Rather more than half of the respondents agreed (40.6 per cent) or agreed strongly (11.6 per cent) that it is now harder for Australia to influence outcomes in world politics. Forty per cent disagreed.

On the whole, DFAT policy officers seem satisfied with their personal capacity to influence foreign policy (these results are heavily correlated with the seniority of the respondent). Seventy-seven per cent believed that they had some influence on foreign policy ("Ministers make policy decisions but I have an opportunity to shape the nature of policy"). Sixteen per cent felt they had not very much influence on foreign policy ("Ministers make policy: I just implement it"). Six per cent felt they had the "capacity to shape the outcomes of foreign policy in important ways".

We have examined these various aspects of DFAT, from its internal administrative structures and cycles of routines to the nature of its staff and their organisational culture and world view, because understanding how foreign policy is made requires a substantive grasp of this core institution in the foreign policy bureaucracy. While other elements of the foreign policy process become involved to varying extents at different times and with differing functions, DFAT remains perennially involved: monitoring, communicating, drafting, filing, reviewing and implementing. And each of the aspects of the department we have reviewed has a significant impact on the nature of DFAT's involvement and influence in foreign policy making: from internal structures, processes and routines that determine how and by whom certain policy issues are addressed, to the training and character of its staff, their acculturation to departmental norms, and their shared outlooks about the nature of world politics. Yet as influential and central as DFAT is, it is by no means the only department of the Australian Federal Government that is involved in foreign policy making. It is to the other departments involved in foreign policy that we now turn.

The rest of the bureaucracy

One of globalisation's most obvious consequences has been to increase greatly the number of issues under the purview of government that have an international dimension. This is not a new phenomenon, but globalisation has increased its scale and changed its form. A much broader range of departments and agencies are engaged in international policy formulation, and these are developing their own direct network of links with external counterparts, often outside centralised channels. Anne-Marie Slaughter has described this process as "transgovernmentalism". Slaughter sees the state

> disaggregating into its separate, fundamentally distinct parts. These parts – courts, regulatory agencies, executives, even legislatures – are networking with their

counterparts abroad, creating a dense web of relations that constitutes a new trans-governmental order [which is] rapidly becoming the most widespread and effective mode of international governance.[28]

This seems like an overstatement, certainly outside Europe, but the trend is clear in Australia.

The networking that supports this process has been made possible by cheap and rapid communications. Officers in departments dealing with, say, disease control in livestock, or pharmaceutical regulation, or competition policy, can be in direct touch by email or telephone with colleagues in counterpart agencies overseas in ways that were impossible a decade ago. DFAT can no longer use its control of the government communications network to keep a coordinating eye on the activities of other agencies. Regional organisations such as APEC have opened up new patterns of international contacts for domestic departments. A process of bureaucratic disintermediation is at work. DFAT officers recognise the changes globalisation has brought about. Seventy-five per cent of policy officers responding to our questionnaire agreed that foreign policy was no longer the exclusive preserve of "specialist" international departments, and 69 per cent agreed or agreed strongly that foreign ministries had less control over sources of advice and information on foreign policy.

Almost all Australian Federal Government departments acknowledge the importance of the international dimension in their work; today there are very few without a branch dedicated to the international aspects of their portfolio. It is important to note that some Federal Government departments have long had international aspects to their work. The Department of Immigration and Multi-cultural and Indigenous Affairs (DIMIA), for example, has always had an external focus because of the job it does and where it does it. (In 2001 it had 157 Australia-based staff overseas and a further 630 locally engaged staff over-seas, employed on its behalf by DFAT.)[29] Every one of the "notable priorities" listed by DIMIA in its business directions document for 2001 to 2003 – relat-ing mostly to illegal arrivals and people-smuggling – had an important foreign policy dimension.[30]

There are other, more clearly domestically focussed departments that have more recently begun paying more attention to the international aspects of their policy responsibilities. For example, of the nine key challenges the Department of Agriculture, Fisheries and Forestry's corporate plan listed for 2001 to 2004, three ("further trade opportunities for our portfolio industries", "provide services to assist Australian exports", and "effective quarantine arrangements")[31] were directly connected with the external environment. The Department of Education,

Science and Training expresses an even broader view of its international responsibilities, describing itself as helping to underpin "Australia's ability to engage in productive dialogue on education issues, *as well as sensitive matters including regional security, environmental protection and trade*".[32] In 2001 the department had counsellors at Australian overseas missions in Bangkok, Beijing, New Delhi, Hanoi, Jakarta, Kuala Lumpur, Paris, Seoul, Taipei and Tokyo, helping to promote Australian education and training (and to sell its own services).

For the most part, the involvement of such domestically focussed portfolios in foreign policy is sporadic and rarely profound. The core foreign policy making institutions are kept relatively well-appraised of their international linkages and initiatives, and the collegial culture that occurs within the foreign policy making process more often than not extends to relationships between DFAT and the other departments. When the policy responsibilities of one of the other departments becomes subject to major international negotiations, DFAT and its overseas network usually become closely involved, often with significant influence on the preparations and negotiations. A good example can be found within the bailiwick of the Department of Environment and Heritage (DEH), which acquired a significant international dimension in the process of negotiating the Kyoto Protocol on global warming and during the ongoing uncertainty in relation to the ratification of that instrument. On such a crucial set of negotiations, DFAT and the other institutions in the foreign policy process were involved from an early stage. Policy and strategy were initially developed by DEH in consultation with DFAT, PM&C and various other departments, and members of DEH were joined by DFAT staff (including the Ambassador for the Environment) during the Kyoto negotiations. On such issues policy coordination becomes crucial: Australia's global-warming policy-making was coordinated through several intra-bureaucratic mechanisms (see below); but also – and most critically – at the highest levels of politics, became subject to repeated Cabinet discussions and the detailed attention of the Prime Minister and his office.

Although most government departments have external interests, the number that can influence the central issues of foreign policy is more limited. The departments of Defence, Treasury, and the Prime Minister and Cabinet are the most important of these. Each becomes involved in foreign policy for different reasons and has a different impact.

The Department of Defence is the largest and costliest of all the Australian government departments.[33] How large and how costly is very difficult to determine. In 2001–02 its annual budget was around $14.6 billion and it employed around 88,000 people. More than 80 per cent of them were in the permanent Australian Defence Force (ADF) or the Reserve. Defence's size and structure have some important consequences. First, the department is highly self-absorbed. It is, in the words of one former senior official, a service-delivery institution not a policy institution. A great deal of its bureaucratic energy is expended inwardly, in the task of managing itself and balancing the different interests and structures of the civilian establishment and the ADF and its individual services. The management "diarchy" – that is, the shared responsibilities of the Secretary of Defence and the Chief of the Defence Force – has generated an elaborate, time-consuming and delicately balanced internal management structure. A consequence of this is that Defence has been less likely than might be thought to be a driver of the general strategic policy debate or to try to shape foreign policy outcomes.

The two principal areas of Defence most connected with foreign policy – the people under the control of the Deputy Secretary, Strategic Policy, and Deputy Secretary, Intelligence and Security – are small in terms of Defence's numbers and cost little more than $250 million. The Strategic Policy group covers divisions responsible for Policy Guidance and Analysis, Strategic and International Policy, and Strategic Command. Its job is to provide strategic policy advice to the government "to enable it to make sound decisions on Australia's strategic circumstances and on specific security issues as they arise". The Intelligence and Security Group is examined in Chapter 7.

At working levels, and especially within the uniformed ranks, the Defence Department's view of itself in relation to DFAT tends towards stereotype (wimpish diplomats versus practical, action-oriented warriors), but that divide is not apparent in the policy debate, and it is hard to identify a distinct strategic-policy culture in that department. Defence finds it easy to dominate policy in areas relating to force structure, but beyond that it has relatively little influence on foreign policy. Defence decisions are made slowly, and strategic policy needs to be revisited only cautiously and over time. Foreign policy decisions are often immediate and require quick responses.

In a different way, defence can have major implications for foreign policy through Australia's various overseas deployments. Defence has played an important part – though in an operational rather than a policy-directing sense – in recent foreign policy issues including East Timor, peacekeeping on Bougainville and Solomon Islands, and border-control issues. In one sense, the Defence role in, say, the Cambodian peacekeeping operation represented crucial support for a decade-long Australian foreign policy initiative, and gave that initiative crucial "weight" in the latter stages of the Cambodia Peace Process. In another sense, the ADF and its capacity to deploy overseas can be a decisive attribute in the influence Australian foreign policy makers are able to wield, whether through the ongoing Australian force commitments to the Five Power Defence Arrangement, or as part of the Coalition forces in Iraq. In yet another sense, defence linkages – from joint exercises and co-training arrangements to "one-and-a-half-track" dialogues with various Asia–Pacific countries – are often fostered as a crucial part of certain bilateral relationships. For many foreign policy makers, the international linkages of the Defence Department provide crucial "ballast" to certain bilateral relationships in the Asia–Pacific.

Defence has an influence on a range of other foreign policy issues, including arms control (a role that has increased as arms-control issues have moved from a focus on weapons of mass destruction to conventional weapons like landmines), peacekeeping and defence cooperation programs. The Defence Cooperation Program – Defence's aid branch – is sometimes seen as an important instrument of foreign policy leverage, especially in the South Pacific. Its effectiveness in this role has been mixed at best, however.

Within government, strategic policy is coordinated through the Strategic Policy Coordination Group (SPCG), which comprises the relevant deputy secretaries and division heads from DFAT, Defence and PM&C. The SPCG meets regularly (at least monthly and often more frequently) to coordinate policy on a range of broadly strategic issues.

Globalisation and growing economic interdependence after the Cold War have also given traditional foreign policy issues a more obvious economic dimension. As problems of coordination during the Asian financial crisis of 1997–98 revealed, this has increased the importance of effective consultation between Treasury, the Department of Finance, the Reserve Bank of Australia and DFAT. On matters ranging from the political impact of the conditionality of IMF loans to Indonesia during the financial crisis of 1997, to ways of tracking and preventing funding for terrorist groups after 11 September 2001, the Treasury and the Reserve Bank have a direct impact on important foreign policy issues. They are the regular participants on behalf of Australia in the annual meetings of major international and regional economic and financial organisations. Treasury and the Finance Department attend to Australia's interests in the World Bank and the IMF, while the Reserve Bank is a member of a regional structure known as EMEAP – the Executive Meeting of East Asian and Pacific Central Banks – which acquired prominence before and during the Asian financial crisis.

All of these organisations have played an increasingly internationalised role since the mid-1980s. To take one example, Treasury's 2000–01 Annual Report identified the links between globalisation, growth, poverty and inequality, financing arrangements within the Asian region, conditionality in IMF programs, encouraging greater transparency, and the implementation of standards and codes and poverty-reduction strategies as among the key debates to which it was contributing.[34] Treasury's Economic Group provides the government with advice on strategic international economic policy issues, manages Australian participation in international financial institutions and international forums such as the IMF, World Bank and Asian Development Bank, and monitors and analyses developments in key global economies. In 2001, Treasury had its own representatives in Washington, London, Paris, Tokyo, Beijing and Jakarta.

After the Asian financial crisis of 1997–98 revealed problems in the co-ordinating of economics-related foreign policy issues within government, an International Economic Coordination Group (an economic equivalent of the SPCG) was established at deputy-secretary level between Treasury, DFAT and PM&C. Given that international economic issues are likely to become more rather than less important in Australia's foreign relations in future, it is likely that such economics-related coordination will continue to be crucial.

Bureaucratic coordination: The role of PM&C

Of all the departments in Canberra, only PM&C has the capacity to mirror DFAT at every point. The department was created in 1911, its Cabinet Office functions date from the mid-1940s, and direct policy-advising functions developed from the mid-1950s, and more directly after 1975 under the Fraser Government.[35] A former Secretary of PM&C, Dr Michael Keating, has described the department's contemporary role in the following terms:

> in the field of substantive policy advising, the Department's aim is to ensure that decision-making is fully informed by providing the Prime Minister with information, analysis and advice on all matters coming to Cabinet and on any matter with which he has to deal. We do not attempt to take over the role of line departments, but we have close links with them and know who to ask for a quick answer. Our essential role is to add value, not to duplicate, and what we aim to bring to the policy process, which is not so readily available from line departments, is:
> • A whole-of-government perspective that comes from our policy coordination role;
> • A nation-wide perspective that comes from our continuing liaison with the States;
> • A developed sense of what the Prime Minister, as the chair of Cabinet, needs and how he wants things done; and
> • Expertise on government processes and how things can be handled.[36]

PM&C is the most protean of the Australian public-service departments. It changes priorities and therefore shape with each new Prime Minister, shifting resources, adjusting structures, taking on new functions and dumping others in accordance with the new Prime Minister's political priorities and interests. So issues – multicultural affairs, youth, women, the environment, families – will settle for a short time in PM&C and fly off elsewhere when political fashion or government preferences change. At the core of the department, however, is a divisional structure that mirrors the other departments of state.

In all its permutations, PM&C has had responsibilities for external policy. Indeed, until the McMahon Government changed the arrangements in 1972, the Prime Minister's Department, not External Affairs, was responsible for relations with Britain, on the grounds that these were not foreign relations. The department's International Division covers the Department of Foreign Affairs and Trade. A new National Security Division was created in mid-2003 to cover Defence, Security, intelligence, counter-terrorism, border protection and law enforcement. PM&C is also responsible for guests of government coming to Australia and for the Prime Minister's overseas visits. The Department's capacity and willingness to act as an alternative source of advice to the Prime Minister and his office on foreign policy matters vary according to the style and preferences of the Prime Minister. In this sense, the department does not have permanent, independent, bureaucratic interests in the way that DFAT, Treasury or Defence do.

Most senior PM&C officials at any given time will define the department's role in terms of coordination, but in practice it can be much more than that, and often is. A good deal depends on the people in it at any given time. Because PM&C is an excellent place for capable public servants to get an overview of the government, and because it is a good place for the same public servants to be noticed and promoted, it tends to attract strong people – and that in turn strengthens its influence within the bureaucracy. Work in PM&C was seen to be a route to promotion and career advancement by 42 per cent of DFAT officers we surveyed in 2001, a higher figure than for any other area except the minister's office, the South and Southeast Asia Division, and the department's Executive Branch. At times DFAT attempts to assert its own influence by seconding senior officials to PM&C. This was the norm at the end of the 1990s. In earlier periods, DFAT staff were required to resign to take up appointments in International Division. Each approach shapes the character of the division's relationship with DFAT in different ways.

The Department's power comes from proximity to the Prime Minister, from the capacity to brief him before Question Time or Cabinet, to draft his speeches, to shape his policy responses through briefing, and to some extent (although his international adviser is more important in this regard) to control the flow of paper and information to him. The Department also provides the secretariat for both the Secretaries Committee on National Security (SCNS), which is considered in more detail in Chapter 7, and the National Security Committee of Cabinet, so it has an important role in interpreting and circulating the government's decisions on foreign affairs. PM&C also has a central crisis-management responsibility. In the Gulf War at the beginning of the 1990s and the East Timor crisis at the end of the decade, PM&C directly managed the government's coordinating process.

The main coordinating mechanism for foreign policy, as for all other issues in government, is personal contact and discussion between different departments. More formally, interdepartmental committees (IDCs) serve this purpose. Some of these are standing IDCs (the SPCG and the International Economic Coordination Group, or IECG), others are formed for special purposes (the East Timor Task Force), and still others are ad hoc.

Australia's foreign and strategic policy community is small. The large institutional rivalries that are familiar in the analysis of policy-making in Washington, DC, are largely absent in Canberra. A substantial proportion – nearly 70 per cent – of DFAT officers responding to our 2001 survey characterise their professional contacts with officers in other Commonwealth departments and agencies as "mostly collegial, but competitive at times", compared with only 2.7 per cent who see them as "invariably competitive/conflictual" and 5.8 per cent who see them as "mostly competitive but collegial at times". "Finance/money" was by far the most common reason seen for any bureaucratic conflicts (17.4 per cent) followed by "turf wars" (12.9 per cent).

Senior officers in DFAT, Defence, PM&C and the intelligence agencies have usually spent time working in other agencies. In 2003 the heads of Defence, Immigration, ONA, ASIS, ASIO and the International Division of PM&C all had backgrounds in DFAT. In the same year, the Secretary of DFAT and the four deputy secretaries had all worked outside the department in other relevant parts of the bureaucracy. This is not so much an indication of a national security establishment closing ranks, but of the small numbers of people in Australia who have made careers in these areas and the inevitable interconnections these have generated. As in any bureaucracy, this does not prevent turf battles, vigorous at times, but it does facilitate the spread of the same consensus, realist view of the world throughout the Australian foreign policy making machine.

Other parts of the bureaucracy are important to foreign policy making in various ways; some of them are involved in the substance of foreign policy in a regular and sustained way. In these realms of foreign policy, DFAT's internal structures, hierarchy, routines and culture no longer have the capacity to impose order and coordination. As we observed in Chapter 3, communication between bureaucratic departments is invariably horizontal, ruling out authoritative styles of communication. Coordination mechanisms therefore become extremely important to the coherence and flexibility of Australian foreign policy. Yet beyond the quality of these coordination mechanisms, the Australian foreign policy machinery runs smoothly for the most part, by virtue of a highly effective lubricant: basically warm, cooperative and collegial relations between a small number of senior officials who know each other well, having often worked together in DFAT or one of the other foreign policy related institutions. This is a very difficult aspect of the process to quantify, yet it is crucial to understanding how foreign policy is made in Australia. It also means that Australian foreign policy making must be understood using models very different to those used to describe the US foreign policy making system, with its higher levels of conflict and rivalry.

Conclusion

A number of participants in the foreign policy machinery of Australia – ministers and bureaucrats – nominated the character of Australia's foreign policy bureaucracy as a major contributor to its foreign policy capacity. The ability to respond quickly to events; to develop imaginative proposals for various international contexts; to master and analyse complex policy issues – all of these are crucial attributes of foreign policy capacity contributed by the foreign policy bureaucracy. In this chapter we have concentrated mostly on DFAT – its structures and processes, its personnel, culture and dominant world views – because of its centrality to the foreign policy bureaucracy itself. Yet we have also noted the important roles played by a number of other Federal Government departments, and the critical coordination role played by PM&C.

Yet important as it is, the bureaucracy in Canberra is not sufficient in itself to make and maintain foreign policy. Other institutions and actors play vital roles in the foreign policy process. Prominent among these are the elected politicians involved in foreign policy making, along with their offices, who play crucial roles in directing, deciding and implementing foreign policy at the highest levels. It is to these that we will turn in Chapter 5.

Notes

1 Max Weber, "Bureaucracy", in H.H. Gerth and C. Wright Mills (eds), *From Max Weber: Essays in Sociology*, trans. H.H. Gerth and C. Wright Mills, London: Routledge and Kegan Paul, 1977, pp. 211, 214.
2 Garrett Mattingly, *Renaissance Diplomacy*, New York: Dover Publications, 1955.

3 Keith Hamilton and Richard Langhorne, *The Practice of Diplomacy: Its Evolution, Theory and Administration*, London: Routledge, 1995, p. 73.
4 Paul Hasluck, *Diplomatic Witness*, Melbourne: Melbourne University Press, 1980, p. 3.
5 P.G. Edwards, *Prime Ministers and Diplomats: The Making of Australian Foreign Policy 1901–1949*, Melbourne: Oxford University Press, 1983, p. 93.
6 ibid., p. 105.
7 ibid., p. 180.
8 Henry S. Albinski, *Australian External Policy under Labor: Content, Process and the National Debate*, Brisbane: University of Queensland Press, 1977, p. 289.
9 Stuart Harris, "The Amalgamation of the Departments of Foreign Affairs and Trade" in *Managing Australia's Diplomacy: Three Views from the Top*, Occasional Paper No. 2, Melbourne: Australian Institute of International Affairs (Victorian Branch) and the School of Social Sciences, Deakin University, 1989, p. 19.
10 Department of Foreign Affairs and Trade Annual Report 2001–02, p. 21.
11 DFAT estimate, November 2001.
12 Department of Foreign Affairs and Trade Corporate Plan 2000–2002, pp. 2, 3.
13 Department of Foreign Affairs and Trade Corporate Plan 1993–1994, p. 5.
14 Harold Nicolson, *Diplomacy*, London: Thornton Butterworth, 1939, p. 113.
15 Hasluck, *Diplomatic Witness*, p. 16.
16 Department of Foreign Affairs and Trade Annual Report 2001–02, p. 21.
17 Foreign and Trade Ministry Best Practice Review, Report to the Secretary by R.C. Smith, August 2000, Restricted.
18 Department of Foreign Affairs and Trade Annual Report 2001–02, p. 197.
19 For an excellent account of the early history of the relationships between ministers and secretaries, see Garry Woodard, "Ministers and Mandarins: The Relationships between Ministers and Secretaries of External Affairs 1935–1970", *Australian Journal of International Affairs*, Vol. 54, No. 1, April 2000, pp. 79–95. Hasluck recounts the problems of Evatt and his First Secretary, Hodgson.
20 Department of Foreign Affairs and Trade Annual Report 2001–02, p. 16.
21 ibid., p. 205.
22 Harold Marshall, *Ignorance to Enlightenment: Fifty Years in Asia*, Australians in Asia Paper No. 18, Brisbane: Centre for the Study of Australia–Asia Relations, Griffith University, September 1997.
23 Sir Walter Crocker, *Travelling Back: Memoirs of Sir Walter Crocker*, Melbourne: Macmillan, 1981, p. 193.
24 On 18 November 1966, the Public Service Act was amended to permit married women to be appointed as permanent officers in the Commonwealth Public Service and to allow female officers to retain their permanent status in the service after marriage. A provision was also included in the Act to allow women to take leave during a confinement and to resume duty afterwards without loss of any rights.
25 For a background account of this period, see Geoffrey Forrester, "Policy Coordination in the Department of Foreign Affairs and Trade" in Patrick Weller, John Forster and Glyn Davis (eds), *Reforming the Public Service*, Melbourne: Macmillan/Centre for Australian Public Sector Management, 1993.

26 See Martin Wight, "Why Is There No International Theory?" in Herbert Butterfield and Martin Wight (eds), *Diplomatic Investigations*, London: George Allen & Unwin, 1966; Hedley Bull, *The Anarchical Society: A Study of Order in World Politics*, Basingstoke: Macmillan, 1977.

27 See also Robert Keohane's concept of cooperation in pursuit of self-interest (*After Hegemony: Cooperation and Discord in the World Political Economy*, Princeton, NJ: Princeton University Press, 1984); and the "possessive individualist" liberal conception discussed by Alexander Wendt (*Social Theory of International Politics*, Cambridge: Cambridge University Press, 1999) rather than the Doyle/Russet, Fukuyama or Moravcsik variants.

28 Anne-Marie Slaughter, "The Real New World Order", *Foreign Affairs,* September–October 1997.

29 http://www.immi.gov.au/annual_report/annrep01/report55.htm

30 ibid.

31 Department of Agriculture, Fisheries and Forestry Corporate Plan 2001–04.

32 http://www.dest.gov.au/iae/Default.htm (emphasis added).

33 How large and how costly is very difficult to determine. The most accessible and useful recent attempt to undertake this task is not in the Defence budget papers but in the Australian Strategic Policy Institute's publication *The Cost of Defence: ASPI Defence Budget Brief 2002–03*, Canberra: ASPI, 2002.

34 http://www.treasury.gov.au/documents/109/HTML/Part2_4.asp

35 Sir Geoffrey Yeend, *The Coordinating Role of the Department of the Prime Minister and Cabinet*, Perth: Royal Australian Institute of Public Administration, 1984; Patrick Weller, *Malcolm Fraser PM*, Ringwood: Penguin, 1989, p. 34.

36 Michael Keating, "The Role of the Department of the Prime Minister and Cabinet in the Policy-making Process: Adding Value", speech to AIC Conference, 17–18 May 1993, p. 10.

The Cambodia Peace Settlement

In November 1989, Michael Costello, then Deputy Secretary of the Department of Foreign Affairs and Trade, was sharing a meal at the home of an old friend, John Bowan, the foreign policy adviser to the Prime Minister, Bob Hawke. The two had known each other for years and had worked together in DFAT and the Office of National Assessments. In the first years of the Hawke Government, Costello had been Chief of Staff to the Foreign Minister, Bill Hayden, and his friendship with Bowan had been an important emollient in smoothing the sometimes uneasy relationship between the Prime Minister and the Foreign Minister, who had been Hawke's predecessor as party leader.

Costello was expressing frustration about his travel program. He was about to leave for Honolulu to take part in regular consultations on politico-military affairs with the United States; then, ten days later, he had to visit Japan. The additional travel time was time wasted. Recalling an exchange earlier in the evening about growing unease within the governing Australian Labor Party about the situation in Indochina, and especially about any possible return to power as part of a peace settlement by the brutal former Khmer Rouge Government, Bowan suggested that Costello fill in those few days by visiting Vietnam. Some good might be done, and it would at least demonstrate to critics that the government was doing something. Costello was receptive: something might come of it.

In an environment as complex as world politics, policy initiatives of any ambition invariably have many antecedents. But the conversation that night was one of the final tumblers dropping to unlock the gate to peace in Cambodia.

Six years earlier, in 1983, the new Australian Prime Minister, Bob Hawke, had proposed to his Foreign Minister, Bill Hayden, that the government should explore the prospects for an international dialogue to help resolve the violence-ridden situation in and around Cambodia. The ALP's opposition to Australian participation in the Vietnam War had been a defining political event for the

party, and there was continuing high party and public interest in the reverbera-
tions of that conflict.

Since 1978, when the genocidal Khmer Rouge regime of Pol Pot had been
driven from power by the Vietnamese army and replaced by a government
supported by Hanoi, Cambodia had continued to be wracked with violence and
instability. An estimated 2 million Cambodians had died in the turmoil. Two
groups of resistance forces – royalist supporters of the former king, Prince
Sihanouk, and nationalists – received support and sanctuary from neighbouring Thailand, the other ASEAN countries and the United States, while
remnants of the Khmer Rouge had continuing military and financial assistance
from China. The strategic aim of these external patrons was largely to contain
the Communist government in Hanoi, which had prevailed against the United
States and its allies in the Vietnam War, and to prevent the Soviet Union, Vietnam's ally, from gaining a larger foothold in the region.[1]

Hayden regarded Hawke's proposal "with some caution".[2] He recognised
that complex external interests, including those of Thailand and the ASEAN
countries, China, Vietnam and the United States were all caught up in Cambodia. Nevertheless, between 1983 and 1986 he made moves towards developing
relations with Vietnam and instituted talks with the principal parties involved
in the conflict. As he expected, he found Australia's room for manoeuvre in the
face of resistance from the ASEAN countries and the United States was
limited. On many of these visits he was accompanied by Costello.

By 1989, however, the international consequences of Mikhail Gorbachev's
radical changes to Soviet policy were opening up new opportunities. Moscow,
Vietnam's principal backer, was no longer willing or able to provide the
economic and military aid that had supported Hanoi, and relations between
China and the Soviet Union, and between the Soviet Union and the United
States, were improving. In the new international environment, the rationale for
the regional proxy conflicts between the great powers which had marked the
Cold War, and of which Indochina was a primary and tragic example, was
disappearing. In January 1989, Vietnam announced that it would withdraw all
its troops from Cambodia, making it easier for Thailand, Vietnam's traditional
rival for power in mainland Southeast Asia, to contemplate change. Each of the
key external parties to the Cambodia conflict now had a greater incentive to
reach a settlement.

In July 1989, France, the former colonial power in Indochina, and Indonesia, the largest of the ASEAN countries, had sponsored the Paris International
Conference on Cambodia, which brought together the four Cambodian
factions, the five permanent members of the UN Security Council, the six

ASEAN countries and others, including Australia, in a month-long effort to broker a comprehensive settlement. Australia's earlier efforts to facilitate dialogue had served to reinforce its standing as an involved participant in the conflict. The Paris conference came close to reaching agreement but stumbled on the issue of the participation of the Khmer Rouge in a quadripartite transitional administration. This prospect had caused considerable public unease, including in Australia, because of the brutal record of the Khmer Rouge.[3]

Not long after this diplomatic impasse, Hayden's successor as Australian Foreign Minister, Gareth Evans, had a conversation in New York with Stephen Solarz, a Democratic Congressman from the United States who had a long interest in Asia. Solarz suggested that one alternative to Khmer Rouge participation in a new Cambodian government might be to set up a UN-supervised administration, a model that had been followed earlier in Namibia. Evans was intrigued and directed his department to examine the idea. The outcome, a general proposal for United Nations supervision of Cambodia until UN-sponsored elections could be held, was set out in a speech by Evans to the Senate on 24 November.[4]

The initial international response to Evans's speech was positive. As he noted later, "It very quickly became clear that the idea was one whose time had come".[5]

It was at this time that Costello, with Evans's agreement, took up Bowan's suggestion and began what Evans described as an "extraordinary feat of diplomatically effective endurance".[6] It was becoming clear that the idea of transferring Cambodian sovereignty directly to the UN – the Solarz model – would be impossible both legally and politically. Some other approach would have to be devised. Costello left on his journey carrying a fairly blank slate. "It was buccaneering stuff. The ideas grew organically as it went along", Costello recalled. Evans's instructions to him had been, "Follow your nose and see where it leads you".[7] He began to explore the idea, drawn in turn from some British comments to the Australian High Commission in London, about the development of some sort of supreme national council to embody Cambodian sovereignty.

In Hanoi, the Vietnamese Foreign Minister, Nguyen Co Thach, remembered Costello from his earlier visits with Hayden. He was receptive to the Australian approach but suggested that Costello put the idea directly to the Hun Sen government. That led to a journey to Ho Chi Minh City for talks with the Cambodian Vice Foreign Minister, Sok An, who was also positive. Then, again at Thach's urging, Costello travelled to Phnom Penh to speak directly to Hun Sen, another contact from the Hayden days.

It was the beginning of an odyssey: a series of thirty meetings with key players in thirteen countries over twenty-one days straddling December 1989 to January 1990. With regular contact between Costello and Evans, the details of the Australian proposal were fleshed out. Costello's interlocutors included ministers and officials from Vietnam, Cambodia, Thailand, the Soviet Union, the United States, China, France and Britain, as well as the UN.[8]

By the end of the trip, it was clear that

the central principle of UN involvement in the administration of Cambodia was acceptable, or at the very least not rejected out of hand, by all factions and major players, with the exception of the Khmer Rouge.[9]

As Evans later described it,

The central concept of the Australian peace proposal was very simple. So as to sidestep the power-sharing issue which had bedevilled the Paris Conference, and constrain the role of the Khmer Rouge in the transitional arrangement, it was proposed that the United Nations be directly involved in the civil administration of Cambodia during the transitional period. Along with a UN military presence to monitor the ceasefire and cessation of external military involvement, and a UN role in organising and conducting elections, UN involvement in the transitional administrative arrangements would ensure a neutral political environment conducive to free and fair general elections. The proposal recognised that a logical consequence of such a role for the United Nations would mean having the Cambodian seat at the United Nations either declared vacant or transferred to a neutral representative Cambodian body for the duration of the transitional period. In other important regards, it preserved the objectives of a comprehensive political settlement as defined at the Paris Conference.[10]

The critical point for Evans was that

the Khmer Rouge could not be effectively isolated and marginalised, and its military influence nullified, so long as it continued to be supplied, especially by China, with arms, money and diplomatic support … Unless and until China was prepared to withdraw from the picture – and only the UN peace plan seemed capable of delivering that – then whatever Australia and other countries might choose to do, the continuation of bloody civil war was inevitable.[11]

Invited by Indonesian Foreign Minister Ali Alatas, who was co-chair of the Paris Conference, to attend as a "resource delegation" an informal regional meeting about Cambodia in Jakarta, Evans sent a delegation of Australian officials to Cambodia to gather information on the country's existing political and administrative structures and the way they would need to be supplemented to enable the UN to do the job. Such details included the practical requirements for the conduct of free and fair elections, and technical and administrative problems that would confront a peacekeeping force. Back in Canberra, Christmas holidays were interrupted by the establishment on 2 January 1990 of a Cambodia Task Force, chaired by Costello, and drawn from relevant geographical desks and from the UN and legal branches of DFAT. Around a dozen Australian public servants were involved in an eight-day, eighteen-hour-a-day drafting session in which Evans participated directly.[12]

In addition to DFAT staff, a Department of Defence liaison officer was appointed to the task force, and was directly involved in its work in Canberra and overseas. Ken Berry judged that

This close cooperation between the two main departments involved in the
Australian effort was a major factor in ensuring that the detailed proposals which
were to emerge were soundly based, practical and thus more likely to be accepted
by the various parties.[13]

The result of the task force's initial efforts was a 154-page series of working papers, later published as *Cambodia: An Australian Peace Proposal*, and known as the "Red Book" after the colour of its cover. The working papers canvassed the creation of a symbolic National Council to embody Cambodian sovereignty during the transitional period, and options for the UN in administering the country, conducting elections and keeping the peace. They also costed the operation. Perhaps the most important impact of the Australian effort was to show to many of the other participants in the search for a settlement "that it was not completely impossible to reduce the complexities of the Cambodian problem to a workable solution given the required political will".[14]

It took a further year after the Jakarta meeting on Cambodia, and many frustrations and setbacks, to develop the plan in meetings involving the permanent five members of the UN Security Council, Indonesia and the UN Secretariat. At many points along the way, the prospects for success looked grim. Then, in August 1990, the Permanent Five agreed on a framework document setting out the elements of the plan, and the four Cambodian parties agreed in September. Finally, in October 1991, the Paris Conference reconvened and the comprehensive settlement was signed.

The final plan was very close to the one Australia had outlined nearly two years earlier. The United Nations Transitional Authority in Cambodia (UNTAC) represented a major challenge for the UN. It involved the commitment of 16,000 troops, 3,600 police and 1,020 administrators from thirty different countries. An Australian military officer, Lieutenant General John Sanderson, was in charge of the peacekeeping force. Following an extensive voter-registration program, elections were held in May 1993 and attracted an overwhelming voter turnout of almost 90 per cent.

The diplomatic solution proposed by Australia did not solve all of Cambodia's problems. Both UNTAC and the new Cambodian Government installed in September 1993 struggled with formidable political and economic challenges. But by resolving the issue of outside support for internal political differences, the Australian initiative set Cambodia on a path towards normalcy.

Australian diplomacy in Cambodia succeeded for a number of reasons. Most importantly, as noted earlier, the timing was propitious. All the major actors were open to diplomatic solutions in a way that had not been true when Hayden had engaged with the problem a few years earlier. But that is not to say that the outcome was inevitable. Perhaps other countries could have provided a similar intellectual foundation for UN involvement, but none did so.

The reason for that underlines the second reason for Australia's success: Australia brought to the task a unique combination of sufficient policy interest in the problem to want to be involved, but sufficient disinterest in the modalities of the outcome to be accepted by the parties principal as an honest broker.

Third, thirty years of diplomatic investment in the region had given Australian diplomatic missions in Asia and officials in Canberra the skills base necessary to advise the policy-makers well and the credibility to advocate the Australian case persuasively in the region. In particular, Australia had developed a close relationship with Indonesia, the most important of the ASEAN countries, whose Foreign Minister, Ali Alatas, it consulted at every step. And, even while pursuing objectives that caused nervousness in Washington, DC, it brought to the diplomatic task the immense asset of the alliance relationship with the United States and the understanding that flowed from it.

These factors were greatly reinforced by Australia's engagement with the problems of Indochina over the preceding six years. In Michael Costello's view, a key factor in Australia's successful diplomacy after 1989 was the level of trust that three of the critical figures – Nguyen Co Thach, Hun Sen and Soviet Vice Foreign Minister Rogachev – had developed in Australia as a result of Hayden's earlier efforts.[15] And, in Evans, Australia had a Foreign Minister of rare energy and intellectual force, who had earned the warm, if occasionally exhausted, admiration of his ASEAN colleagues.

Finally, the Australian Government was willing to spend the extensive human, financial and political capital necessary to pursue the settlement. This capital included the time of the Foreign Minister and his senior officers, the money for the diplomatic effort, aid, and eventually the peacekeeping operations, and, just as importantly, the political will to persevere with a course of policy that at times seemed likely to deliver far more political costs than benefits to its proponents. The initiative demonstrated how effective a skilled and cooperative foreign policy bureaucracy could be in supporting ambitious foreign policy aims. While Evans played a major role in driving the initiative and catalysing important high-level support in Australia and overseas, the quality of the Red Book proposals for a peace settlement in Cambodia were directly attributable to the efforts of the members of the foreign policy bureaucracy who worked on them.

Evans's own assessment of the Australian policy initiative seems justified: it showed, he wrote,

> how effective middle power diplomacy could be. Our United Nations peace
> initiative was not taken at anyone's behest. It was not the kind of "good offices"
> role that Australia had undertaken in the past … It was neither front- nor back-seat
> driving, but the more demanding, but less visible, role of mapmaker and
> persuader. It was much more an intellectual than a political or military role.[16]

A number of the lessons learned in Cambodia would a few years later have application to the UN role in East Timor.

Notes

1 For a broad account of the peace initiative in the context of Australia's relations with Cambodia, see Frank Frost, "Labor and Cambodia" in David Lee and Christopher Waters (eds), *Evatt to Evans: The Labor Tradition in Australian Foreign Policy*, Sydney: Allen & Unwin, 1997, pp. 196 ff. See also Gareth Evans's account of the background to the peace initiative in *CPD Vol. 142 Senate,* 6 December 1990, pp. 51656–75.

2 Bill Hayden, *Hayden: An Autobiography*, Sydney: Angus & Robertson, 1996, p. 380.

3 Keith Scott, *Gareth Evans*, Sydney: Allen & Unwin, 1999, p. 266.

4 A comprehensive account of the whole Australian peace initiative is given by one of the participants in the process in Ken Berry, *Cambodia – From Red to Blue: Australia's Initiative for Peace*, Sydney: Allen & Unwin, 1997.

5 Gareth Evans and Bruce Grant, *Australia's Foreign Relations: In the World of the 1990s*, 2nd ed., Melbourne: Melbourne University Press, 1995, p. 229.

6 ibid.

7 Interview with Michael Costello, December 2002.

8 For details see Berry, *Cambodia – From Red to Blue*, p. 29.
9 ibid., p. 41.
10 Evans and Grant, *Australia's Foreign Relations*, pp. 225–6.
11 ibid., p. 227.
12 Berry, *Cambodia – From Red to Blue*, p. 58.
13 ibid.
14 ibid., p. 63.
15 Interview with Michael Costello, December 2002.
16 Evans and Grant, *Australia's Foreign Relations*, p. 234.

CHAPTER 5

The Executive

Responsibility for the content of foreign policy is almost invariably ascribed – by the public, by the media, by other states, and by historians – to members of the executive: elected members of Parliament given foreign policy roles in the government in power. So, for example, the "turn to America" during the Second World War is attributed to Prime Minister John Curtin, the signing of the Australian–Japanese trade agreement to Trade Minister John McEwen, the Cambodia Peace Settlement to Foreign Minister Gareth Evans – not to the other members of the foreign policy bureaucracy or the diplomatic or intelligence personnel who were undoubtedly involved in these policies. A statement made by a Prime Minister, a Foreign Minister, or a Trade Minister becomes policy as soon as it is uttered. It remains policy until it is retracted or overtaken by events. When a policy misstep occurs, ministers are blamed; when a success is registered, credit and kudos accrue primarily to them.

Members of the executive preside over the foreign policy machinery because they are ultimately accountable to the electors for the conduct of foreign policy. This is the reason that theirs is the final, authoritative decision on policy questions and that all other parts of the foreign policy machinery work to support them.

This chapter examines the particular type of involvement and influence of different members of the executive on the foreign policy process. It begins with the role of the Prime Minister, a non-continuous but powerful influence on the process, before moving on to the roles of the Foreign and Trade ministers, who have ongoing carriage of the executive functions in relation to foreign policy. It also examines the structures and support mechanisms that are an indispensable part of the roles of members of the executive. One of these is Cabinet and its National Security Committee, which play a vital co-ordinating role among the different parts of the foreign policy machinery. The other is the role of ministerial offices, an increasingly influential factor in contemporary foreign policy making.

The Prime Minister

When a visiting head of government arrives in Canberra, he or she is formally welcomed by the Prime Minister at the main entrance to Parliament House on Capitol Hill. The visitor's motorcade draws up at the pillared veranda and fore-court, which look out across Lake Burley Griffin to Anzac Avenue, the great monument-lined parade that ends with the domed National War Memorial at the foot of Mount Ainslie. A guard of honour is reviewed. A salute is fired. Then a remarkable thing happens. All the doors along the central axis of Parliament House are thrown open to reveal a direct passage through the centre of the massive building. The Prime Minister escorts the visitor past the marble entrance vestibule and the ceremonial Great Hall, through the core of the build-ing – the Members' Hall, dominated by a skylight with the Australian flag flying on its 81-metre-tall flagpole directly above – through the wood-panelled Cabi-net Room and directly into the Prime Minister's suite. Looking back, the visitor can see right through the building to Mount Ainslie, framed against the sky.

It is a powerful message to the overseas visitor that in the Australian system the Prime Minister is the most influential individual in Australian foreign policy making. That influence comes with the job. It applies whether the particular Prime Minister is directly and heavily involved in policy-making, as Gough Whitlam and Malcolm Fraser were, or is less engaged, like Ben Chifley. Either way, the tone and direction of Australian foreign policy are set from the top. Russell Trood has described the capacity of Australian prime ministers to secure and maintain a degree of control over foreign policy as "unique in government".[1] For Peter Edwards, "the Australian political culture not only accepts but expects a far more prominent role for the Prime Minister" in foreign affairs.[2] Patrick Weller says, "Prime Ministers often dominate their nation's foreign policy".[3]

The central role of the Prime Minister in external affairs has been present from the start. Apart from the short-lived Labor Government of John Watson in 1904, all prime ministers until 1908 also held the position of External Affairs Minister.[4] In the late 1940s the Opposition criticised Evatt because he and his department challenged the established norm of the Australian Prime Minister's dominance in foreign policy.[5]

In Australia's modified version of the Westminster system, the Prime Minister enjoys relatively unconstrained authority in most areas of policy, but the fetters are nowhere looser than in foreign policy. Foreign policy and broader issues of strategic policy do not rank high on lists of voters' concerns most of the time, but the electorate has a general expectation that the Prime Minister will deal competently with them.

The Prime Minister's influence on foreign policy flows from his or her general responsibility for setting the strategic agenda for government and for articulating its vision; for interpreting the country to itself and to others. Part of any such vision is a view of how Australia relates to the outside world. The Prime Minister alone speaks with the ultimate authority of the government at two different levels: for the Australian Government to other governments, and for the Australian nation to other nations. In the first of those tasks, the Prime Minister's role derives from the hierarchical traditions of diplomacy and from its historical development as machinery to enable sovereign to negotiate with sovereign. At the second level, the Prime Minister's role is broader and symbolic. It involves articulating the values and qualities of Australia to an audience beyond government; first to overseas elites like businesspeople and investors, the media and opinion-makers, and through them to the broader international public. The Prime Minister represents Australia for this wider constituency more effectively and comprehensively than the Foreign, Trade or Defence ministers can do.

And because the nation's constitutional arrangements do not permit the monarch to travel to another country as the Australian head of state – she always represents Great Britain when outside Australia – the Prime Minister's responsibility for expressing a national identity (or, more crudely, burnishing a national brand) weighs more heavily than it might do under a republican constitution.

The nature of contemporary media reinforces this trend. Overseas visits by the Prime Minister are an important point of intersection between foreign policy and domestic politics. Australian foreign ministers and trade ministers can wander the world alone (or alone apart from the requisite number of personal and departmental staff), but prime ministers invariably take with them an entourage of senior press-gallery journalists. Their visits are among the most visible manifestations of government foreign policy. The choice of destination has a symbolic purpose as well as a practical one. Paul Keating deliberately chose to go to Indonesia on his first overseas trip.[6] John Howard did the same.

Over time in office, prime ministers grow familiar with their overseas counterparts in a way their officials can not, and become more confident of their capacity to make decisions. The role of personal relationships in foreign policy making has been an irritant to some theorists. The general view during the Cold War has been summed up as one in which "incorporating leaders and leadership into general theories of international relations is unnecessary since such knowledge adds little to our understanding of the dynamics of conflict, cooperation and change in international affairs".[7] This is one of the areas where the gap between the experiences of foreign policy practitioners and the views of international relations theorists seems widest. Practitioners have a natural tendency to emphasise the role of the personal. They want to say, "These are the things that happened on my watch, and they happened in the way they did in part because of me". But even discounting this temptation, it is hard to argue that Menzies's particular personal views of Australia's place in the world, or Whitlam's or Fraser's, or Keating's or Howard's, did not set the tone for Australia's view of itself in the world and did not alter, in one way or another, the outside world's view of Australia.

Of course, in the absence of mutual national interests, personal relationships will not go far to shape policy. Hawke's friendship with Kenneth Kaunda or Malcolm Fraser's with Michael Manley were never going to lead to a dramatic growth in Australia–Zambia or Australia–Jamaica relations (although they did have useful multilateral implications within the Commonwealth debates over southern Africa). But it is very difficult to argue from the Australian example that Hawke's relationship with US Secretary of State George Shultz did not make the handling of the MX missile crisis[8] easier, or that Keating's relationship with Suharto was not instrumental in securing Indonesia's willingness to host the second APEC Leaders' Meeting, thereby institutionalising the process.

Even prime ministers such as John Howard, who do not come to office with great enthusiasm for foreign policy, become caught up in it. Foreign policy is intrinsically interesting. It involves many of the skills – negotiation, psychological insight, judgement, the ability to articulate a case – that any politician who reaches high office feels he or she possesses (and usually does). Menzies reflected these considerations in conversation with the Secretary of the Department of External Affairs, Sir Alan Watt, in the early 1950s:

> Any Prime Minister had to handle a wide range of domestic policy matters, many of which were dull and boring. Menzies said he would like nothing better than to be able for a time to give his whole attention to foreign policy.[9]

Compared with health or transport or education, foreign policy is also easy for the Commonwealth Government to do. Section 51 of the Australian constitution places the external-relations function unambiguously in the hands of the Federal Government (see Chapter 8). Policy-making is free of the sniping of resentful state governments, or of the need to balance difficult domestic trade-offs, and for the most part it comes without the fiscal price tags of social programs or defence. And of course, the Prime Minister exercises substantial authority over the policy of the Federal Government.

Foreign ministers can and have wielded great power and influence, as Evatt, Casey, Hayden and Evans did. But when Foreign Minister and Prime Minister differ, as Menzies did with Casey over support for Anthony Eden during the Suez crisis (with disastrous results),[10] or Fraser did with Peacock over Cambodia policy in 1980–81, the Prime Minister's will almost always prevails. This is in part the result of the Prime Minister's greater political authority in Cabinet, but, in a negative sense, it also reflects the grim political consequences that flow from any perceived rebuff to the Prime Minister from his Cabinet colleagues.[11] The Prime Minister's involvement in foreign policy making can best be characterised as sporadic but profound. John Howard's Defence Minister, Robert Hill, described him as a "unilateral superpower": "I think it works that way with most prime ministers, it's been my observation – a weighted voting system".[12]

As in other areas of policy-making, prime ministers have considerable freedom to decide the foreign policy issues in which they will or will not involve themselves. As Paul Keating has written:

> The Prime Minister of Australia has no job description. The constitution doesn't even mention the position, and it can be performed in ways as different as the people who occupy the position. That is especially true of its external dimensions. Apart from turning up to shake hands with visitors and attending a couple of more-or-less compulsory international meetings (at which there is no particular need to do more than express enough politely bland sentiments to keep the press at bay) there is nothing the Prime Minister must do in the area of foreign policy. Some have done little more.[13]

Russell Trood has pointed out that

> Prime Ministers have been inclined to mark out one or two areas of policy as being of special personal interest ... The reasons for these choices have varied considerably, but they all have the effect of identifying the Prime Minister with a particular area of policy, both publicly and within government, and isolating that area, except for the unwary or incautious, from concerted ministerial or bureaucratic interference.[14]

Each Prime Minister will focus on particular matters that are important to him or her. Hawke records, "From the beginning of my Prime Ministership I used the Commonwealth Heads of Government Meetings (CHOGM) as an instrument to give effect to Chifley's philosophy of Labor's universal mandate".[15] Keating focussed on the centrality of Asia.[16] Howard personally coordinated the proposal for a free-trade agreement with the United States.

Some issues, however, tend to fall naturally into the orbit of all prime ministers. The relationship with the United States is pre-eminent among them. The alliance engages the direct interests of the Defence Minister, his department and the Australian Defence Force, as well as Foreign Affairs and Trade. The US relationship is also critical in domestic political terms. The political costs of mismanaging it are substantial and no Australian Prime Minister can permit them.

During the 1990s, Asia also assumed a more prominent place in the Prime Minister's portfolio of issues. This reflected not just the growing economic and political importance of the region, but a significant structural shift as well, with the development of APEC Leaders' Meetings (see the case study on page 114).

All prime ministers have cut their political teeth on, and established their credentials through, domestic politics. Most of them experience foreign policy in an operational sense for the first time when they take up the prime ministership. They often come to enjoy it and sometimes to believe in its capacity to serve domestic political ends. According to Stephen Mills, who worked in his office, Bob Hawke was "acutely aware of the domestic political benefits he gained from being a successful international figure".[17] But the evidence that excellence in foreign policy confers much domestic political advantage is ambiguous at best, and most prime ministers understand (and, if they do not, their political colleagues remind them) that their government's political success or failure will rest on different policy and political assets.

To perform the external policy role, the Prime Minister needs sources of advice and support apart from the departments of Foreign Affairs and Trade, and Defence. In the thirty years since the newly elected Gough Whitlam, according to one who was present, walked into his initial meeting with senior Foreign Affairs officials in 1972 to introduce his Principal Private Secretary, Dr Peter Wilenski, as "My Kissinger", successive prime ministers have continued to develop this support capacity. Malcolm Fraser did much to institutionalise the Prime Minister's place at the centre of the process,[18] strengthening the policy-advising capabilities of the Department of the Prime Minister and Cabinet (PM&C) and creating an intelligence structure under which the Director-General of the Office of National Assessments reported directly to him. Hawke, as discussed further below, strengthened the role of the Prime Minister's office in foreign policy agenda-setting. It was under Howard, however, that most significant steps were taken to increase the Prime Minister's control over foreign policy making, and the presidential style of the Prime Minister's involvement in foreign policy making became more firmly established. The creation of the National Security Committee of Cabinet, with a broader agenda than any of its predecessors, the greater political as well as administrative role taken by the Secretary of PM&C, and the Prime Minister's increased influence over the staffing of Australia's overseas missions all made Howard more influential in this area than any of his predecessors. After 1996, appointments of all ambassadors and high commissioners (rather than just key appointments like Washington, DC, and London) were for the first time vetted and approved by the Prime Minister and Cabinet rather than being sent directly by the Foreign Minister for endorsement by the Executive Council.

One of the keys to successful foreign policy making lies in effective coordination between Prime Minister and Foreign Minister.[19] Gareth Evans wrote about his period in office that

> The main focus of the day-to-day effort has been to ensure that neither the Prime Minister nor the Foreign Minister springs surprises on the other – that each can go into the Parliament or face an impromptu "doorstop" media conference knowing what the other is likely to be saying about the current issue of the day; and that any significant policy initiative that either is inclined to float has been the subject of prior discussion.[20]

Underlying this quote is the particular role differentiation that occurs between the members of the executive involved in foreign policy. The Foreign Minister, Trade Minister and Defence Minister are all charged with the ongoing management of their portfolios, but in a way constrained by the areas of the Prime Minister's particular interest and the general political values of the party. This in turn defines the way the different members of the executive are involved in the policy process: for the Prime Minister, sporadic involvement but decisive influence; for the ministers, ongoing involvement but influence constrained by the interests of the Prime Minister.

The Minister for Foreign Affairs and the Minister for Trade

Whatever the Prime Minister's influence on the strategic direction of foreign policy and on particular issues, most of the weight of day-to-day decision-making at the operational level, and a good deal of the responsibility for the general direction of policy, lies with the ministers for Foreign Affairs and for Trade. They handle the bulk of the routine decision-making (whether to vote one way or another on a UN resolution, how to respond to a development overseas), representational work with foreign visitors, and defence of the government or attacks on the Opposition in parliamentary Question Time. They are first port of call for media demands early in the morning or late at night. The Prime Minister can choose when to intervene. The Foreign or Trade ministers cannot.

This means that the working days of ministers are shaped by the executive's role in responding to the incessant flow of events through the foreign policy space. According to Gareth Evans,

> In a given year – to take a departmental average of the last three – the foreign minister has to sign nearly two thousand items of more or less routine correspondence; read and digest over seven hundred "information" submissions, some of considerable length and complexity; and deal with over twelve hundred other submissions requiring substantive consideration and decision of some kind – whether it be a new policy strategy, a voting position in the United Nations, the appointment of an ambassador, the terms of reply to a ministerial counterpart, the text of a statement or whatever. In addition there are myriad matters not in the shape of formal submissions, originated by the department or by other ministers or parliamentary colleagues or whoever, which nonetheless require ministerial attention. There are speeches to prepare – a major one perhaps every two weeks, and a number of minor ones in between. And there are the daily cables to read, seven days a week – culled of the trivial and pre-sorted by the minister's staff, but still amounting to an average reading for him of 150 each day, and rather more than that when a major crisis is running.[21]

The Foreign and Trade ministers also have a heavy program of overseas commitments. Gareth Evans, again, "made in his first five-and-a-half years in office 65 separate visits totalling 656 days, to 94 countries (or 223 countries if one includes return visits)".[22] Of course the Foreign and Trade ministers also have the usual requirements to prepare for parliamentary sessions and to contribute to the collegial work of the government through the Cabinet process.

The Foreign Minister has traditionally been one of the most senior members of the government, although sometimes (for example, Hayden, McMahon, Barwick and Hasluck) is a figure who, through either personal desire or prime ministerial preference, has been placed on the sidelines of the domestic political competition. Under Coalition governments, the trade ministry has been the preserve, and at times the impregnable citadel, of the Country Party and later the National Party. John McEwen, during his long tenure in the portfolio, was the most politically and policy-dominant occupant of the position, using it to shape policy across government.

For most of the period since the amalgamation of the departments of Foreign Affairs and Trade in 1987, the portfolio has had two Cabinet ministers within the one portfolio. This makes it unique among government departments. Under Coalition and Labor governments, the Minister for Foreign Affairs has been the portfolio minister, taking overall responsibility for the administration of the department (even during the period when the Minister for Trade, Tim Fischer, was also Deputy Prime Minister). At various times the two ministers have been supported by junior ministers or parliamentary secretaries. These support positions have usually involved aid and administrative responsibilities, although for the period between 1993 and 1996 the junior minister, Gordon Bilney, was delegated specific area responsibility as Minister for Pacific Island Affairs, as well as Minister for Development Assistance. The joint responsibilities place heavy demands on the Foreign and Trade ministers to consult and communicate effectively with each other. According to Alexander Downer, "How it works depends on the personality of the two ministers".[23] It also depends on the relationships of the staff of the offices, which is discussed later. On the whole, over the period since the amalgamation of the department in 1987, the relationship between the two Cabinet ministers seems to have worked quite effectively, no matter how close or distant the personal relationship between them has been. In part this is because the division between Trade and Foreign Affairs, including in the structure of the department, is reasonably clear (although the geographic desks in the department handle bilateral trade issues). And in part it reflects the fact that the demands of work are heavy enough on both sides to ensure that neither minister is treading too obviously on the toes of the other.

More than the Minister for Foreign Affairs, the Minister for Trade has a domestic constituency to deal with – those advantaged by his work and those potentially damaged by it. The constituency is active, voluble and comparatively wealthy. Quite specific damage done to particular companies in narrow areas (for example, automotive leather exports to the United States, or potential imports of apples from New Zealand) will always have a deeper political impact than will the general support of those advantaged by trade liberalisation. As a result, compared with the Foreign Minister, the Minister for Trade spends a good deal more of his time selling the government's external policies domestically. This is done partly through the lobbying activities of particular companies, partly through policy dialogue with industry groups like the Australian Industry Group, the Australian Chamber of Commerce and Industry, or the National Farmers' Federation, and partly through the role of formal consultative bodies such as the appointed Trade Policy Advisory Council or the WTO Advisory Board, formed in April 2001 to advise on Australia's position on multilateral trade negotiations.

As important as the relationship between ministers is their relationship with their department. The core of this relationship lies in the communication of information. The department and the ministerial office need to make sure that the minister is informed about all significant policy issues, events or initiatives, so that he or she is not surprised in the course of a parliamentary question, a media inquiry or a visit from the diplomatic representative of another state. On the other hand, the capacity of ministers to absorb information is not unlimited. Because people take in information in different ways, the working style of ministers varies greatly. Some (among whom Evans was legendary) want massive amounts of information on paper. Others (Tim Fischer was an example) prefer oral briefing and discussion. Because most officials come from a bureaucratic culture that emphasises and rewards writing, they tend to prefer and to elevate the former and to be less effective at the latter.

The Foreign and Trade ministers play substantial roles in the foreign policy process at two predominant levels of policy: the strategic and the operational. At the strategic level, ministers are constantly establishing the government's position in relation to a range of foreign policy situations, issues and initiatives. These work as the general guidelines of policy-making for other levels of foreign policy making: they provide the limits and directions for foreign policy in relation to any particular issue (see Chapter 2). Beyond this, there seems to have been a recent trend towards setting an overarching, integrated framework for foreign policy in general. Both Gareth Evans and Alexander Downer felt the need to develop such a framework upon assuming office. Evans recalls that he spent much of his early months in the portfolio taking briefings from senior officials and academics, and trawling through recent international relations literature for elements of a general framework. The result was two lectures delivered to the Fabian Society in early 1989, which provided the initial basis for a coherent view of Australia's place in the world, and which was then moderated and elaborated in a regular series of speeches. Downer's approach was different, but his intent the same. He appointed a committee of former policy-makers, academics and businesspeople to begin work on a foreign and trade policy White Paper, coordinated by a DFAT official. The White Paper was released in September 1997, and according to many in the department, provided much of the "policy cover" or "policy hooks" for subsequent Australian foreign policy. (A similar document was issued in 2003. It had been promised in 2002, but was delayed after the unexpected impact of the Bali bombings. As was the case with the equally unexpected impact of the Asian financial crisis soon after the first White Paper was issued, the delay underlined the inherent conceptual difficulty in trying to force a fluent and contingent process like foreign policy making into a long-term conceptual framework.)

The Foreign and Trade ministers, as well as the Prime Minister, also play significant roles at the operational level of policy-making. Their regular rounds of meetings with representatives of other governments – and also with the Australian electorate – are a part of the detailed implementation of foreign policy and the monitoring of the positions and views of significant interests. This is a qualitatively different part, but nevertheless a part, of the operational level. With the growing ease of travel, the Foreign and Trade ministers spend substantial amounts of time overseas, conferring with counterparts from other states, and attending multilateral or regional meetings. While bilateral visits and multilateral and regional meetings are subject to significant preparatory work by diplomats and officials, the preparation, the negotiating skills, the personality and the rapport of the minister with his or her hosts can make a significant difference. In organisations like APEC, for instance, the importance of commitments made between ministers (or heads of government, in the case of APEC) was important in moving the organisational agenda along, as "agreement from the top" could override potential months of bureaucratic wrangling about a certain issue.

Sitting at the top of the foreign policy machinery, the Foreign and Trade ministers, along with the Prime Minister, set the general directions of policy, are the ultimate decision-makers, and are important implementers of bilateral and multilateral diplomacy. Yet the picture is not complete without considering the mechanisms by which their work is coordinated, or the vital support they receive from ministerial offices.

Cabinet and foreign policy

In most areas of government the process for dealing with major policy issues is established and clear. Ministers bring policy submissions, appropriately coordinated within the bureaucracy, to Cabinet, chaired by the Prime Minister, where their recommendations are debated and decisions taken and recorded as Cabinet minutes. The dissemination of these minutes to the relevant areas of the bureaucracy establishes the policy parameters for action. The bulk of such work involves decisions by ministers about new legislation or new spending programs. Foreign policy fits uneasily into this framework. Most foreign policy decisions do not involve legislation or require financial support for new programs. Usually they do not engage the responsibilities of more than one or two departments outside DFAT, so there is less need for bureaucratic coordination. Decisions must sometimes be taken hour to hour, so the deliberately formal and considered processes of Cabinet – which are in part designed to prevent the government from making hasty, uncoordinated decisions – are useless. In addition, the sensitivity of the issues and the security classifications involved often make foreign ministers reluctant to distribute papers widely.

Until 1996 the Cabinet process was used by ministers principally to seek endorsement of the strategic settings of foreign policy (such as Gareth Evans's 1989 regional security statement or Bob McMullan's work in 1995 on strategic approaches to APEC), or to secure agreement to the negotiating positions for trade or other treaty negotiations. Gareth Evans estimated that during the Hawke and Keating governments an average of sixteen such submissions were considered by Cabinet each year.[24] For most working purposes, however, the Hawke and Keating governments' decisions on day-to-day matters of external policy were considered in informal meetings of ministers, especially the Prime Minister, Foreign Minister, Trade Minister and Defence Minister.[25]

For ease and speed of handling, Australian governments regularly use committees of Cabinet as well. These involve smaller groups of ministers, dealing with particular issues, and which, under the Howard Government, often include participation by officials and ministerial advisers as well.

Cabinet had a Foreign Affairs and Defence Committee under the Menzies Government, but this fell into disuse under his Liberal Party successors. Such a committee was re-established by the Whitlam Government under the Prime Minister's chairmanship in 1972, although it met infrequently. One senior committee member recalled only a single meeting.[26] For most of the period thereafter, the committee was used essentially to oversee the work of the security and intelligence agencies. In 1996, however, the Howard Government instituted a significant structural change with the creation of a National Security Committee (NSC), which had a broader mandate than its predecessors, including international security and international economic issues. The NSC is chaired by the Prime Minister. Its members after 2000 were the Deputy Prime Minister, Foreign Minister, Treasurer, Defence Minister, Immigration Minister and Attorney-General, with others coopted as required. The committee meets with officials and staff present and participating actively. The secretaries of PM&C, Foreign Affairs and Trade, Defence, Treasury and the Attorney-General's Department, as well as the Commander of the Defence Force and the Director-General of ONA, attend all meetings. Other officials and agency heads are brought in as required. The Prime Minister's international adviser, and staff from the offices of the Foreign Minister and the Defence Minister, also sit in. The Trade Minister, however, is not an ex officio member, and most trade issues (which often involve the interests of a wider range of domestic portfolios and interests) are taken by the full Cabinet.

Participants in the NSC describe the meetings as informal and unstructured, with considerable freedom for officials to participate. In part, no doubt, because it involves them structurally in high-level decision-making rather than leaving them to rely on the ad hoc arrangements of the past, officials speak enthusiastically about the innovation. An agenda and formal submissions are circulated, but ministers and officials are free to raise other issues. The Prime Minister can ask for issues to be brought to the committee. His chairmanship of this committee has strengthened the Prime Minister's influence over the foreign policy process. The NSC meets on average about once a month, but more frequently during crises such as the East Timor deployment, or in intense periods of policy-making such as the formulation of the 2000 Defence White Paper. Because a greater range of issues were referred to the NSC under the Howard Government, rather than being handled by individual ministers, the creation of this structure raised the level of coordination of foreign policy issues generally throughout the government.

The principal bureaucratic support mechanism for the NSC is the Secretaries Committee on National Security (SCNS). SCNS (pronounced as 'scones') is chaired by the Secretary of PM&C, and comprises the secretaries of Foreign Affairs, Defence, the Attorney-General's Department, Immigration and Treasury, the Commander of the Australian Defence Force and the Director-General of ONA. Other agency and departmental heads (such as those of Finance and ASIO) are coopted where necessary. The committee vets most submissions intended for the NSC, although ministers retain the right to go directly to the NSC if they wish. It also considers issues that require coordination but might not pass the threshold for ministerial consideration. SCNS has been used not just for policy coordination, but also for a limited amount of policy development. The Prime Minister has commissioned SCNS, rather than individual ministers or departments, to prepare reports for the NSC.

The secretariat for both SCNS and the NSC is provided by the Cabinet Division in the Prime Minister's Department. This structure has reinforced at the bureaucratic level the Prime Minister's policy dominance at the political level. Even more importantly, it has strengthened the domestic political influence over foreign policy by increasing the degree of control of officials from PM&C, whose interest and responsibility are primarily domestic.

Crisis handling

One clear marker of the growing importance of the executive in foreign policy decision-making has been the centralisation of crisis handling in the Ministerial Wing at Parliament House. Unlike their counterparts in Britain or the United States, who work primarily from offices in their executive departments,

Australian ministers operate primarily out of Parliament House. The 1991 Gulf War was the first security-policy crisis handled almost exclusively out of the then new building, with officials providing daily intelligence and policy briefings for ministers in the Cabinet suite. The trend was strengthened by the handling of the East Timor crisis in 1999. Individual crisis task forces at the official level still operate in departments, but the high-level handling has drifted to the Hill. This has been facilitated by technological change – with secure communications making it easier to distribute intelligence and policy papers directly to policy-makers. It also reflects the greater ease of coordinating the government's media interests, with the press gallery located in the same building.

The ministerial offices

One of the most important changes in Australian policy-making over the past decade has been in the growing role of ministerial advisers. This development has affected the national security portfolios as much as others. The Whitlam Government began the innovation, partly because of its distrust of a public service that had served a conservative government for more than twenty years.[27] The number and seniority of such advisers have increased markedly in the 1980s and 1990s, however. Alexander Downer reflected that as Minister for Foreign Affairs he had thirteen ministerial staff, including three at the level of the senior executive service. In the 1950s his father, as Minister for Immigration, had the support of one middle-ranking clerical officer and two typists.[28]

The first prime minister to have a designated senior adviser on international affairs was Hawke, who in 1983 appointed John Bowan, a senior public servant who had worked in Foreign Affairs and the Office of National Assessments, and subsequently became Ambassador to Germany. (Fraser had used consultants.) The adviser draws heavily on the support of the International Division of PM&C. (Between 1983 and 2002, several occupants of the position – Allan Gyngell, Michael Thawley, David Ritchie and Miles Jordana – had previously served as head of International Division.) The creation of the position of senior adviser in turn also strengthened International Division's role and influence in the bureaucracy.

The growth in the size and responsibility of ministerial offices is a response to the great increase in the volume of information that ministers must handle. As Howard's first foreign policy adviser, Michael Thawley, commented: "There's a vast blow-out in information, but the funnel still leads to only one man".[29] Each office is organised in the way that best suits the minister, within general guidelines laid down by the government. In general, however, the office performs the functions of personal support for the minister (coordinating programs and travel arrangements), media relations, support for the minister's electorate responsibilities, coordination within the government – with other ministers and with backbenchers – and with Parliament, and advice on policy. Advisers to most ministers have the right to add personal comments to submissions from the department if they disagree with the departmental advice. Alexander Downer estimated that in his office this occurred perhaps one time in twenty.[30]

The influence of ministerial staff depends above all on their relationship with the minister, but access – not least the capacity to be the last person to see the minister before a Cabinet meeting, to choose which telegram or article to draw to the minister's attention, to suggest lines as the minister goes into a press conference or to do a final edit on a speech – gives staffers considerable power. (The nature of foreign policy means that much of it is made at the declaratory level in speeches or interviews: control of words means control of foreign policy.) In a study of ministerial policy advisers in the Keating Government, Maria Maley has pointed out that advisers can enable ministers to engage with the complexity of the policy process. They can enhance ministers' capacity to influence policy as it is shaped through multiple interactions of policy actors in different organisations.[31] She suggests advisers have access to two important resources:

> information and relationships. Advisers have access to information about agendas
> and policy opportunities, as well as knowledge of the positions and interests of
> stakeholders. They are linked in relationships with key players, both within the
> executive and the wider political environment. In their dealings with others they
> carry not only the authority of the minister, but also the power to control
> information flowing to the minister.[32]

Personal staff can act as proxies for ministers in a way public servants cannot, so they tend to carry the weight of responses to representations by interest groups. Senior staff members also perform a general advisory function, usually of a strategic nature.

The growth in the numbers and influence of ministerial staff has changed the power relationships between the executive and the public service. The capacity of advisers to monitor the department's activities and interpret its actions has helped shift power to the executive wing and away from the departments. Of course, departments also see advantages in gaining access to the minister's ear by appointing their own officers to staff positions, but the power benefits are heavily in favour of the minister.

The staff of ministerial offices are employed not as public servants, but under the *Members of Parliament (Staff) Act 1984*. Public servants who take such positions resign from the public service for the duration of their appointment (which is at the minister's pleasure). The purpose of these arrangements is to make clear that the primary responsibility and loyalty of staff lie to the minister and government, rather than to the department they have come from. Most staff dealing with external policy and working for the Prime Minister and the other external ministers have been drawn from the ranks of the public service and return there, although this has been less true during the terms of Coalition governments than those of Labor.

By the late 1990s, however, it was clear, in the words of Patrick Weller, that,

> Ministerial staff have grown in influence and importance over the past twenty
> years, to the extent that they have long outgrown existing procedures for
> accountability and responsibility. They are now the black hole of government,
> unaccountable in practice, even if not in theory.[33]

This "accountability vacuum"[34] was present in the role of ministerial advisers during the "Children Overboard" Affair in 2001, and generated heavy pressure for reform of these accountability mechanisms.

Conclusion

In our 2001 survey of DFAT policy officers (see the Appendix), we asked respondents to nominate certain positions in terms of their influence on foreign policy. The results were revealing about the importance of members of the executive: 54 per cent saw the Prime Minister as most important; 47.8 per cent saw the Foreign and Trade ministers as next most important, followed by the Secretary of DFAT, the Secretary of PM&C, the Prime Minister's international adviser, and the Foreign Minister's senior adviser. Significantly, 42.9 per cent of respondents felt that ministerial staff had gained more influence on the content of Australian foreign policy compared with the time when they first joined the department. These figures confirm our belief in the highly influential roles of members of the executive and their staff in the making of Australian foreign policy. As discussed in Chapter 3, it is a different sort of influence from that possessed by the bureaucracy, but in a range of ways it is more decisive. Yet our examination of the institutions of foreign policy making cannot stop with the bureaucracy and the executive; we must also understand the roles of diplomats and the intelligence community.

Notes

1 Russell Trood, "Prime Ministers and Foreign Policy" in Patrick Weller (ed.), *Menzies to Keating: The Development of the Australian Prime Ministership*, Melbourne: Melbourne University Press, 1992, p. 156.
2 P.G. Edwards, *Prime Ministers and Diplomats: The Making of Australian Foreign Policy 1901–1949*, Melbourne: Oxford University Press, 1983, p. 189.
3 Patrick Weller, *Malcolm Fraser PM*, Ringwood: Penguin, 1989, p. 313.
4 Edwards, *Prime Ministers and Diplomats*, p. 193.
5 David Lowe, "Divining a Labor Line: Conservative Constructions of Labor's Foreign Policy, 1944–49" in David Lee and Christopher Waters (eds), *Evatt to Evans: The Labor Tradition in Australian Foreign Policy*, Sydney: Allen & Unwin, 1997, p. 70.
6 Paul Keating, *Engagement: Australia Faces the Asia–Pacific*, Sydney: Macmillan, 2000, p. 131.
7 Margaret Hermann and Joe Hagan, "International Decision Making", *Foreign Policy*, Fall 1998.
8 R.J.L. Hawke, *The Hawke Memoirs*, Melbourne: Mandarin, 1994, pp. 290–1.
9 Sir Alan Watt, *Australian Diplomat: Memoirs of Sir Alan Watt*, Sydney: Angus & Robertson, 1972, p. 171.
10 Alan Watt, *The Evolution of Australian Foreign Policy 1938–1965*, London: Cambridge University Press, 1967, p. 303.
11 See Weller, *Malcolm Fraser PM*, for an interesting account of foreign policy making under Fraser.
12 *Canberra Times*, 14 December 2002, p. C1.
13 ibid.
14 Trood, "Prime Ministers and Foreign Policy", p. 163.
15 Hawke, *The Hawke Memoirs,* p. 315.
16 Keating, *Engagement*, 2000, p. 15.
17 Stephen Mills, *The Hawke Years: The Story From the Inside*, Melbourne: Viking, 1993, p. 196.
18 Trood, "Prime Ministers and Foreign Policy", p. 173. See also Tony Kevin, "Our Man in Purgatory", *Australian's Review of Books*, October 2000, p. 21.
19 The way this happened during Gareth Evans's term as Foreign Minister is described in Gareth Evans and Bruce Grant, *Australia's Foreign Relations: In the World of the 1990s*, 2nd ed., Melbourne: Melbourne University Press, 1995, p. 47.
20 ibid.
21 ibid., p. 53.
22 ibid., p. 49.
23 Interview with Alexander Downer, 5 August 1999.
24 Evans and Grant, *Australia's Foreign Relations*, p. 45.
25 ibid., p. 47.
26 T.B. Millar, *Australia in Peace and War: External Relations 1788–1977*, Canberra: ANU Press, 1978, p. 28. See also Henry S. Albinski, *Australian External Policy under Labor: Content, Process and the National Debate*, Brisbane: University of Queensland Press, 1977, p. 288.

27 See T.B. Millar, *Australia in Peace and War*, p. 31.
28 Interview with Alexander Downer, 5 August 1999.
29 Interview with Michael Thawley, November 2000.
30 Interview with Alexander Downer, 5 August 1999; correspondence with his office, 8 November 2002.
31 Maria Maley, "Conceptualising Advisers' Policy Work: The Distinctive Policy Roles of Ministerial Advisers in the Keating Government, 1991–96", *Australian Journal of Political Science*, Vol. 35, No. 3, 2000, p. 469.
32 ibid.
33 Patrick Weller, *Don't Tell the Prime Minister*, Melbourne: Scribe, 2002, p. 70.
34 Meredith Edwards, "Ministerial Advisers and the Search for Accountability", Australian Institute of Administrative Law Seminar, 16 June 2002, p. 4.

Developing Regional Architecture: The APEC Leaders' Meetings

A significant structural change – and power shift – in the process of Australian foreign policy making took place in the 1990s with the establishment of APEC Leaders' Meetings. These meetings now bring together annually the heads of government of all the APEC economies, including the President of the United States, the President of China, the Prime Minister of Japan, the President of Indonesia and the Prime Minister of Australia.

The proposal and advocacy of these meetings by Australia illustrate in two ways the importance of the executive – the Prime Minister, the portfolio ministers, and their immediate staff – in foreign policy. First, the initiative was developed because of the perceived need to establish regular face-to-face meetings between the Australian head of government and the leaders of Australia's most important diplomatic partners. Second, the progress of the initiative demonstrates the impact a Prime Minister can have on a foreign policy initiative when he or she decides to make it a personal policy priority.

Before the first Leaders' Meeting in 1993, Australian prime ministers had been regularly involved in only two sets of international meetings: biennial gatherings of Commonwealth heads of government, and annual summits of island leaders in the South Pacific Forum, which they did not always attend. The result was a serious disjunction between Australia's general foreign policy and trade priorities, which centred on Asia and North America, and the allocation of the Prime Minister's energy and time.

With the end of the Cold War, a desultory debate about regional architecture, which had dragged on for many years, gained fresh urgency. In part, this was because new opportunities were opening up. The relative economic weight of Asia in the world was growing. East Asia's share of world GDP had risen from 12.3 per cent in 1970 to 21.3 per cent in 1991. China was more actively engaging with the region. The division between Indochina and the ASEAN countries, which reflected in part the divergent interests in the region of the United States, the Soviet Union and China, was eroding. All these factors had underpinned Australia's sponsorship of the Asia–Pacific Economic Cooperation organisation (APEC), whose first ministerial meeting had been held in Canberra in 1989.

A second, more strategic imperative was also driving Australian policy-makers, however. That was the fear that with the end of the Cold War the United States might heed the siren call of neo-isolationism, as some in Washington were urging, and step back from its political and military engagement with Asia to consolidate its position in the Western Hemisphere. The premonition of a world divided into three blocs – a larger and more integrated European Union, a US-dominated Western Hemisphere and a Japan-led yen bloc in Asia – was unsettling Australian policy-makers. Such a world would have negative strategic consequences for Australia, and, especially under Bob Hawke's prime ministership, ways were being sought to re-engage the United States institutionally in the region. APEC was a start, but it had a limited agenda of economic cooperation. Asia was the only major part of the world not to have any formal structure under which heads of government could meet regularly.

The process that would eventually result in the establishment of annual APEC Leaders' Meetings began within the bureaucracy. In December 1991, President George Bush was to visit Australia. This was to be the first visit to Australia in a quarter of a century by the head of state of the country's closest ally. In preparation for the visit, the head of the International Division of the Prime Minister's Department[1] made a preliminary visit to Washington to discuss the agenda. In an internal memorandum for colleagues in the department and the Prime Minister's office, he reported that he had raised the idea of regular meetings of Asia–Pacific heads of government in discussions with senior US officials on the National Security Council staff and in the State Department, "making it clear that I was speaking personally". He had suggested that either APEC or the ASEAN Post Ministerial Committee meetings might provide a framework.

The response from the United States had not been hostile, and the report recommended that when Hawke met Bush in Australia,

> The Prime Minister should tell President Bush that he sees the absence of a Head of Government Forum in the Asia Pacific region as an impediment to more effective cooperation and something on which regional leaders should be actively working.

After endorsement within the department and by the Prime Minister's office, this suggestion was incorporated into a brief for Hawke. (Although most drafts for the Prime Minister's briefing papers are commissioned from relevant line departments, the final edit is in the hands of PM&C. It is a source of considerable power. Before each meeting the Prime Minister usually receives a cut-down list of talking points, always overseen by, and usually prepared by, the international adviser in his office.)

Before Bush's arrival in Australia, however, Hawke had been displaced as Prime Minister by Paul Keating. The meeting with Bush would be Keating's first opportunity to shape foreign policy, and he was looking for a large idea to leave with his visitor. He embraced the suggestion of regional heads-of-government meetings enthusiastically. He saw it, partly, as a tangible manifestation of his desire to integrate Australia more closely with the region around it, to win Australia, as he put it, a "seat at the table".[2] But partly he saw the direct involvement of leaders as a way of getting quicker and more ambitious action on the regional economic agenda than would happen if the organisation moved at the pace of its slowest ministers and officials. (This was the reason Australia pressed hard and successfully to have officials and advisers excluded from the Leaders' Meetings, and for the greatest possible informality in their structure.) Keating's support for the idea drove it forward with greater force and speed than officials could ever have accomplished. Because the proposal concerned other heads of government, the Prime Minister had to be directly engaged. This was not just for reasons of protocol: foreign ministers and their officials can be particularly impermeable to suggestions that might give larger roles in their policy space to heads of government.

Keating put the idea to President Bush at their first meeting at Kirribilli House.[3] He was listened to with interest and later received a polite but non-committal written reply from the President that did not rule out the idea but made it clear that it was up to Australia to deliver it. (It would have been a waste of time and energy for Australia to pursue the proposal in the face of a United States veto.)

Within government there was debate on how the meetings should be framed. Some officials were sceptical that APEC would be a workable forum for a heads-of-government meeting. To get around the fact that two of the core participants in the Asian economy, Hong Kong and Taiwan, were both claimed by China, a claim accepted by most other countries, APEC defined itself as a meeting of regional economies rather than of states. China might refuse to allow leaders of the other 'Chinese economies' to participate in a meeting designated for heads of government, or decline to attend if they were there.

Keating believed – and persuaded the sceptical Foreign Minister, Gareth Evans – that China would eventually agree to hold the meetings under APEC auspices, with Hong Kong and Taiwan represented at lower levels. In Keating's view, the meetings needed to be firmly tethered to an existing institution like APEC. One-off or free-floating meetings of heads of government would have had too precarious an existence.

After meeting Bush, Keating wrote to the leaders of some other key APEC countries (Japan, China, Indonesia and Korea) to sound them out informally before floating the idea publicly in his first foreign policy speech on 7 April 1992:

> Another way of promoting cooperation in the Asia Pacific region would be to establish a process of periodic heads of government meetings, say every two or three years. The absence of such a process is conspicuous in a region whose weight in global affairs is steadily increasing. Various formulas for participation are possible, but I personally would find most attractive a mechanism based on APEC membership, because it embraces the most important economic linkages throughout East Asia and across the Pacific.[4]

An intensive burst of diplomacy followed as Australia tried to sell the idea to its fellow APEC members. Keating wrote and spoke to other leaders, including those he had not contacted in the first round, Evans lobbied hard at ASEAN meetings, and DFAT posts around the region sought to identify potential allies and to pursue the idea with other governments.

Initial replies were positive but guarded. Throughout 1992 it looked as though Indonesia, which was to take over the rotating chair of APEC in 1994, would be the likely first site for such a meeting. It did not seem that Australia could hope for such meetings more than every two or three years. Then came a stroke of luck. In November 1992, Bill Clinton was somewhat unexpectedly elected as President of the United States. He, too, was looking for some way of establishing his own foreign policy credentials. In particular, he wanted to emphasise the links between foreign policy and trade and economic policy. And the United States was to chair APEC in 1993.

Seizing the opportunity, Keating wrote the incoming President a letter that was much more substantive than the usual letter of formal congratulations from one leader to another: "I said, in effect, 'Have I got an idea for you!'"[5]

Clinton's national-security team took up the idea, and by late June 1993 the President wrote to Keating saying that he intended to invite APEC members to attend an "informal meeting" of APEC leaders (language designed to reassure China that its sovereignty was not at issue) in Seattle in November, following the planned APEC Ministerial Meeting.

For Australia, however, a one-off meeting in Seattle would be of little use. Australian interests were only served by a more regular and routine series of meetings that would institutionalise contact between regional leaders and give the Australian Prime Minister a permanent place in the regional dialogue. That meant that Australia had to work out a way of keeping the momentum going. Because Indonesia was to chair APEC the following year, President Suharto's attitude would be critical. Keating wrote to him urging him to respond positively to Clinton's initiative, and directly addressing fears by the members of the Association of Southeast Asian Nations (ASEAN) that this would somehow detract from ASEAN's importance. He said he hoped that the Seattle meeting of leaders would be followed by one in Indonesia.[6]

He then made a personal decision to visit Suharto in October on his return from a Commonwealth meeting in Cyprus. In their one-and-three-quarter-hour meeting, Suharto made it clear to Keating that he was rather more favourably inclined to the idea of APEC Leaders' Meetings than was his own foreign ministry, although the continuing opposition from Prime Minister Mahathir of Malaysia (who preferred a model of regional cooperation that would exclude the United States and Australia) was obviously a source of concern for him. Keating told Suharto that he had extracted from Clinton a personal promise to attend any further APEC Leaders' Meeting that might be held in Jakarta in the following year.

Invitations from the President of the United States are not often turned down, and in November 1993, less than two years after Keating had first floated the idea with his predecessor, Clinton hosted the historic first meeting at Blake Island, off Seattle. As Keating had surmised, China's President Jiang Zemin did attend, along with officials from Hong Kong and Taiwan. Only the "recalcitrant" Dr Mahathir was not present. And largely as a result of a plan orchestrated by Keating, President Kim Young Sam of Korea proposed, and Prime Minister Goh Chok Tong of Singapore supported, a proposal that President Suharto should convene a follow-up meeting the following year in Jakarta. Suharto duly accepted.[7]

In his book *Engagement*, Keating sets out some telling statistics. In the nine months between a meeting held with officials from DFAT and PM&C, and advisers from the offices of the Foreign and Trade ministers, in his office in February 1994 to discuss the steps beyond APEC and the next Leaders' Meeting hosted by Suharto in Bogor, near Jakarta, on 15 November,

> my diary records around thirty six meetings or telephone calls, mostly with other
> APEC heads of government, focussing on the meeting, and seventeen letters to

other leaders about APEC. This was in addition, of course, to the constant work done by Bob McMullan and Gareth Evans with their own colleagues and the enormous effort put in by the public service and my own office.[8]

The Bogor meeting, hosted by Suharto, was followed the next year by one in Japan, and the meetings became institutionalised. Each new chair of APEC saw advantages in hosting a meeting of world leaders, and participants increasingly found value in attending, not just for the formal sessions, but for the opportunities quickly and effectively to conduct bilateral meetings in the margins of the meeting. The meetings began to take on an increasingly political dimension as leaders became more comfortable with each other and the pressures of the regional agenda intruded. Issues like China's membership of the World Trade Organisation, the international response to East Timor's independence, and the regional reaction to terrorism have all been more easily and effectively handled because of the APEC Leaders' Meetings.

For Australia, the meetings have provided a sharper alignment of the Prime Minister's activities with the foreign policy interests of the country. They have ensured that the Australian Prime Minister is in personal contact at least once a year with the key leaders of North America, and North and Southeast Asia. They have increased the Prime Minister's more active role in foreign policy making.

As with the Cambodia Peace Settlement discussed earlier, Australia succeeded because it was pressing its case in a receptive environment: that is not to say one in which the outcome was inevitable, but one in which it was possible. Luck, an under-analysed factor in international diplomacy, was also on its side. The United States was chairing APEC in 1993, the incoming President was looking for an initiative, China was diplomatically on the defensive after the international reaction to the killing of protesting students in Tiananmen Square in 1989, and Australia's close neighbour Indonesia would chair APEC the following year. The Australian initiative succeeded, above all, because it had a Prime Minister and Foreign and Trade ministers who were prepared to invest a large part of their time and energy into selling the proposal, and because both Prime Minister and Foreign Minister had developed close relations with their key interlocutors. The Australian journalist Greg Sheridan described Keating's diplomacy between Clinton and Suharto about the Leaders' Meetings as "one of the few occasions in Australian diplomatic history when an Australian Prime Minister has engaged in effective shuttle diplomacy with the leaders of the world's largest and fourth largest nations".[9] Australia also had, in PM&C and DFAT, officials who were skilful advocates for the Australian position.

Notes

1 Allan Gyngell, later Keating's foreign policy adviser, and one of the authors of this book. See also Don Watson, *Recollections of a Bleeding Heart: A Portrait of Paul Keating PM*, Sydney: Knopf, 2002, pp. 77–8.
2 John Edwards, *Keating: The Inside Story*, Sydney: Viking, 1996, pp. 524, 525.
3 ibid., p. 19.
4 A comprehensive account of Keating's APEC diplomacy is given in Paul Keating, *Engagement: Australia Faces the Asia–Pacific*, Sydney: Macmillan, 2000, pp. 76 ff.
5 ibid., p. 86.
6 ibid., p. 88.
7 Watson, *Recollections of a Bleeding Heart*, pp. 446 ff.
8 Keating, *Engagement*, p. 100.
9 Greg Sheridan, *Tigers: Leaders of the New Asia–Pacific*, Sydney: Allen & Unwin, 1997, p. 113.

CHAPTER 6

The Overseas Network

Diplomacy is the oldest form of any of the foreign policy institutions of the state, predating foreign ministries, foreign ministers and ministerial offices by centuries. Remarkably, given its age, diplomacy is an institution that preserves the basic forms of its core functions – communication, representation, information-gathering and negotiation – and the basic set of diplomatic privileges and immunities (now codified in the 1961 Vienna Convention on Diplomatic Relations) substantially intact from the fifteenth and sixteenth centuries. Few institutions in contemporary Australian life have older antecedents than diplomatic missions, and few have changed so little in their basic structure: ambassadors and staff are sent to live abroad under the protection of diplomatic status to represent the government and speak on its behalf. The designations of staff overseas – ambassadors, counsellors, first, second and third secretaries, and so on – has remained largely immune from the fashions of management re-engineering in home-based departments. The form has endured for 500 years or so because it is simple, replicable and comprehensible across cultures and countries, and has been able to adapt effectively to profound changes in technology, social values and the form and norms of the international system.

Australia's overseas posts range in size from tiny outposts in micro-states like Kiribati to complex operations like the Australian Embassy in Washington, DC. The conditions of living for staff can vary from an apartment in Paris overlooking the Eiffel Tower to a guarded security compound in Port Moresby. The focus of the work differs enormously. It ranges from the multilateral trade negotiations of the Mission to the World Trade Organisation (WTO) in Geneva, to the aid-centred work of the tiny embassy in Kathmandu, to the work in Wellington of monitoring and maintaining a mature and deep bilateral relationship, most of it operating well outside the control of government.

However frustrating it is for foreign policy practitioners, the public image of diplomacy seems stuck in a caricature of pinstriped men gliding their way around a never-ending global cocktail party. It is an image as remote from contemporary reality as that of the friendly family physician making house calls, but it underlines the fact that the public still sees foreign policy making, when it sees it at all, as a remote, elite and secretive activity.

If the entire foreign policy system of a state can be thought of as a large central nervous system, the diplomatic posts represent the nerve endings and motor functions of the system. It is the overseas posts that pick up substantial disturbances in the policy space, transmitting them back to the other institutions for contextualisation, analysis and decision; they are then the ultimate recipients of a large proportion of policy responses, which they operationalise in the context of the bilateral or multilateral post. Without these posts, Australian foreign policy making would have only a fraction of its current capacity to monitor, understand and act in the outside world. In this chapter, we explore three crucial aspects of the overseas posts: their purpose, where they are located, and the basic functions they perform within the foreign policy system.

The purpose of the posts

A former Secretary of DFAT, Stuart Harris, neatly summarised the functions of Australia's diplomatic missions in his 1986 *Review of Australia's Overseas Representation*:

> The purpose of Australia's overseas representation is to protect and promote
> Australia's national interests. It does this by seeking to influence the decisions of
> countries, their governments and institutions, and those of the international bodies
> to which they belong, where they impinge in any way on matters of concern to
> Australia.[1]

In 2001–02, Australia had eighty-four overseas posts,[2] the generic name given to Australian missions abroad. These may be embassies or high commissions (the term used for an embassy in a Commonwealth country) accredited to sovereign states. They may be permanent missions accredited not to governments but to international bodies like the United Nations. Posts can also be consulates-general or consulates, which are generally located outside capital cities and which issue visas, help Australians and provide advice about Australia, but which are not formally involved in the work of government-to-government interaction. (The Australian trade-promotion agency, Austrade, manages and staffs seventeen consulates, which are primarily involved in trade promotion and facilitation but provide some limited consular services.) In addition,

Australia has forty-eight honorary consuls. These are unpaid members of the local community – often expatriate Australian businessmen – who can provide a limited range of consular functions (for example, certifying documents, providing initial information and advice to Australians) on behalf of the Australian Government.

Australia has diplomatic relations with far more countries (161) than those in which it has diplomatic representation. Most Australian ambassadors and high commissioners are accredited to several different governments. The Australian High Commissioner in Harare, for example, lives in Zimbabwe but is also accredited as Australian Ambassador or High Commissioner to Angola, Malawi, Mozambique and Zambia. In most cases, non-resident accreditation involves little more than one or two visits each year to the country concerned, but the fact of accreditation gives Australian officers diplomatic rights and standing to conduct business there. This can be critical in getting access to other governments in the event of a crisis, whether political or consular. DFAT also ascribes to its posts a range of other responsibilities ("visiting responsibility", "reporting responsibility", "consular responsibility" or – the lowest, post-box, level – "bilateral liaison responsibility") for other countries in which Australia is not represented.

Some posts (the permanent missions to the UN in New York or to the WTO in Geneva, for example) are exclusively multilateral. That is, the head of mission is accredited to the organisation rather than a government. Because multilateral bodies tend to cluster, New York and Geneva are home to several of them. So the Mission to the WTO also has responsibility for working with multilateral organisations as diverse as the International Union for the Protection of New Varieties of Plants and the World Intellectual Property Organisation. In other cases the mission is partly bilateral and partly multilateral. The Australian Ambassador in Vienna, for example, is accredited to the Government of Austria, but also to the International Atomic Energy Agency. The High Commissioner in Suva is also responsible for the South Pacific Forum and the South Pacific Economic Commission (SPEC). In a further twist, diplomats at posts such as Brussels, where the European Union is headquartered, spend most of their time liaising with multilateral organisations of which Australia is not a member.

In the past, ambassadors were appointed to places and to institutions, but during the 1980s and 1990s they began to be appointed for functions. Such appointments served a political purpose as much as a diplomatic one. An Australian Ambassador for Disarmament, for example, was first appointed in 1983, partly in response to widespread public unease about nuclear dangers.

The initial appointees to the position spent a considerable amount of their time liaising with a domestic Australian constituency. Similarly, an Ambassador for the Environment was first appointed in the early 1990s, partly, at least, to placate and influence home-based green groups. In March 2003, the government announced the appointment of a new Ambassador for Counter-Terrorism.

Australia's overseas representation

Although the popular image of Australia's overseas diplomatic premises is of something like the grand Edwardian bulk of Australia House, the Australian High Commission on the Strand in London, much more typical are the rented rooms in an office building of one of the smaller Australian posts.

The pattern of Australia's overseas representation is focussed on Asia but is global in scope (if only just). In 2001–02, Australia had twenty-four posts in Europe, eighteen in South and Southeast Asia, thirteen in the Middle East and Africa, thirteen in the Americas, ten in New Zealand and the South Pacific, and six in North Asia.[3] About 40 per cent of DFAT officers posted overseas were serving in Asia, 25 per cent in Europe and 13 per cent in the Americas.[4]

Compared with other countries, Australia has a relatively small number of overseas posts, and the trend has been downward in recent years. In 1986, DFAT had 101 posts;[5] in 1990, ninety posts; a decade later, eighty-four. The Netherlands, with an economy about the same size as Australia's, has twice the number of overseas missions. Sweden has 104 missions, Canada 131, and the United Kingdom 223.[6] In addition, the total number of Australians posted from Canberra to these missions has also fallen sharply. The reduction in the total number of posts in the 1990s was largely the result of financial cutbacks compounded by a relatively weak Australian dollar, which affected DFAT more immediately than most departments. However, technological change has also made it easier to cut staff overseas. Computerised management systems and easier, cheaper communications have enabled DFAT to reduce sharply the number of administrative assistants, communications specialists and other support staff at its posts.

Such financial pressures prompted DFAT to look for cheaper ways of maintaining an overseas presence. One response was to establish micro-posts like the Australian High Commission in Bridgetown, Barbados, where a sole Australian diplomat raises a flag, but is accommodated within, and dependent for administrative support on, an existing Canadian mission. Canada was chosen because it has a complementary pattern of overseas representation to Australia's. It also offers the obvious advantages of a common language, similar scale and a longstanding partnership in intelligence matters, which eases security concerns.

Another way in which the pattern of overseas representation is being remoulded is in the enhanced role in posts of "staff recruited overseas". These are staff employed from the local community (but frequently including Australians living overseas, such as the spouses of Australia-based staff) on local conditions of employment. By 2001 the cost of sending even a very junior Australia-based officer overseas was typically between $375,000 and $500,000, depending on the city. A locally engaged staff member could be employed for less than a quarter of the cost. And, by facilitating the employment of partners of Australian officials overseas, local employment also helped to address one of the most serious problems DFAT faced in getting officers to go overseas – the loss of a second household income. In the past, locally engaged staff were recruited only for routine administrative functions or specialist jobs like inter-preting and translating. They are now being used much more broadly in support and research positions formerly occupied by Australia-based officers.[7] This process has a limit, however. Locally employed staff cannot speak authorita-tively on behalf of the Australian Government, and are not used in jobs that have advocacy or representational functions. Already, when measured against bench-mark overseas services, DFAT has the second-lowest proportion of its home-based staff overseas and the second-highest proportion of locally engaged staff of total staff employed overseas.[8]

Each diplomatic post is headed by an ambassador or a high commissioner. Most of them are career appointments from within DFAT, but a handful of posts are still used for political patronage or because the government of the day believes that its message can be more effectively put by one of its own. In a mission like Washington, DC, strong personal relationships within the Australian Government add credibility to the Ambassador's position and can make operating with senior levels of the Administration and Congress easier. Good political appointees in these circumstances can be as effective as the best professionals. Heads of mission are chosen by the government but are appointed by the Executive Council, and their credentials (that is, the official documents of appointment) are issued by the Governor-General in the name of the head of state. This method of appointment underlines the fact that heads of mission represent not just DFAT but the government as a whole. They have overall responsibility for the full management of the bilateral relationship with the country of accreditation. In administrative terms, the Ambassador's role in the post is formally set out in a 1985 directive, the Prime Minister's "Guide-lines for the Management of the Australian Government Presence Overseas".[9]

The head of mission's authority within the post rests, however, far more on his or her personal qualities of leadership than on any formal document.

Most Australian missions include representatives of other departments and agencies. AusAID officers are at many developing-country posts, and defence attachés are posted in most regional countries and other important capitals. Other departments and agencies represented overseas include Immigration, Education, Treasury, Industry, Health, the Australian Federal Police, Industry, and the intelligence and security agencies. DFAT provides common services (that is, local administrative support, security services, communications, and so on) for all officers at posts and recovers costs from their home departments. But apart from the Immigration Department, the general trend of overseas representation by other departments is on the decline, a result of increasing overseas costs and easier and more rapid communications. The Defence Department and some of the intelligence agencies now have direct communications links with their principal allies. Other departments also find it easier to deal with their opposite numbers directly from their headquarters, a process that has been aided by the growth of regional organisations. The trend of the late 1980s and early 1990s towards an expansion of overseas representation by other departments in Asia was reversed in the late 1990s and early 2000s. In 2002, for example, the Industry Department withdrew its representatives from Jakarta and Seoul.

The work of the posts

Much of the work of Australia's overseas missions has little to do with foreign policy making. The functions of smaller posts, in particular, are limited and carefully targeted: supporting Australian travellers, providing on-the-spot advice for Australian businesspeople and promoting Australia's international image through cultural or public diplomacy. All posts carry responsibility for the sometimes onerous but important job of arranging programs and providing support for visits by ministers and senior officials. The career paths of heads of mission insufficiently sensitive to this task have been precarious and sometimes abruptly cut short. Consular issues – that is, support for Australian citizens – are increasingly important for DFAT and its minister. More Australians are travelling abroad, and the number getting into trouble of some sort while overseas is increasing in proportion. In 2000–01, around 3.6 million Australians travelled abroad, and more than 99,000 of them required some form of consular assistance.[10] To meet this need, DFAT had 160 "points of consular service", including DFAT posts and honorary consulates, Austrade posts and Canadian missions, which, under a reciprocal deal with Australia, serve the interests of Australian visitors in parts of the world like Africa and Latin America, where Australia is not heavily represented. More than most issues in the DFAT portfolio, consular problems are easily personalised. They engage the attention of tabloid (and, increasingly, broadsheet) newspapers, television and talkback radio, with all the implications this has for politicians. The priority given to consular matters increased markedly when Alexander Downer became Foreign Minister in 1996.

Information

Notwithstanding the growth of these other tasks, overseas posts retain a central role in traditional foreign policy making. They provide its nerve ends. They are part of the beginning and the end of each loop in the continuous process through which foreign policy is made. Diplomats in posts collect information about issues that could affect Australian interests and report it to Canberra, often with advice about how Australia should respond. Then, once any policy response has been decided in Canberra, posts also have a major responsibility for implementing it. Their job at this point in the cycle is to convey, in the most persuasive way possible, the views of the Australian Government to the governments to which they are accredited and, in doing so, to try to convince those governments to act in ways that suit Australian interests. Of course, in practice the foreign policy process does not work so neatly. Foreign policies do not often begin and end in such a usefully clear-cut way. The environment in which they are operating and to which they are responding keeps changing. US diplomat Richard Holbrooke aptly described diplomacy as being less like chess than like jazz – "improvisations on a theme".[11]

If the institution of the overseas mission has not greatly changed in form in over 500 years, the way it does its work has altered radically. It is becoming much harder for posts to act autonomously. The days when Thomas Jefferson could write to his Secretary of State, "We have not heard from our Ambassador in Spain for two years. If we do not hear from him this year, let us write him a letter",[12] are long gone. Secure communications systems, emails and mobile telephones can track down and instruct the most reclusive head of mission. Posts can be in no doubt about what the department in Canberra is thinking about a given issue. Compared with the past, ministers are also more inclined, and more able, to pick up a telephone and speak directly to an ambassador. This does not necessarily mean a decline in the policy influence of diplomatic missions. The same technology in reverse gives posts the capacity for more immediate input into the policy-making process in Canberra. Submissions to the minister about policy changes, draft speeches or press releases, or simply back-channel conversations – say from desk officers to their colleagues in missions – are far easier to manage and exchange with secure and cheap communications. Secure email has transformed the contact between posts and the department. It enables more personal contact than the formal cablegram, with its wide distribution and impersonal style (and is less likely to be leaked).

Reporting

Reporting by posts has altered radically in form and content over the past twenty-five years. It is less descriptive and more policy-oriented. Longer-term, longer-form policy advice such as diplomatic dispatches – formal communications from the head of mission to the Foreign Minister – have been abandoned. Changes in information technology mean that posts are no longer the principal conduits to government for general information about what is happening overseas. It has been suggested, including at times by the Australian Department of Finance, that the reporting role of posts might be better left to journalists or outsourced to commercial operations. It is true that diplomats, for the most part on three-year postings, will usually be unable to compete for knowledge of the local scene in, say, Vietnam or India with academics who have spent a lifetime studying it, nor move around as freely and flexibly as the best journalists (or convey the situation with as much power). But that is not really the task of diplomatic reporting. The reporting function of diplomats is to understand and analyse the way developments in the country they are covering will affect Australian interests, broadly interpreted. For that to happen they need to bring to their job at least as much knowledge of Australian foreign policy as insight into the country they live in.

In one way, in any case, DFAT has already outsourced reporting. One of the authors of this book, who served in Rangoon in the early 1970s, recalls the difficulty of finding variations on the words "It was a quiet month in Burma" with which to begin a monthly political report for the department. His report, covering such weighty matters as the visit of an Indian trade delegation or a reorganisation of local government structures in Mandalay, was sent by diplomatic bag to an equally junior officer in Canberra, who may have glanced at it quickly before consigning it to a file where it rested, no doubt undisturbed, until consigned to some archival graveyard. Now the chronicle of day-to-day events is available to the department – and just as importantly to ministers – from a wide variety of other sources, including satellite television and the internet.

Some posts are instructed to do no reporting at all, and for almost all others reporting has become limited to issues of direct concern to Australian foreign policy. For the most part, Australian diplomats now provide commentary and glosses on accounts of events that are already known to Canberra. (There are exceptions. Posts in Asia, like the Australian Embassy in Jakarta, with a political and economic branch of around sixteen officers, still undertake extensive and high-quality reporting of the traditional kind.)

In a further development, DFAT has established an Open Source Collection Unit to collate, translate and distribute within government news reports from the South Pacific and Indonesia, where it employs two translators. These translated press reports are fed into the regular cable-distribution network and relieve the Jakarta embassy of the need to report separately on these issues unless it has a separate comment to make. Priorities for translation are set by the National Intelligence Collection Priorities (see Chapter 7). The reporting priorities of posts are increasingly set less by events on the ground than by the media and political environment in Australia. If the newspapers are running with an issue that has the potential to embarrass the minister or expose him to question, the issues are set. So the great majority of embassy reporting is event-driven. But, whatever the form, reporting is not the end of the job for posts. At the other end of the policy cycle is advocacy work; that is, the job of persuading other governments to take actions that suit Australia, or to avoid taking actions that might harm its interests.

Advocacy

Effective diplomatic advocacy has three dimensions to it: clarity of objectives (that is, knowing what you want to achieve and the tactics most likely to deliver it), the personal skills of the diplomat, and the power of the country he or she represents. Objectives (or foreign policy goals) are largely the government's to set. Canberra will usually send instructions to the post. But decisions on tactics – who needs to be influenced, what will best persuade them, who are potential allies and who adversaries, and how it can be done – are for the diplomats overseas to make.

In this operation, the intelligence, integrity, cultural understanding and energy of individual diplomats are critical. If they are any good at their jobs, they will have developed relationships grounded in trust and mutual understanding with influential members of the country in which they are accredited. They will (and here the situation is no different from any negotiations) have worked hard to understand the motives, thought patterns and culture of the other side. In 1837, Talleyrand, by then an old man, described the qualities of diplomacy:

> there is one thing that I must say in order to destroy a widely spread prejudice: No. Diplomacy is not a science of deceit and duplicity. If good faith is necessary anywhere it is above all in political transactions, for it is that which makes them firm and lasting. People have made the mistake of confusing reserve with deceit. Good faith never authorizes deceit but it admits of reserve; and reserve has this peculiarity that it increases confidence.[13]

Talleyrand, of course, knew a great deal about reserve.

This basic requirement of diplomats – the need to understand the interests of others in order to pursue better the interests of the government for which they work – lies at the base of some of the mistrust of the profession, and the belief that diplomats are too easily seduced by the country in which they are living, too willing to dump the national interest in the cause of "good relations". The writings of journalist Brian Toohey provide a good example:

> Diplomatic postings ... often induce a tendency to defend the behaviour of host governments rather than deliver tough messages about human rights or the virtues of financial probity ... As one official puts it: "Invitations to presidential cocktail parties are less likely to be forthcoming if an Ambassador insists on delivering yet another sermon."[14]

Stuart Harris offers a different interpretation:

> The Anglo-Saxon culture and institutions are commonly adversarial, whereas representational work involves compromise and mediation: international representation is biased towards resolving conflicts, to mitigating and civilising differences between nations and ambiguity is at times of great value. This distinction is often most clear in contrasting what is seen as the Australian blunt, direct, at times aggressive style judged to be characteristic of domestic dealings, against the style judged necessary in dealing with other cultures.[15]

This is not to diminish the danger to diplomats of becoming disconnected from their own country and culture. Even one of their number, Sir Harold Nicolson, acknowledged that diplomats can become "denationalized, internationalized and therefore dehydrated, an elegant empty husk".[16] However, more regular postings, easier communications with Australia and more open recruitment processes within DFAT make this a much less likely outcome than it has been in the past.

The final dimension of successful diplomatic advocacy is the power of the state. In fact "clout" is probably a better word than power, because it is vaguer and more subjective, and better reflects the imprecise, immeasurable and fluid mix of economic strength, military weight, political influence, national image and cultural influence that make it more or less possible for a particular nation, at one time or another, and in one place or another, to have its interests accommodated. This relationship is never fixed in time or place. In general, however, it will always be true that the Australian High Commissioner to Nauru can bring far more weight to bear on the Nauruan Government than his or her counterpart in Brasilia can achieve with the Government of Brazil. As was seen with the 2001 "Pacific solution" to the flows of asylum-seekers arriving in Australia by boat, Nauru itself, and the particular ministers and officials being lobbied, have far greater interest in Australia and more reason to accommodate its policies than do Brazilian ministers. So the most able Australian Ambassador in Brasilia will always have less influence than even a mediocre high commissioner to one of the smaller South Pacific posts. Similarly, the views on the situation in the Middle East of a junior US diplomat in Tel Aviv will be listened to with more rapt attention than will those of the Australian Ambassador. It is difficult for embassies to influence governments. Domestic pressures will usually play on the government Australia is trying to influence far more forcefully than any persuasive power Australia can bring to bear. And other governments – as well as business interests or non-governmental organisations – may be applying counterpressures in an effort to bring about different results.

Most of its practitioners (a sizeable 68 per cent of respondents to our 2001 survey) believe that a distinctly Australian style of diplomacy has emerged, and they characterise it in positive terms. The most frequently used adjectives were: energetic (37 per cent), informal (35 per cent), direct (26 per cent), imaginative (20 per cent) and well-prepared (20 per cent).

Conclusion

The cost of Australia's network of overseas posts is substantial, a fact that has not escaped successive iterations of federal razor gangs over the years. Yet no government, however budget-minded, has been willing to dismantle this major piece of Australia's foreign policy architecture. Even in the era of globalisation and instantaneous media reporting of overseas news, it is plain that the network of diplomatic posts plays a crucial series of roles in the national interest. Most of these we have discussed in this chapter. Yet a major role of the overseas posts falls into the ambit of the intelligence community, the last major piece of foreign policy architecture yet to be discussed, which will be considered in the next chapter.

Notes

1 Stuart Harris, *Review of Australia's Overseas Representation,* Canberra: AGPS, 1986, p. xiv.
2 Department of Foreign Affairs and Trade Annual Report 2001–02, p. 348.
3 ibid. Offices in Taiwan and Ramallah were managed separately.
4 Department of Foreign Affairs and Trade Corporate Plan 2000-2002, p. 13.
5 Harris, *Review of Australia's Overseas Representation*, p. xix.
6 Figures drawn from Foreign and Trade Ministry Best Practice Review, Report to the Secretary by R.C. Smith, August 2000, Restricted.
7 Ashton Calvert, "Secretary's Speech: The Role of DFAT at the Turn of the Century", address to the Canberra Branch of the Australian Institute of International Affairs, 4 February 1999.
8 Foreign and Trade Ministry Best Practice Review, pp. 25, 26.
9 ibid., p. 6.
10 Department of Foreign Affairs and Trade Annual Report 2000–01, p. 143.
11 Quoted in Michael Ignatieff, *Virtual War*, London: Chatto and Windus, 2000, p. 17.
12 Quoted in Abba Eban, *Diplomacy for the Next Century*, New Haven, CT: Yale University Press, 1998, p. 92.
13 Quoted in Duff Cooper, *Talleyrand*, London: Phoenix, 1997 (originally published 1932), p. 358.
14 *Australian Financial Review*, 13 December 1997.
15 Harris, *Review of Australia's Overseas Representation*, p. 3.
16 Harold Nicolson, *The Evolution of Diplomacy*, New York: Collier, 1962, p. 107.

CHAPTER 7

The Australian Intelligence Community

It is probably not surprising that much of the limited amount of writing on Australia's intelligence agencies has concentrated on what is most distinctive about them – their secrecy and culture – rather than their place in public administration. Most analysis has focussed on their technical capabilities, their external links, their relationship with politicians and the political process, and the culture of intelligence.[1]

This way of looking at the agencies has been reinforced by the mystification and sometimes excessive secrecy in which they have traditionally wrapped themselves, and by the media's willing suspension of disbelief when reporting on many intelligence matters. As commissioners Samuels and Codd commented in their 1995 report of the Commission of Inquiry into the Australian Secret Intelligence Service: "The fascination which journalists apparently feel for secret organizations tends to expel judgment and restraint".[2]

This chapter looks at the intelligence agencies in a different way, as part of the Australian foreign policy making machinery. It describes their structure and functions, their links with overseas agencies and their relationships with Australian policy-makers in order to answer the question, "How do the intelligence agencies influence the formulation and implementation of Australian foreign policy?" Would Australian foreign policy be different if we did not have this particular intelligence community?

Australia has been in the intelligence business since the beginning of its nationhood. The new Federal Government sent a French-speaking agent under cover as a businessman to gather intelligence in New Caledonia in 1901.[3] But most of the principal Australian intelligence agencies were created at the end of the Second World War and the beginning of the Cold War, during the years when the national government was grappling for the first time with the development of a comprehensive Australian foreign policy. The intelligence agencies, in other words, grew in parallel with Australia's foreign policy institutions almost from the beginning.

Definitions of intelligence and its various subsets abound, but in the context of its contribution to foreign policy it is best thought of as another word for information. "Useful information" is one of the simplest but most accurate definitions. In his first royal commission report into the Australian security and intelligence agencies in 1977, Justice Hope quoted approvingly the US scholar Sherman Kent's definition of intelligence as knowledge: "The kind of knowledge our state must possess regarding other states in order to assure itself that its cause will not suffer nor its undertakings fail because its statesmen and soldiers plan and act in ignorance".[4]

Such knowledge does not have to be secret or covertly collected. Open sources – newspapers, radio, television, the internet, the reporting of Australian embassies, the analysis undertaken inside the Department of Foreign Affairs and Trade in Canberra and its overseas posts – provide the overwhelming bulk of intelligence available to the Australian Government at any time. Any good diplomat will from time to time persuade sources to impart confidential information. At least so far as foreign policy making is concerned, Australia's most powerful and comprehensive intelligence agency is DFAT. Its day-to-day capacity to gather information and shape policy with its analysis outweighs the others by a large margin.

But some information cannot be obtained from open-source or diplomatic reporting. By its nature it can be critically important. (Is Iraq likely to attack Kuwait? How far has North Korea got in developing nuclear weapons? Have the military forces in country X begun moving overnight, and does the government need to prepare for the evacuation of Australian civilians?) Or, if not critical, such information can still be very valuable to the national interest. (What is Australia's opponent's negotiating position on a particular trade question?)

Secret intelligence is also important in filling in gaps when ordinary forms of diplomacy fail, or look like failing. Australia experienced this problem when diplomatic access to Bougainville became impossible after the unilateral declaration of independence there. Similarly, during the violent days immediately after the independence referendum in East Timor in 1999, when diplomats, aid workers and UN personnel had been evacuated, intelligence information was almost the only source of information Australia had about what was happening on the ground. Even in cases where governments are currently open (in the Southwest Pacific, for example), it cannot be assumed that this will remain the case.

In answering broad questions about the political, economic or strategic outlook (will Indonesia hold together or fragment? will ASEAN remain a core part of the Southeast Asian regional architecture? will Japan further open its agriculture markets?), experienced diplomats, analysts or academic specialists will usually have more to contribute to government assessments than will specific pieces of secret intelligence.

Justice Hope commented:

> Australia cannot hope to know everything that is going on in every part of the world. But we can try to keep informed about what people are doing and planning in areas of special significance to us. That requires us to be discriminating in choosing subjects for intelligence collection and assessment.[5]

Such discrimination is essential because secret intelligence is an expensive and sometimes risky way to gather information. It is difficult to estimate Australia's expenditure on foreign intelligence, and not only because of the limited amount of public information available about the agency budgets. Much of the intelligence budget of the Department of Defence, for example, also covers the military intelligence aspects of ADF operations. In the 2001–02 Australian budget, the Defence Department's intelligence output was costed at $385 million, ASIS's one-line appropriation was given at around $55 million, ONA's at $7.1 million and ASIO's at $70 million (only part of which was related to foreign intelligence). Thus, a reasonable estimate of Australia's annual foreign-intelligence expenditure in that year was around $350 million to $400 million. This amounts to almost half the $805 million allocation for DFAT in the same year.

The six agencies that form the Australian intelligence community (AIC) divide broadly between those whose job is to collect information, and those that analyse it, providing context and interpretation for what is termed the "raw" data of collection. The foreign-intelligence collectors are the Defence Signals Directorate (DSD), the Australian Secret Intelligence Service (ASIS), the Defence Imagery and Geospatial Organisation (DIGO) and, in one particular regard, the Australian Security Intelligence Organisation (ASIO). The analytical organisations are the Office of National Assessments (ONA) and the Defence Intelligence Organisation (DIO). (ASIO also has an analytical responsibility for security intelligence.)

The contribution intelligence makes to the formulation and implementation of foreign policy is by no means its only role. The agencies under the aegis of the Defence portfolio (as well as ASIS) make vital contributions to the operational capabilities of the ADF. ASIO's principal role is counter-terrorism and counter-espionage.

The collection agencies

Defence Signals Directorate

The Defence Signals Directorate is the oldest, largest and costliest of the Australian secret intelligence agencies. Its functions, set out in the *Intelligence Services Act 2001*, are:

a) to obtain intelligence about the capabilities, intentions or activities of people or organisations outside Australia in the form of electromagnetic energy, whether guided or unguided or both, or in the form of electrical, magnetic or acoustic energy, for the purposes of meeting the requirements of the Government, and in particular the requirements of the Defence Force for such intelligence;

b) to communicate, in accordance with the government's requirements, such intelligence;

c) to provide material, advice and other assistance to Commonwealth and State authorities on matters relating to the security and integrity of information that is processed, stored or communicated by electronic or similar means; and

d) to provide assistance to Commonwealth and State authorities in relation to cryptography and communications technologies.[6]

When Prime Minister Malcolm Fraser acknowledged the agency's existence for the first time in October 1977, he told the House of Representatives, more simply, that:

> the Defence Signals Directorate is an organisation concerned with radio, radar and other electronic emissions from the standpoint both of the information and the intelligence they can provide and the security of our own Government communications and electronic emissions.[7]

The advent of large electronic databases and the explosion of email communications have opened up new areas of opportunity for DSD.

Unlike its British or US counterparts, DSD operates as an integral part of the Department of Defence, reporting through the department to the minister. Its director (like the heads of the other agencies under the Defence umbrella) is appointed by the Secretary of the Defence Department. And unlike ONA, ASIO or ASIS, it does not have statutory independence.

DSD has an important role in providing operational, technical and strategic intelligence for the ADF (around one-third of its staff are uniformed personnel), but in foreign policy terms its most relevant task is intercepting and decrypting communications from other governments and individuals. Access to such communications can throw invaluable direct light on the intentions of others.

DSD was created as the Defence Signals Bureau in November 1947 from the Australian wartime communications intelligence operations. It was renamed the Defence Signals Directorate in 1978. Its foundation was overseen by the British Government Communications Headquarters (GCHQ), but following Australia's participation in the 1948 UKUSA security agreement, it developed an increasingly close relationship with the United States National Security Agency. By 1948 a US liaison group had arrived at DSB's Melbourne headquarters.[8]

The secret UKUSA agreement grew out of the shared Allied communications intelligence cooperation during the Second World War. It brought under a single umbrella the signals intelligence (SIGINT) organisations of the United States, Britain, Canada, Australia and New Zealand.[9] The UKUSA members developed standardised terminology, code words, intercept-handling procedures and secrecy provisions. The agreement remains the foundation of the close SIGINT relationship between Australia and the United States. But, more extensively, it underpins the intelligence relationship as a whole. It facilitates an openness and ease of communication in shared intelligence analysis, for example, that would otherwise be impossible. Without the SIGINT partnership, Australia would simply be one of a number of small allies with ad hoc intelligence liaison relationships with the United States.

Australia's most visible direct contribution to burden-sharing within the UKUSA partnership is the important joint collection facilities at Geraldton and at Pine Gap, near Alice Springs, although the integrated work of collection through Shoal Bay is more important.

DSD moved its headquarters from Melbourne to purpose-built premises in Canberra in 1992. As a result of the move, it has become much more effectively integrated into the rest of the intelligence community as well as the Defence Department.[10]

DSD has been at the centre of the information revolution for intelligence. Appearing before a parliamentary select committee on intelligence in August 2001, the then Director of DSD, Ron Bonighton, described DSD's contemporary operations in the following terms:

> We all know we are in the middle of an information revolution, and that is
> predicated on the new communications technologies that are abroad in the world.
> The old days of low volume, wireless communications and Morse code are long

gone, but that is the sort of environment for which DSD was established. Increasingly in the future we are going to be in a world of infinitely varied and complex communications systems where the velocity of those communications will be at speeds that would not even be countenanced 10 or 15 years ago and where the volumes are exponentially increasing. DSD's job can be described as looking for nuggets of intelligence in mullock heaps of information.[11]

Australian Secret Intelligence Service

The Australian Secret Intelligence Service collects human intelligence in ways familiar to any reader of espionage novels, if often less glamorously. The then Director-General of ASIO may have been stretching the definition of the word "mundane", however, when he described ASIS's work to the Joint Parliamentary Select Committee on Intelligence. "There's not much Ian Fleming in it?" asked the Chair. "Very little," Allan Taylor responded. "It is mundane. Meeting people and collecting intelligence is basically what it is."[12]

Human intelligence (known as HUMINT) refers to intelligence gathered from people by people, rather than intelligence gathered by machines. Developing secret sources is a time-consuming and often frustrating business. For intelligence purposes, however, it can be invaluable because agents have a flexibility – a capability for interrogation – that signals intelligence and imagery do not possess.

ASIS's remit goes beyond traditional political and economic intelligence. It provides some direct operational assistance to the ADF, for example, as well as invaluable support for other forms of intelligence like SIGINT and computer network attack. More recently, it has been asked to play a role in monitoring people-smuggling.[13]

ASIS headquarters in Canberra are co-located with the Department of Foreign Affairs and Trade. Most of its overseas staff operate under diplomatic cover. It is a small organisation, with staff in the hundreds. Its budget is set out as a one-line item in the DFAT budget. In 2001–02 it was more than $55 million.

Like all Australian intelligence agencies, its principal focus is Asia and the South Pacific. Its first foreign station was established in Jakarta in September 1954. Japan followed in 1955.[14] According to press reports, it now maintains about eighteen stations overseas.[15]

The Director-General is appointed by the Governor-General on the recommendation of the Prime Minister, after consultation with the Leader of the Opposition. He or she is responsible to the Minister for Foreign Affairs (but not the Secretary of DFAT) for the operations and activities of the agency.

ASIS is precluded by legislation from planning for, or undertaking, "paramilitary activities or activities involving violence against the person or the use of weapons".[16] ASIS was originally given limited capabilities in the area of "special political action"; that is, covert operations backed by lethal force. This capability was removed after a training incident at a hotel in Melbourne went badly wrong in February 1984.[17]

Under its Act, the service's functions are:

a) to obtain, in accordance with the Government's requirements, intelligence about the capabilities, intentions or activities of people or organisations outside Australia;

b) to communicate, in accordance with the Government's requirements, such intelligence;

c) to conduct counter-intelligence activities;

d) to liaise with intelligence or security services, or other authorities, of other countries; and

e) to undertake such other activities as the responsible Minister directs to relating the capabilities, intentions or activities of people or organisations outside Australia.[18]

In May 1950 the Australian Government of R.G. Menzies decided to accept an invitation from the British Secret Intelligence Service (MI6) to pay for and train a small group of Australians in London.[19] Menzies wrote in his own hand to advise his British counterpart, Clement Attlee, of the decision:

I have decided to establish a Secret Intelligence Service which, when organised, will operate in Southeast Asia and in Pacific areas adjacent to Australia. Recent developments in Asia and our "near north" make this a prudent and urgent measure … I trust that the establishment of an Australian Service may in some small measure reduce the onerous world-wide commitments of the United Kingdom.[20]

After two years of study and planning, ASIS finally was created formally by executive direction on 13 May 1952. It continued to receive active support from its British mentor.[21] The service's existence was not acknowledged publicly for another twenty-five years.

In the report of their 1995 Commission of Inquiry into ASIS, Justice Samuels and Michael Codd repeated earlier recommendations that ASIS be brought under legislative cover to affirm its existence and provide authority for its activities. They noted:

ASIS carries out important functions in the national interest. Its operations are usually sensitive and potentially controversial. It is no longer appropriate that the authority for the exercise of these functions should be conferred exclusively by the executive arm of government. It is appropriate that, in a parliamentary democracy, the existence of an agency such as ASIS should be endorsed by the Parliament and the scope and limits of its functions defined by legislation.[22]

This was finally done in the *Intelligence Services Act 2001.*

ASIS's value to its customers shifts from time to time, according to the quality of its product and the needs of its consumers. But Samuels and Codd concluded that ASIS's operational management was

well structured and its tactical decisions are thoroughly considered and, in major instances, subject to external approval. Its operational people are skilled and discreet, and the product it gathers is well regarded by its customers and professional assessors.[23]

ASIS's contribution to foreign policy making does not lie exclusively in its collection activities. It also maintains a wide range of liaison contacts through "declared" officers posted to the overseas capitals of friendly countries. In 1977, Justice Hope reported that it maintained intelligence liaison relations with Japan, Singapore, Malaysia, Thailand and Indonesia, in addition to its partners in the United States, Britain, Canada and New Zealand.[24] The number of such countries is now greater.

Defence Imagery and Geospatial Organisation

The Defence Imagery and Geospatial Organisation is the newest of the intelligence agencies. It was created in November 2000 to bring together the Australian Imagery Organisation (formerly DIO's imagery-analysis arm), which was established in 1964,[25] the Directorate of Strategic Military Geographic Information and the Defence Topographic Agency.[26] Like DSD, it is an integrated part of the Department of Defence.

DIGO's staff of more than 200 collect – or, more accurately, collate and interpret – overhead (principally satellite) imagery, as well as providing geospatial information to support advanced weapons systems.[27] Imagery is also collected principally by manned aircraft and, increasingly, by UAVs (uninhabited aerial vehicles).

DIGO was established in response to rapid technological changes in satellites and digital imaging that were making imagery collection and analysis one of the great growth areas for intelligence. Imagery is obviously vital to ADF operations, but it also has an important national-security dimension. All recent arms-control agreements, for example, have depended upon it for verification.

This is the area of the Australian intelligence community where dependence on the United States is the highest. As the US investment in imagery intelligence grows, DIGO is likely to require considerable resources in order to keep up.

Australian Security Intelligence Organisation

The Australian Security Intelligence Organisation is primarily concerned with gathering intelligence on activities or situations that might endanger Australia's national security (defined in the *Australian Security Intelligence Organisation Act 1979* as the protection of Australia and its people from espionage, sabotage, politically motivated violence, the promotion of communal violence, attacks on Australia's defence system, and acts of foreign interference).

A simpler definition is given in ASIO's own description of what it does:

> ASIO focuses on terrorists, people who may act violently for political reasons and people who may clandestinely obtain sensitive government information (spies) or otherwise harm Australia's interests in order to further their own causes or the interests of foreign governments.[28]

Its job is to collect information on these areas and to analyse it. Unlike its US counterpart, the FBI, it has no powers to charge or arrest. For this reason it works closely with the state and federal police forces.

ASIO also performs a particular foreign-intelligence role. It is authorised to collect foreign intelligence inside Australia on behalf of the foreign-intelligence collection agencies, ASIS and DSD. The reason for this is that ASIO alone can operate under a single authority and legal framework inside Australia. ASIO can only collect such intelligence at the request of the Minister for Defence (for DSD) or the Minister for Foreign Affairs (for ASIS).

The analytical agencies

The product of the collection agencies – the SIGINT, imagery and secret reporting – is distributed directly to security-cleared individuals who need to know about the information. Recipients include ministers and ministerial offices, the relevant areas of DFAT, Defence and PM&C, and other departments and agencies whose interests are involved (information on people-smuggling to Immigration, on financial issues to Treasury, and so on).

But the principal customers for the product of the collection agencies are the analytical agencies, ONA and DIO. These agencies – ONA for a national audience, DIO primarily for Defence customers – combine the raw intelligence with the information available from open sources and diplomatic reporting, sift it through the filter of experienced analysts and turn it finally into intelligence reporting.

Unprocessed intelligence can be seductive and therefore dangerous. Its colourfulness can have a distorting effect on policy. Heavily code-worded documents purporting to reveal the private thoughts or communications of adversaries or friends are intrinsically interesting, but without being put in context or against the total background they can be deeply misleading. A former Prime Minister, Paul Keating, records

> I was a more sceptical and disinterested consumer of secret intelligence than some other Prime Ministers have been. Very sceptical in fact. It is easy to be seduced by documents stamped with code-words and handled through special channels and easy to forget to ask, "Yes, but does it matter?" For this reason I did not usually see, or want to see, unassessed intelligence but preferred it properly assessed and put in the context of what we knew from all sources.[29]

Office of National Assessments

The Office of National Assessments was established by the *Office of National Assessments Act 1977*, following the royal commission established by the Whitlam Government in 1974 under Justice Robert Hope to report on Australia's intelligence and security services.[30]

Hope found an intelligence-assessment process that was the subject of a tug of war for control between the powerful departments of Defence and Foreign Affairs, each of which was suspicious of the other's intentions. He concluded that Australia needed to take a new, more national approach to intelligence analysis. To elevate the assessment process beyond the debilitating bureaucratic rivalry he found, he recommended the creation of a new assessments office to undertake short-term (current intelligence) and longer-term assessments. The Fraser Government accepted the recommendation, and the new office was created under the Prime Minister's portfolio and reporting to him.

ONA's functions under its Act are to assemble and correlate information relating to international matters that are of political, strategic or economic significance to Australia, and to prepare reports and longer-term national assessments about them. The ONA website puts it more concisely. The office's role, it says, is "to enhance the basis for Australian government policy-making by anticipating and analyzing international change and its implications for Australia and to ensure coordination of the national intelligence effort".[31]

ONA has no policy responsibilities; that is, its functions are to describe, analyse and (so far as possible) anticipate international developments, not to prescribe actions to change the world. Reviewing his creation in his second royal commission report in 1984, Hope noted:

> the very purpose of having an independent body like ONA in the centre of an assessment process is to facilitate the preparation for the government of informed assessments that are not circumscribed by the policy perceptions of departments.[32]

In more direct words, ONA exists because of the dangerous but ingrained tendency of policy-makers to interpret the world in terms of the policies they have already prescribed to deal with it.

What matters most about ONA is its capacity to look freshly at the world from a perspective outside the policy framework; to bring an outsider's dispassion to the rapidly changing world of the policy-maker. In the words of one senior Australian policy-maker, ONA operates as an "independent reality check". To make its assessments, it works in an all-source environment; that is, it draws on all the information – overt and covert – available to the Australian Government.

Like the other agencies, ONA's value to Australian foreign policy at any given time depends on the quality, timeliness and relevance of its work to the policy-making community. Its product is distributed in several different forms – Warning Notes to alert policy-makers to a looming crisis, Watch Reports to provide regular updates during a crisis, Intelligence Notes, dealing with less pressing issues, and Current Assessments, which are longer-term analyses, usually no more than two pages long.

Hope's original vision of ONA was that it would undertake a higher proportion of broader National Assessments, which would try to look ahead at Australia's political and economic environment. Like almost all intelligence structures, however, ONA has found that the day-to-day demands of policy-makers for information about what is happening right now tend to diminish the market for, and the capacity to prepare, such longer-term assessments.

Within government, ONA has a reputation for writing directly and colourfully rather than in flat bureaucratic prose. This style occasionally irritates (and sometimes distorts), but it has the advantage of sharpening and dramatising choices for decision-makers.

Headed from the beginning by former diplomats, it draws its staff from within the public service and from academic specialists. Its 2000–01 budget was $6.7 million, and it has a staff of around sixty. ONA's focus, for political and economic assessments, has always been heavily on Asia and the Pacific, but it has also sought to maintain a limited capability for global assessment, especially on strategic issues.

The Director-General also has a general overview role within the intelligence community, which is discussed below.

Defence Intelligence Organisation

The Defence Intelligence Organisation is a collation and analytical organisation serving the Defence Department and the Australian Defence Force. Its staff of more than 200 is drawn from civilians and serving members of the ADF. It has a small intelligence-collection capability, in that Australian military attachés, who are tasked by DIO, also collect information, as diplomats do, in the normal course of their work.

Founded as the Joint Intelligence Bureau in 1946 to bring together the wartime service intelligence directorates, it became the Joint Intelligence Organisation after a review in 1969. In earlier forms, it incorporated some of the national assessment responsibilities of ONA, and since ONA's establishment in 1977 has sometimes had difficulty deciding where its focus lies. The slow pattern over recent years, however, has been for a steadily greater integration of DIO into the Defence Department and ADF structures. This has not always been easy.

DIO's contribution to the national foreign policy process has been greatest during crises such as the Iraq war and the peacekeeping operation in East Timor.

With frequent changes at the top, and personnel and security problems that received extensive media coverage, over the 1990s DIO was probably the least stable of the intelligence agencies.

Accountability and oversight

Writing about the Australian intelligence agencies in 1978, a prominent critic, Richard Hall, described them as "a self-perpetuating intelligence elite which too often looks for the approval of its accepted peer group, the international intelligence club".[33] His outsider's criticism was hardly more damning than Hope's conclusion a year earlier:

The Australian intelligence community is fragmented, poorly coordinated and organized. The agencies lack proper guidance, direction and control. They do not have good or close relations with the system of government they should serve.[34]

It is difficult to put in place proper accountability and oversight arrangements for organisations which are necessarily secret, and some of which operate illegally in other countries. That difficulty, however, makes it even more important that the Australian people, through Parliament, can be assured that the institutions their taxes are funding are doing what they are supposed to do – but only that – and that they are doing it well enough to justify the money that is being spent on them. As the Director-General of ASIO, Dennis Richardson, told the *Australian Financial Review*:

> When you are an organisation doing work that is mostly secret, the accountability arrangements are essential in giving confidence to the community that the powers of the organisations will not be abused.[35]

Accountability arrangements are also important in ensuring the protection of the privacy of Australian citizens.

External accountability and oversight are also important to the intelligence agencies for internal reasons, however. Without them, small agencies, operating in a climate of secrecy, are particularly vulnerable to losing perspective on the outside world and drifting away from the community in which they operate.

The period from the first Hope Royal Commission report in 1977, through his second report 1984, to the Samuels and Codd Commission of Inquiry into ASIS in 1995 and the *Intelligence Services Act 2001*, was a story of the gradual integration of the intelligence agencies into the Australian foreign policy process, a growing movement to accountability and greater, though inevitably limited, transparency.

The reforms adopted after the Hope royal commissions improved coordination and oversight. Lines of accountability through individual ministers and Cabinet were made clearer. The Office of the Inspector-General of Intelligence and Security was created. The opaque intelligence world became slightly clearer as the existence of agencies was publicly acknowledged. ASIO, and later ASIS and DSD were brought under limited parliamentary oversight. Agency recruitment became more open and broadly based.

Perhaps equally importantly, the key collection agencies were physically relocated from Melbourne to Canberra (ASIO in 1982, ASIS in 1984, and DSD in 1992). These moves caused significant short-term disruption (ASIS lost 50 per cent of its staff in the move),[36] but they also opened the agencies up to fresh blood and, most importantly, integrated them much more effectively into the work of government and into the foreign policy making process. The moves ended an era in which the agencies thought of themselves as separate from the Australian Government.

At the top of the accountability pyramid for the intelligence agencies sits the National Security Committee of Cabinet (NSC). This was established in its earliest form as the National and International Security Committee in 1977, following Justice Hope's criticisms of government coordination and control of the intelligence agencies. (The Cabinet committee does not replace the responsibility of individual ministers for the agencies under their control, a point emphasised by Hope in 1984 and re-endorsed by Samuels and Codd in 1995.)[37]

In relation to the intelligence agencies, the NSC's main functions are to set broad intelligence priorities, review and approve the budgets, and approve outlines for the operation of the agencies.[38] (A fuller account is given in Chapter 5.) Samuels and Codd reported in 1995 that the Security Committee of Cabinet met between three and six times a year. Under the Howard Government, the committee met more frequently and with greater direct participation by the agency heads as well as ministers. During crises (for example, the East Timor deployment and the Iraq war), the committee meets almost every day, with the intelligence agencies providing updates.

At officials level, the senior coordinating mechanism for the intelligence community is the Secretaries Committee on National Security (SCNS). This was also part of the package of changes introduced after the first Hope Royal Commission. SCNS is chaired by the Secretary of the Department of the Prime Minister and Cabinet and comprises the secretaries of Foreign Affairs, Defence, Attorney-General's Department, Immigration and Treasury, the Commander of the Australian Defence Force and the Director-General of ONA. Other agency and departmental heads (such as that of Finance) are coopted where necessary. All the work of Cabinet's NSC in the intelligence area – especially the annual round of reporting, forward estimates and budget estimates – is filtered first through SCNS.

The secretariat for both SCNS and the NSC is provided by the Defence, Intelligence and Security Branch of the International Division in the Prime Minister's Department.

External monitoring of the agencies is undertaken by the Inspector-General of Intelligence and Security (IGIS). This position was established in February 1987 as a result of recommendations of a second royal commission into the intelligence and security agencies, conducted by Hope. The Inspector-General monitors the activities of the intelligence and security agencies (ASIO, ASIS, DSD, DIO, ONA and DIGO) to provide an

> independent assurance to the government, the parliament and the people that the agencies conduct their activities within the law, behave with propriety, comply with ministerial guidelines and directives and have regard to human rights.[39]

The IGIS is appointed by the Governor-General for a fixed term of up to three years and cannot be dismissed by the government. He or she has extensive powers, and can require any person to answer questions and produce relevant documents, and take sworn evidence, and regularly enters agency premises to review operational files. The office of the IGIS is, in the words of one journalist, essentially, a "standing Royal Commission".[40]

Parliamentary oversight takes place through the Parliamentary Joint Committee on ASIO, ASIS and DSD. The joint committee can review the administration and expenditure of the agencies, including their annual financial statements, and review any matter in relation to them referred to it by the responsible minister or as a result of a resolution of either house of Parliament. The committee's functions, are, however, heavily circumscribed. It cannot review intelligence priorities or operational methods.[41]

Coordination and tasking

The usefulness of the intelligence agencies for foreign policy making purposes depends directly on the relevance and quality of the information (or assessments) they produce and the timeliness with which they can provide it. Intelligence analysis provided thirty minutes after a policy decision is taken is worse than useless. Timeliness is usually synonymous with speed, but not always. Intelligence can arrive too early for the policy-makers – and therefore be lost or forgotten – as well as too late.

If the agencies are to get the issues of relevance and timeliness right, they need to have a clear view of what the government is interested in, as well as a broad enough grasp of the general policy environment to be able to recognise and disseminate to policy-makers intelligence that they might not yet know they need.

It takes time to get collection systems in place. With human intelligence, for example, it can take years to recruit agents, without any guarantee that they will have appropriate access when the time comes to call on them. Technical collection systems need to be pointed in the right direction (metaphorically, but sometimes also literally), and can also require years of work, often involving human collection, and big dollars to put into place.

To try to ensure that the agencies are actually producing the product the policy-makers need, and in the most effective way, the coordination of the Australian intelligence agencies has become increasingly refined in recent years.

The Director-General of ONA was given coordinating responsibilities under Section 5(1)(d) of the ONA Act,

> to keep under review the activities connected with international intelligence that are engaged in by Australia and to bring to the notice of relevant Departments and Commonwealth authorities any inadequacies in the nature, the extent, or the arrangements for coordination of those activities that become apparent from time to time and suggest any improvements that should be made to remedy those inadequacies.[42]

This function is exercised through Part 2 of ONA's annual report to government, which deals with the achievements of the intelligence community, and through the triennial Foreign Intelligence Planning Document (FIPD) (see below).

This requirement to report on the activities of the other agencies has not always been a comfortable one for ONA, given its small size and the over-whelmingly greater size and resources of the agencies under the Defence umbrella. One of the ways in which the Australian intelligence structure differs most markedly from that of its intelligence allies is in the greater power of the Defence Department over the management and budget of the agencies. DSD, DIGO and DIO all form part of the Department of Defence. Because the great-est proportion by far of the intelligence community budget is in the hands of the Defence Department and funded from its global appropriation, it has been difficult to balance the needs of the smaller agencies outside the Defence umbrella. Under successive governments, ASIS, ONA and ASIO have been subject to the same stringent "efficiency dividends" and other cost-cutting measures as larger government agencies. Yet because, for budgetary purposes, they are part of smaller portfolio groups (DFAT, PM&C and Attorney-General's Department, respectively) and are less central to the priorities of those portfolios, they lack the financial flexibility of the Defence agencies.

Partly because of this difficulty, a 1992 review of the intelligence commu-nity at the end of the Cold War, conducted by D.J. Richardson, at that stage a senior official in PM&C, and later Director-General of ASIO, recommended the introduction of a new, regular, long-term planning document – the Foreign Intel-ligence Planning Document (FIPD). Cabinet agreed and the FIPD was introduced to provide "a long-term strategically-oriented view of Australia's foreign intelligence needs, integrating judgments about changes in the international environment with resource planning and programs". The document aims to look ahead over a five-to-seven-year period and is reviewed, on a rolling basis, every three years.[43]

ONA has principal responsibility for the preparation of the FIPD, which is then submitted through SCNS to the NSC for approval.

The FIPD's underlying objective was to give the government the opportunity to make strategic decisions about the allocation of resources to the intelligence community as a whole, rather than having the outcome determined by the capacities, resources and skills at bureaucratic budget maintenance of individual agencies. (In theory, for example, the government might decide that it needed more information about what was going on in the Southwest Pacific, but that this could be done better by funding more staff at DFAT's regional posts than by spending large amounts on a new technical collection capability.)

If the FIPD is intended to set the overall strategic framework for the intelligence agencies over the medium term, their general work program – the targets to which they should be directing their capabilities – is set out in another document, the National Foreign Intelligence Assessment Priorities (NFIAPs). These describe the principal subjects, geographical and functional, likely to be of interest to Australia's national security policy over the following two years. The NFIAPs are also drafted by ONA and submitted through SCNS to the NSC.[44] (ASIO coordinates a process parallel to the FIPD and the NFIAPS for security intelligence purposes.)

Then, at a more tactical level, specific tasking for the collection agencies is coordinated by the National Intelligence Collection Requirements Committee (NICRC), which meets under ONA's chairmanship each month – and more frequently during crises – and assigns key subjects on which collectors should focus their attention in the coming period. (The Prime Minister of Thailand is making an official visit to Australia next month; Cabinet will be considering legislation to deal with illegal arrivals and needs to understand whether neighbouring governments are being truthful when they say they are trying to impede the flow; the government is preparing a proposal for closer coordination between monetary authorities in Southeast Asia for a meeting later in the year.) The committee is chaired by ONA and comprises representatives of DFAT, Defence, the ADF, ASIS, ASIO, DIO and DSD, and the Australian Federal Police and Customs for transnational issues.[45]

For the agencies that are part of the Department of Defence (DSD, DIGO, DIO), coordination is exercised by a Defence Intelligence Board, chaired by the department's Deputy Secretary, Intelligence and Security. The board's membership also includes the Director-General of ONA from outside Defence.

The coordination structure for the intelligence community as a whole seems elaborate (and certainly lacks memorable acronyms). Some of those involved at both the policy and the intelligence ends of the process question its effectiveness. Some participants report that the attempts via the NSC to establish a global intelligence budget have not been a success, generating, in the words of one of them, "large quantities of opaque paperwork". Defence, unsurprisingly, vigorously repels efforts to establish more than cursory outside oversight of its intelligence budget.

Yet there is no doubt that coordination works more effectively than when Hope first studied it in 1977. Together with a more client-oriented culture on the part of the agencies, it has led to a more policy-responsive and therefore useful role for the intelligence agencies in the policy process.

An informal but powerful element in the coordination of the intelligence community is provided by the Heads of Intelligence Agencies Meeting (HIAM). This meeting acts as a forum for the exchange of information and experiences (and an informal caucus for community interests). It meets roughly monthly, and has no formal constitution. It is coordinated by the Director-General of ONA and comprises the heads of ASIO, ASIS, DSD, DIGO, and DIO, the Chairman of the Defence Intelligence Board and a relevant deputy secretary from DFAT.

Change and challenges

From the early 1990s onwards, intelligence agencies had to cope with new challenges. The disintegration of the Soviet Union and China's faster opening up to the outside world meant that the days in which any scrap of information from inside the Kremlin or from the Chinese politburo could feed a Sovietologist or Sinologist for a month had gone forever. At the same time, the revolution in communications – especially the role of the internet, satellite-television networks and mobile communications – meant that the agencies faced new competitive pressures.

For the collection agencies, technical developments, with the increasing use of fibre-optic cable rather than radio communications, and the availability of commercially available encryption, created new challenges, but technological developments like the creation of electronic databases also offered prospective new avenues for collection. Meanwhile, the analytical agencies faced much greater pressure from policy-makers for timely responsiveness. Much more often than in the past, the agencies found themselves responding to news that policy-makers had already seen on television, rather than breaking the news to them. The 1991 Gulf War was the first time CNN had been piped into the Australian Parliament House. It was clear that this new technology demanded a different sort of briefing from ONA and DIO, which found themselves with the additional task of providing ministers with commentary on the CNN reporting. The tidal wave of open-source information opened up by the internet meant that the collection and collation of such material became an increasingly urgent task. The importance of open sources was recognised in 1999 when DFAT was given funding to establish an Open Source Collection Unit, focussing on information about the South Pacific and, later, Indonesia. Open Source collection also became a way of filling in the gaps left for the intelligence agencies as DFAT's traditional diplomatic reporting capabilities were squeezed out in favour of other priorities, such as trade advocacy.

Meanwhile, for collectors and assessors, information technology opened up new electronic distribution channels and enabled product to be targeted much more precisely to the requirements of individual clients.

The formal response of the Australian agencies to the end of the Cold War was that because they had never been focussed on the Soviet target, nothing much had changed except that the world in which Australia was operating had become even more complex (and, by implication, more resource-intensive).

It was true that the Australian agencies had always focussed on Asia and the Pacific, and that the end of the Cold War did contribute to the creation of a much more fluid situation in Southeast Asia in particular. It was also true that governments were tasking agencies to provide intelligence on issues like terrorism, drugs and people-smuggling that were outside their traditional ambit.

Some intelligence officials saw a new product stream opening up for the collection of commercial intelligence, in addition to the general economic intelligence they had always gone after. The Australian Government considered these questions of commercial intelligence collection in reports on the intelligence community in the post-Cold War era prepared in 1992 for the Secretaries Committee on Intelligence and Security (later renamed the Secretaries Committee on National Security). It concluded that this area was fraught with difficulties. In addition to questions about whether the agencies could actually collect commercially useful information, it was by no means clear in a globalising world of increasingly multilateral corporations how you could define an Australian company, or an Australian commercial interest, or how you could possibly distinguish between the interests of companies competing in the same areas. As a result, Australian agencies have eschewed commercial operations, although collectors and assessors continue to target economic information.[46] Section 11(1) of the Intelligence Services Act says: "The functions of the agencies are to be performed only in the interests of Australia's national security, Australia's foreign relations or Australia's economic well-being".

With a population and economy the size of Australia's, an intelligence community with comprehensive ambitions always operates on the edge of viability. Intelligence collection, especially through ASIS, always has the potential to embarrass the government, and sometimes to put at risk the liberty and lives of others. It needs to be handled by people who are carefully chosen, well-trained and fully supported. Maintaining such professional capability and skills with the limited financial and personnel resources of the Australian agencies is difficult. All the agencies have problems identifying, clearing, training and providing appropriate career structures for staff who are performing jobs that are often highly specialised – whether a DSD linguist or an ONA country analyst – or else, as in the case of information technology jobs, in heavy demand elsewhere in the economy.

It was also becoming clear by the late 1990s that maintaining a comprehensive intelligence structure would be an increasingly expensive business. As in the area of defence, the anticipated post-Cold War peace dividend proved short-lived. Technology and collection platforms were becoming increasingly expensive to build and maintain. Australia's informal dues to the intelligence club were rising fast.

The relatively small size of the Australian intelligence community does have some advantages, however, in terms of its contribution to foreign policy. A high degree of interaction exists between the agencies.[47] In 2003, three of the major intelligence organisations (ASIO, ONA and ASIS) were headed by former diplomats, and the heads of DSD, DIO and DIGO all had experience in other areas of Defence. The agencies and the policy-makers interact more effectively than in other countries with larger intelligence structures. Even the Defence Department's centralised control has benefits in constraining too strong a sense of autonomy on the part of the agencies under its umbrella.

Intelligence and foreign policy

Australia has an unusually highly developed intelligence structure for a middle-sized power.[48] This architecture reflects some distinctive Australian ways of looking at the world, as well as, perhaps, the enduring philosophical influence of British empiricism on the Australian view of government. There is a belief, for example, that intelligence is important – that the truth is out there and that assiduous effort will ferret out the information others are trying to hide. There is a conviction that Australia has global, not just regional, interests, and that its foreign policy needs to include a developed understanding of the international outlook. There is a belief, among the foreign policy elite at any rate, that more information makes governments more responsible. As one official noted, "Data is dangerous only when you don't have structures robust enough to put it in".

Australia also draws clearer distinctions than do other countries between intelligence and policy, and between collection and analysis. Just as Australia created a distinctly indigenous political structure out of the Westminster and Washington models on which its constitution drew, so the intelligence agencies have developed their own characteristics. The Australian intelligence agencies are less collegial and consensus-based than their counterparts in Britain, but less directly competitive than those in the United States. ONA, for example, has no counterpart in either Britain, which adopts a committee-based structure for its intelligence analysis, or the United States, where the CIA combines both a collection (Directorate of Operations) and analytical (Directorate of Intelligence) component, and where the analytical component faces direct competition from the State Department's Bureau of Intelligence and Research, as well as the Defence Intelligence Agency.

The Australian agencies are also more integrated than those of their counterparts, including those in the United States, into the Defence establishment. This may reflect the high public standing of the ADF compared with the professional military forces in, say, Germany or France, as well as an important budget reality.

Another deep-seated Australian trait reflected in the intelligence structure is the perennial national sense that the country needs, and wants, to build relationships with more powerful friends and allies.

The relatively ambitious scope of Australian intelligence and the fact that successive governments have been willing to spend large amounts of money over half a century to sustain those ambitions suggest that political leaders have valued what it has to offer them. Alexander Downer reflected a general view from ministers, especially under the Howard Government, when he said:

> In over five years as foreign minister I have found the information provided by our intelligence agencies to be invaluable. The service that the agencies provide is essential to our approach to key foreign relations and defence issues.[49]

But what exactly is that service? At its most general, the intelligence community is an important content provider for foreign policy making. It delivers data and helps to build a conceptual framework for policy. A good deal of data and analysis would be there anyway, of course, in DFAT and other parts of government. But accurate, timely intelligence improves the chances of success for particular foreign policies. It helps to give policy-makers greater confidence in the positions they have adopted. Intelligence can alert policy-makers to new developments and greatly facilitate crisis management, and has done so.

Australia's own intelligence product, as well as the material policy-makers receive as a result of liaison exchanges with the United States, Britain and many Asian countries, increases the range of interpretations of international developments available to the government. This makes it easier for dissident opinions to get a voice in the system (at least in principle; other conditions must also be present) and lessens the danger of groupthink. It helps provide Australia with an expanded global framework for looking at the world, which its diplomacy alone could not deliver.

Commentators have sometimes charged that the intelligence assessment process has been distorted to make it more consonant with the views of the government:

> The security and intelligence agencies are themselves competing for access to the Prime Minister and to other senior ministers. They want to be the ones that make sure that their material is sitting with the Prime Minister when he's having his cornflakes in the morning … You've got to give [the Prime Minister and other senior ministers] stuff which continues to sustain their interest, and often that means telling them the sorts of things that you know they want to hear. And there's no doubt that in recent Australian history there's been many instances of that, to the detriment of the Australian intelligence community itself in the long run.[50]

Hope found nothing to sustain such a charge in his 1984 report on ONA. Even so, Henry Kissinger's observation that, "In the real world, intelligence assessments more often follow than guide policy decisions",[51] is probably as true of Australia as of the United States.

Australian intelligence agencies also provide the Australian Government with an additional foreign policy instrument. Intelligence exchanges with important regional partners like Indonesia and Japan function as reinforcing mechanisms for general Australian foreign policy. They provide an additional avenue for the dissemination of Australian views of the world and a useful way of ensuring that our neighbours understand the foundations of Australian foreign policy.

In times of friction in the diplomatic relationship, the intelligence agencies can be used for crypto-diplomacy.[52] For example, during *Konfrontasi* (President Sukarno's effort to "confront" the creation of the new state of Malaysia in the mid-1960s), service-to-service links were used as back-channel communications between the Indonesian and Australian governments. Such links have been less important in recent years as the internal structures of Asian governments have changed and the network of other relations between Australia and the region has become denser.

Intelligence is not always one step back from foreign policy, providing discreet background support. It can itself become a foreign policy issue, or can be used to try to shape particular foreign policy outcomes. Some prominent examples have been the ongoing issue of how much Australia knew from signals intelligence about the shooting of five Australian journalists in Balibo, East Timor, in 1975, and whether Australian intelligence predicted, or could have predicted, the massacres and looting there after the independence referendum in 1999. In neither case, however, could it be argued that the Australian policy positions were determined by the intelligence (although it is true that protecting the source of the intelligence was the principal issue guiding the policy response).

Since the mid-1990s, under the Howard Government, Australian intelligence agencies have played a more overt and direct role in policy-making. This was probably in part an outcome of the structures of the National Intelligence Committee and SCNS, which, by intensifying the coordination of foreign policy issues, brought intelligence agency heads more directly into the policy process. On at least three key occasions – East Timor's independence referendum, the Sandline Affair and the Bali bombings (see the case studies in this volume) – the heads of ASIO and/or ASIS were brought in to undertake diplomatic or quasi-diplomatic tasks.

The most obvious way in which the intelligence community affects Australian foreign policy is through the close links to the United States and Britain. Speaking about the reasons for Australia's commitment to the conflict in Iraq in March 2003, John Howard described the intelligence relationship as "a priceless component of our relationship with our two very close allies. There is nothing comparable to be found in any other relationship – nothing more relevant indeed to the challenges of the contemporary world".[53]

The Australian agencies were nurtured by the British and Americans, and the British SIS intervened to save ASIS in 1957 when the Australian Government had decided to disband it.[54] Fifty years later, the relationship with the United States remains as strong as ever and the degree of dependence, at least for technical collection, is even greater. The relationship with Britain has diminished as the foreign policy interests of the two countries have shifted, but language, history and a similar world view still give it a high degree of intimacy.

The UKUSA relationship is the core of the alliance relationship with the United States. It is the daily, routine manifestation of the commitments in the ANZUS Treaty. A former Chief of the Australian Defence Force, General John Baker, describes the intelligence relationship as adding "substance and immediacy" to the relationship.[55] (Speaking privately, another official commented that it weighs more heavily than it should in the US relationship because it is the most vivid and immediate element in it.)

Critics, especially those writing in the 1970s, saw aspects of the Australia–US intelligence relationship as constraining Australia's capacity to operate independently in the world.[56] Certainly a vast volume of intelligence is exchanged between the UKUSA partners. Australia is linked with the United States, Britain and Canada through a secure communications network that permits rapid dissemination of intelligence reports.[57] The overwhelming bulk of raw and assessed intelligence reaching Australian policy-makers from non-Australian sources comes from the United States.

But volume does not necessarily equal influence. Australian assessments of international (and especially Asian) developments differ sharply at times from those of the United States as a result of Australian diplomatic reporting, or specialist expertise, or the force of national or political interests. In any case, access to intelligence product is a very minor element in the influence Washington can bring to bear on the policy decisions of the Australian Government. Of much greater importance are direct and overt channels of interaction. According to one senior official, "The central question is whether we have pulled back from policy for fear of affecting the US [intelligence] relationship. It is hard to think of examples". In his view, Australian ministers on both sides of politics have been more worried by the domestic political reactions to any perceived downturn in Australia–US relations than by any fear that the intelligence flow might diminish.

Nevertheless, it is probably true that the UKUSA intelligence relationship does affect Australian foreign policy making in a different and more subtle sense. In the language of the 2000 Defence White Paper, US–Australia intelligence cooperation and sharing "play a central role in enhancing our understanding of the world around us".[58]

The intelligence links contribute to the construction of a shared model of the global strategic and political environment. The fact that the UKUSA governments begin their analyses working from a basis of evidence more closely aligned than is the case with other countries often helps to shape similar conclusions. The confidence that intelligence can provide can make it easier for the Australian Government to give firm support to US policy positions. (US policy-makers are not, of course, immune from the temptation to display such intelligence selectively, a danger of which most Australian governments have been quite conscious.)

In addition to the direct influence of the data exchanged with the allies, the day-to-day management of that volume of information itself generates a high degree of interaction and intimacy. Australian liaison officers in Washington, DC, and London have excellent access to their counterpart organisations (Australians sit in meetings of the British Joint Intelligence Committee, for example) and, in some instances, agencies exchange personnel.

The UKUSA intelligence community is, in fact, an early and highly developed example of the process that Anne-Marie Slaughter has described as "transgovernmentalism".[59] One senior Australian official described the Allied intelligence community as the "world's first governmental multinational organisation".

Summing up his work on the United States intelligence community, the American scholar Walter Laqueur wrote:

> after much research and discussion with the leading consumers of intelligence, I have concluded that, far from being an invisible government, far from wielding great influence in the councils of state, intelligence has frequently been disregarded or ignored by decision makers. No-one claims that intelligence has been of major importance in the conduct of affairs of state, which, while it may be unfair or inaccurate, certainly shows that intelligence is not held in very high esteem by those in high places.[60]

The situation in Australia is probably not very different. Australian officials interviewed for this book tended to see intelligence as a useful adjunct to the formulation of foreign policy, but not a determinant. But the product of the intelligence agencies does help to give that policy an additional breadth, confidence and robustness.

Notes

1 See, for example, Richard Hall, *The Secret State: Australia's Spy Industry*, Melbourne: Cassell, 1978; Desmond Ball, *A Suitable Piece of Real Estate: American Installations in Australia*, Sydney: Hale & Iremonger, 1980; Brian Toohey and William Pinwell, *Oyster: The Story of the Australian Secret Intelligence Service*, Melbourne: William Heinemann, 1989; Jeffrey T. Richelson and Desmond Ball, *The Ties That Bind: Intelligence Cooperation Between the UKUSA Countries*, Sydney: Unwin Hyman, 1990.

2 Gordon J. Samuels and Michael H. Codd, *Report of the Australian Secret Intelligence Service Commission of Inquiry into the Australian Secret Intelligence Service*, Canberra: AGPS, 1995, p. 17.

3 P.G. Edwards, *Prime Ministers and Diplomats: The Making of Australian Foreign Policy 1901–1949*, Melbourne: Oxford University Press, 1983, p. 8. For an extensive coverage of the origins of the Australian intelligence community, see Christopher Andrew, "The Growth of the Australian Intelligence Community and the Anglo-American Connection", *Intelligence and National Security*, Vol. 4, No. 2, April 1989.

4 Quoted in Justice Robert Hope, *Third Report of the Royal Commission on Intelligence and Security: Abridged Findings and Recommendations, April 1977*, Canberra: Government Printer, 1977, p. 3.

5 ibid., p. 14.

6 *Intelligence Services Act 2001*, Part 2(7).

7 Quoted in Richelson and Ball, *The Ties That Bind*, p. 36.

8 Andrew, "The Growth of the Australian Intelligence Community and the Anglo-American Connection", p. 234.

9 James Bamford, *The Puzzle Palace: A Report on America's Most Secret Agency*, Boston: Houghton Mifflin, 1982, p. 309.

10 For a useful summary of the collection capabilities on which DSD (and DIGO) draw, see Alan Dupont, "Intelligence: Strategic Trends, Issues and Implications for Australia" in Desmond Ball (ed.), *Maintaining the Strategic Edge: The Defence of Australia in 2015*, Canberra: Strategic and Defence Studies Centre, Australian National University, 1999, p. 355.

11 *Official Committee Hansard, Joint Select Committee on the Intelligence Services*, 1 August 2001, pp. IS57–8.

12 ibid., p. IS78.

13 ibid., p. IS73.

14 Andrew, "The Growth of the Australian Intelligence Community and the Anglo-American Connection", p. 233.

15 Hamish McDonald, "Head Spy a Diplomat with Dash", *Sydney Morning Herald*, 23 November 2002, p. 11.

16 *Intelligence Services Act 2001*, Section 6(4).

17 See Justice Robert Hope, *Report on the Sheraton Hotel Incident, February 1984, Royal Commission into Australia's Intelligence and Security Agencies*, Canberra: Government Printer, 1984.

18 *Intelligence Services Act 2001*, Section 6(1).

19 Toohey and Pinwell, *Oyster*, pp. 24–5.

20 Quoted in ibid., p. 27.

21 See Andrew, "The Growth of the Australian Intelligence Community and the Anglo-American Connection", pp. 231 ff.

22 Samuels and Codd, *Report of the Australian Secret Intelligence Service Commission of Inquiry*, p. 11.

23 ibid., p. 5.

24 Justice Robert Hope, *Fifth Report of the Royal Commission on Intelligence and Security* (confidential), c. 1978, Appendix 5e, paragraphs 29–45.

25 Andrew, "The Growth of the Australian Intelligence Community and the Anglo-American Connection", p. 237.
26 John Moore, "New Defence Imagery and Geospatial Arrangements", Media release, MIN 332/00, 8 November 2000. http://www.minister.defence.gov.au/Mooretpl.cfm?CurrentId=430
27 See Dupont, "Intelligence", p. 355.
28 http://www.asio.gov.au/about/content/what.htm
29 Paul Keating, *Engagement: Australia Faces the Asia–Pacific*, Sydney: Macmillan, 2000, p. 14.
30 Hope, *Third Report of the Royal Commission on Intelligence and Security*, pp. 22 ff.
31 http://www.ona.gov.au/corporate.htm
32 Justice Robert Hope, *Report on the Office of National Assessments and Joint Intelligence Organization Royal Commission on Australia's Security and Intelligence Organisations*, Canberra: AGPS, 1985, p. 27.
33 Hall, *The Secret State*, p. 209.
34 Hope, *Third Report of the Royal Commission on Intelligence and Security*, p. 16.
35 Geoffrey Barker, "The Spying Game", *Australian Financial Review*, 28 March–1 April 2002, p. 52.
36 Samuels and Codd, *Report of the Australian Secret Intelligence Service Commission of Inquiry*, p. 3.
37 ibid., pp. 72, 75.
38 ibid., p. 71.
39 http://www.igis.gov.au/about.html
40 Barker, "The Spying Game".
41 *Intelligence Services Act 2001*, Sections 28, 29.
42 *ONA Act 1977*, Section 5(1)(d).
43 Samuels and Codd, *Report of the Australian Secret Intelligence Service Commission of Inquiry*, p. 77.
44 ibid., p. 77.
45 ibid., p. 86.
46 See, for example, DIO's "Defence Economic Trends in the Asia–Pacific". http://www.defence.gov.au/dio/
47 See, for example, Richelson and Ball, *The Ties That Bind*, p. 30.
48 It is by no means the norm for such countries to organise their intelligence apparatus in this way. See, for example, Douglas Porch, "French Intelligence Culture: A Historical and Political Perspective", *Intelligence and National Security*, Vol. 10, No. 3, July 1995, pp. 486 ff.; Jeffrey T. Richelson, *Foreign Intelligence Organizations,* Cambridge, MA: Ballinger, 1988; Walter Laqueur, *The Uses and Limits of Intelligence*, New Brunswick, NJ: Transaction Publishers, 1993, Chapter 7, "Secret Services in Open Societies".
49 *CPD, House of Representatives*, 27 June 2001.
50 Desmond Ball, interview with Terry Lane, "The National Interest", ABC Radio, 31 October 1999. http://www.abc.net.Australia/rn/talks/natint/stories/s64305.htm
51 Henry Kissinger, *Diplomacy*, New York: Simon & Schuster, 1994, p. 303.
52 See H. Bradford Westerfield, "America and the World of Intelligence Liaison", *Intelligence and National Security*, Vol. 11, No. 3, July 1996, p. 536.

53 John Howard, "Address to the Nation", 20 March 2003.
54 Andrew, "The Growth of the Australian Intelligence Community and the Anglo-American Connection", p. 235.
55 John Baker and Douglas H. Paal "The US Australia Alliance" in Robert D. Blackwill and Paul Dibb (eds), *America's Asian Alliances*, Cambridge, MA: MIT Press, 2000, p. 88.
56 Ball, *A Suitable Piece of Real Estate*, p. 147.
57 Tom Mangold and Jeff Goldberg, "The Near Perfect Spy", *Sunday Age*, 17 June 2001.
58 Department of Defence, *Defence 2000: Our Future Defence Force*, Canberra: Defence Publishing Service, 2000, p. 35.
59 Anne-Marie Slaughter, "The Real New World Order", *Foreign Affairs,* September–October 1997.
60 Laqueur, *The Uses and Limits of Intelligence*, p. 4.

The Bali Bombings: Foreign Policy Comes Home

On the evening of 12 October 2002, just two days before his official departure from Jakarta, his bags packed and his thoughts turning to the challenges of his new job in Canberra, the Australian Ambassador to Indonesia, Richard Smith, was relaxing at a farewell party hosted by his New Zealand counterpart. Soon after 11 p.m., local time, he received a call on his mobile telephone from the Australian Consul-General in Bali, Ross Tysoe. Tysoe reported that he had just heard a large explosion near the tourist area of Kuta and was now making his way there. Another guest at the party, the Australian Defence Attaché, Brigadier Ken Brownrigg, had received a similar call a few minutes earlier from Captain Jon Steinbeck, another member of the embassy's defence staff, who was holidaying in Bali.[1]

For the next half hour or so, Smith and Brownrigg received regular telephone reports as Tysoe and Steinbeck made their separate ways towards the scene of the devastation. As often happens in the early stage of any crisis, the news was fragmentary and uncertain. Was this a bomb attack? A gas explosion? What was the target? How many people had been injured? How many were Australians?

The Australian intelligence organisations had for some time been directing government attention to the dangers of radical terrorist groups in Southeast Asia. The general security-threat levels for Australians in Indonesia were rated as high, but no specific warning of any action had been received. Indeed, the Deputy Head of the embassy, Neil Mules, was spending the weekend in Bali after attending a conference there. (The issue of what the government knew, and when it knew it, would later become a public issue. A report commissioned by the government from the Inspector-General of Intelligence and Security concluded after reviewing all the intelligence information available that the government had no intelligence warning of the Bali bombings.)[2]

The closer Tysoe and Steinbeck came to the bombsite, the more ominous the news became. Speaking on his mobile telephone as he ran down the main thoroughfare of Jalan Legian towards the ruins of the Sari Club about thirty minutes after the first explosion, Tysoe told Smith that he had already passed four or five burned-out cars with charred bodies inside, but that worse was still ahead. Steinbeck reported that he had encountered a metres-wide crater across the road. Smith and Brownrigg looked at each other and knew that this was a major disaster, that large numbers of Australians were likely to be involved, and that the Australian Government's response would have to be comprehensive and immediate.

Preliminary messages about the explosion had already been passed through to ConOps, DFAT's twenty-four-hour Consular Operations Centre in Canberra, but Smith now telephoned the experienced head of the DFAT Consular branch, Ian Kemish (who had overseen the consular response to the World Trade Centre attacks a year earlier). Smith advised him that Australia was facing a fundamental consular crisis and that DFAT would require enormous additional resources, including defence assets, to handle it.[3] Brownrigg rang Defence Headquarters at the same time with a similar message.

The other Australia-based officer in the Consulate-General, David Chaplin, had already made his way to one of the medical clinics in the area of the nightclubs. He helped to comfort the first of the injured and dying victims there. A number of other Australian officials were also in Bali, many, like Mules, taking a break from the stresses of Jakarta. Some heard the explosion and made their way to the small Australian Consulate; others were contacted from Jakarta. They were joined at the Consulate by large numbers of Australian volunteers, some of them Australians resident in Bali, others visitors, especially medical professionals. Many of those who offered their services that night would still be working two weeks later. They would provide vital assistance in the hours and days ahead.

In Jakarta, the embassy's crisis response committee met at about 1 a.m. local time to begin coordinating efforts to help in Bali and to protect Australians in Jakarta: it was by no means clear that similar attacks might not be made elsewhere in Indonesia. Smith immediately ordered the embassy's "fly-away team" of defence and consular officials, a standing part of its contingency plans, down to Bali on the earliest commercial flights on Sunday morning. More officials followed on Sunday afternoon.

In Canberra, senior departmental and agency officials were being woken by telephone calls from about 3 a.m., Canberra time, about fifty minutes after the first explosion. Few of them went back to bed. In addition to DFAT and Defence, other government agencies received the news separately at about the same time. ASIO's media-monitoring centre, which had been established after the 11 September 2001 attacks in the United States, notified the Director-General, Dennis Richardson. The Australian Federal Police (AFP) was first contacted by members of its own force holidaying in Bali. PM&C and the offices of the Prime Minister, the Foreign Minister and the Attorney-General were also advised. There followed several hours of intensive and at times frustrating information-gathering as officials tried to form an accurate picture of the scale of the tragedy.

At 5 a.m., DFAT activated its Crisis Centre, a small suite of rooms with secure communications systems on the fourth floor of the R.G. Casey Build-ing, to coordinate the whole-of-government response to the crisis and to ensure that information was flowing properly to other government agencies.

The most urgent need was for consular assistance – help for the injured and for the families of those who had died. That was clearly DFAT's responsibility. Just over a year earlier, DFAT had established an Emergency Call Unit. The unit gave the department the capacity during a crisis to respond to high volumes of inquiries from the public. Telephone operators, who were all volun-teers from the department, could enter details of inquiries into a consular data-base that was linked to relevant overseas posts. Staff were called in, and talking points prepared, and the telephones went online at 6.30 a.m. At the same time, the number of the help line and details of what was known about the bombings were posted on the DFAT website. By the end of its first twenty-four hours of operation, the call unit would handle 10,000 telephone calls. Over the follow-ing two weeks it would take 30,000 calls and the staff of Consular Branch would help to resolve 5,000 individual consular cases.

At 9 a.m., the first meeting of an Interdepartmental Emergency Task Force was held in the Crisis Centre. Defence, PM&C, the Protective Security Coordi-nation Centre of the Attorney-General's Department, and the intelligence and security agencies – ASIO, ONA and ASIS – were represented. It was clear by now that two bombs had exploded at the Sari Nightclub and the nearby Paddy's Pub. An entire block of the main tourist area of Kuta had been destroyed, and the dead and injured numbered in the hundreds. The meeting focussed almost entirely on evacuation plans for the wounded, the identity of the likely suspects and the security implications of the bombings. Defence had already arranged for the first two C-130 Hercules aircraft to leave for Bali with seven medical staff at 10 a.m. On a twelve-hour standby, the RAAF had got its planes in the air in eight hours.

Even by the time of the first Task Force meeting, it was clear that an adequate response to the tragedy would have to involve a much wider range of government departments. The impact was national in scale. In the course of Sunday morning, Family and Community Services, Australian Protective Services, Immigration, Customs, Transport and Regional Services, Health and Ageing, Emergency Management Australia, Treasury, Finance and AusAID were also brought in to the response effort. Private companies like Qantas were also heavily involved. DFAT had to operate with Commonwealth and state agencies with which it would not normally deal. Inevitably there was a good deal of work on the run. As Kemish commented later, "We had no national plan for this sort of incident".[4] Nevertheless, so far as the outsider could see (and no participants suggested otherwise to us), there was remarkably little dispute about turf, and considerable flexibility in the response.

In Bali itself, staff from the Consulate-General had been joined by Sunday evening by an additional sixteen DFAT staff. A further Orion aircraft, carrying DFAT, AFP and ASIO staff, had left Australia in midafternoon. Together with some of the volunteers, they were engaged in the emotionally devastating work of caring for the injured and the dying, preserving the bodies of the dead, and providing what help they could to distraught relatives who wanted, understandably, immediate answers in a situation in which they were not available. Hospitals, airports and hotels were checked to try to identify the number of Australians injured. Within twenty-four hours, 113 had been identified. A temporary office was set up at Denpasar Airport to facilitate the departure of Australians and the arrival of relatives and friends of the victims. An international disaster-recovery company, Kenyon International, was contracted to assist with the return of bodies to Australia.

Meanwhile, a second, though interlinked, group of agencies was grappling with the issue of Australia's security and law-enforcement response to what had happened. What were the implications for Australian security? Who was responsible? How could they be brought to justice? Was this the beginning of a wider series of attacks?

By 8 a.m. on Sunday, the AFP and ASIO had agreed that they should put investigators on the ground in Bali that day. Nine AFP investigators, with three ASIO officials to give intelligence support to the law-enforcement effort, were in place by that evening. ASIS also moved an officer to Bali for the same purpose.

Throughout Sunday, ASIO had a team of people at work reviewing all its intelligence holdings over the preceding six weeks to see whether any information it held could throw light on the event.

ASIO shares responsibility for intelligence assessment of terrorism issues with the Office of National Assessments (ONA). ASIO's mandate is narrower and derives from its legislative responsibility to advise the government on threats to Australian security (as defined in its Act), whether those threats come from inside Australia or outside. ONA's responsibility is only external to Australia. Its job is to provide a broader contextual analysis of terrorism and its impact on other countries and regions. After 11 September 2001, the two agencies had increased the level of their cooperation on terrorism intelligence analysis and had begun to jointly badge some of their reporting to government. (They share the same Canberra building near the Defence complex at Russell Hill.)

Responsibility for coordinating security responses within the government and between the Commonwealth and the states rests with the Protective Security Coordination Centre (PSCC) in the Attorney-General's Department. On Sunday, the PSCC briefed state and territory governments, and at 3.30 p.m. it held a meeting of the Commonwealth's Special Incident Task Force.

At the political level, the Foreign Minister had been woken at about 5 a.m. and the Prime Minister at 6.40 a.m. at his Sydney residence. Both of them spoke to Smith in Jakarta. Throughout the morning the Prime Minister was briefed on the growing scale of the tragedy by intelligence and policy officers. He made it clear to officials that the Australian response needed to be full and effective, and unconstrained by concern about resources: those questions could be sorted out later.

On the international front, Howard spoke to Indonesian President Megawati Sukarnoputri at 2 p.m., and to Britain's Tony Blair and Helen Clark of New Zealand later in the day. (President George W. Bush telephoned early on the Monday.) After returning to Canberra from Sydney, he held a meeting at the Lodge late on Sunday night with his personal staff and the heads of ONA and ASIO to look at the questions of who might be responsible and what the next steps should be.

Howard had spoken to the Leader of the Opposition, Simon Crean, at about midday, and the heads of ASIO and ONA briefed Crean about the situation later that evening.

From Sunday night, consideration was being given within government to the need to send a minister to Bali urgently. It was recognised that effective linkages between Australia and Indonesia would be critical to the success of any investigations into the bombings.

A meeting of the National Security Committee of Cabinet on Monday afternoon confirmed that a delegation would travel to Indonesia that day. It would be led by Foreign Minister Downer, and would include Justice Minister Chris Ellison, ASIO Director-General Dennis Richardson, AFP Commissioner Mick Keelty, ASIS Director-General Allan Taylor (a former Ambassador to

Indonesia) and DFAT Deputy Secretary David Ritchie (who was also Ambassador-designate to Indonesia).

The delegation's objectives were to give government support at the highest levels to the victims of the bombings and their families, to make high-level contact in Jakarta, and to encourage the Indonesian Government to take the investigation forward vigorously, regardless of where it might lead. Australian policy-makers believed it was important for the Indonesian Government to accept that an important line had now been crossed: that the threat of militant Islamic groups like Jemaah Islamiyah had to be faced and dealt with. The delegation's immediate practical objective, however, was to secure Indonesian agreement to a joint investigation of the crime. In the light of traditional Indonesian sensitivity about sovereignty, and of the Indonesian Government's political nervousness about issues involving radical Islam, such agreement could certainly not be assumed. It was decided that rather than seeking an umbrella agreement at government-to-government level, it would be easier and more effective to try for a working-level agreement between the police agencies, with a broad endorsement of this process from the national government.

The delegation flew to Bali to inspect the damage and talk to the victims and their families. It then went on to Jakarta, where Downer met President Megawati and senior Indonesian ministers and officials. The Indonesians agreed to a joint three-year investigation between the AFP and the Indonesian police. This was a significant achievement for the AFP. It was also the first and most important indicator that the Indonesian authorities were committed to a substantive and sustained response to the bombings. The agreement bore fruit for both governments in subsequent effective police work.

For the foreign policy and security agencies, and for the Australian political leadership, the pace remained intense for the next three weeks. The task of identifying the Australians who died in Bali, transporting their remains, treating the injured and counselling grieving families continued. Young DFAT consular and policy officers found themselves undertaking the most harrowing tasks of victim identification and consular support for grieving friends and families. Most of them knew that, as with the survivors and the families of those who died, the experience would always be with them.

Australian Defence Force C-130 aircraft shuttled medical stores to Bali and assisted with evacuations to Australia. Five ADF aero-medical evacuation teams, including Reserves, were involved. By 2.30 a.m. on Monday, just twenty-four hours after the bombings, the first fifteen Australian evacuees had arrived back in Australia on an RAAF C-130. Within thirty-six hours, all the injured Australians who wanted to return to Australia were back in the country. Within three days, all the Australians who wanted to leave Bali had been able to do so.

In Canberra, more than 420 DFAT officers – about half the department's Canberra-based staff – were rostered as volunteers on a twenty-four-hour basis through the crisis call-unit and operations centre, in addition to their normal duties. DFAT offices in the states worked long hours to help coordinate the return of remains to families. In New York, the Australian Mission to the United Nations was successfully pressing the Security Council to add Jemaah Islamiyah to its consolidated list of al-Qaeda-related terrorist entities so that all UN member states would be obliged to take measures against it, including freezing its funds and assets.

The police investigation moved into full operation and made some excellent early progress. By Monday, 21 October, more than 109 Australian law-enforcement officers from every state and territory were in Bali, including members of the Disaster Victim Identification team.

On Thursday, 17 October, Howard himself visited Bali with Deputy Prime Minister John Anderson and Opposition Leader Simon Crean.

The essential pattern of the Australian response had been established within the first forty-eight hours after the tragedy, however. Indeed, the direction had been mostly set by the decisions taken in the first couple of hours. Crises take different forms. The Sandline Affair, discussed earlier, was a crisis of prevention: Australian policy was directed towards preventing an otherwise inevitable action (the introduction of mercenary soldiers to Bougainville) that would be contrary to Australia's interests and dangerous for the region. Bali, on the other hand, was a crisis of response. The bombings had taken place and the critical decisions had to be made immediately, and often with incomplete information.

In this regard, the timing of the bombings, in the early hours of a Sunday morning, Australian time, made it easier for government and officials to handle. That is perhaps the one time of the week that the twenty-four-hour media cycle slows down. And unlike the drama of the attack on the World Trade Centre, the media were not there from the beginning. Television crews and journalists took time to arrive in Bali. Ministers and officials therefore had a longer than usual period to come to terms with the events, and to understand them and formulate responses out of the glare of public attention and journalists' questions. That made for easier and arguably more effective policy-making.

The tragedy was undoubtedly easier to handle because it happened in Bali, a place many Australians knew well, with regular transport and communications links to Australia and an existing infrastructure of support that could be drawn upon. In a place more remote from Australian connections, the response would have been much more difficult.

This was, of course, more than just a foreign policy issue. It was a disaster-relief issue, a law-enforcement issue and a community-safety issue as well. A post-Bali review of Commonwealth counter-terrorism arrangements resulted in significant organisational changes, with the lead role in counter-terrorism policy response (though nor operational coordination) passing from the Attorney-General's Department to the Department of Prime Minister and Cabinet.

But the foreign policy dimensions of the bombings were central: the event took place outside Australia's borders; Australia's capacity to respond depended upon its ability to influence other governments; and the main coordinating agency was DFAT, under its traditional consular responsibilities.

And as a foreign policy issue, it drew together a number of the trends that had been transforming foreign policy making over the decades of the 1980s and 1990s. From the growth of mass tourism to the changing role of the nation-state, globalisation was a thread that stitched the tragedy together. Many of the challenges of globalisation to be discussed in Chapter 10 were present. The terrorist groups responsible were transnational, non-state actors. Extremist Islamist groups like Jemaah Islamiyah were, in part at least, a manifestation of the reaction to globalisation (drawing some of their support from popular fear of the speed of social change and growing westernisation), and their actions were made possible by globalisation's technologies (easy travel, effective communications to plan operations, and use of the internet to spread their message).

The bombings underlined the way in which non-traditional issues such as terrorism, money-laundering, and people- and arms-smuggling were forcing their way onto the security agenda. This process had been under way since the end of the Cold War, but 11 September and 12 October gave a new urgency and new political legitimacy to the task of rethinking aspects of the links between internal and external security policies, and about the way the national security institutions responded to terrorism.[5]

Reflecting on the impact of Bali, the Labor Party's Shadow Foreign Minister, Kevin Rudd, said:

> There is a temptation in policy elites to regard foreign policy and security policy
> as high policy, removed from the influences, the impact and the impulses of the
> general community. Just as that is no longer true of the United States after
> September 11, so too it is no longer true of Australia after October 12. For
> Australians, foreign and security policy have become personal, relevant and
> immediate ... It has become central to everyday life – and death. As a
> consequence it is a realm of policy which now moves from the periphery to the
> centre of the national political debate.[6]

As a proportion of the country's population, the eighty-nine Australians who died as a result of the Bali bombings represented about half the number of those who died in New York in the World Trade Centre attacks. If 11 September marked the end of the post-Cold War period elsewhere in the world, Bali brought this home to Australia.

The immediate impact was, therefore, to increase the public expectations of the foreign policy and security agencies. Before 11 September 2001, the travel advisory pages on DFAT's website were receiving roughly 30,000 hits per week. After 11 September this became 140,000. Three days after Bali the figure at times reached more than 500,000. The responsibility of government to provide meaningful travel advisory notifications to its citizens became a sensitive political issue. With 10,000 Australians resident in Indonesia and 300,000 tourists a year travelling there, what was the most effective way of keeping Australian citizens advised of risk? These were issues that would be heavily canvassed in the period ahead.[7]

How to deal with the media was one of the key questions facing the government. This was not primarily from a desire to 'manage' the news (although political elements were inevitably present: political leaders knew that they would be held politically accountable if the humanitarian and consular response was handled badly), but because the way information was released would have a profound impact on the public reaction within Australia. Most of this work was coordinated out of DFAT's Parliamentary and Media Branch and, in Bali, by the embassy's Counsellor (Public Affairs), Kirk Conningham, with a colleague from the AFP.

Yet 12 October also underlined the constant elements in Australia's foreign policy. The terrorists might have been thinking globally, but they were acting locally. Without the cooperation of its neighbours, Australia could not ensure an effective police response to the bombings and bring the perpetrators to justice. It needed to intensify its bilateral and multilateral cooperation on terrorism with all the states in our region. As Foreign Minister Alexander Downer commented:

> in the main, the campaign against terrorism is going to be won by sovereign states, including the sovereign states of our region taking specific action to cut off the capacity of terrorists to operate.[8]

The intensity of the regional response to security raids by ASIO and state police forces, and to some careless words from Prime Minister Howard about Australia's right to pre-empt terrorist attacks on its citizens, underlined how sensitive the relationship between Australia and its neighbours continued to be, and how difficult it would be to manage the sometimes divergent strands of Australia's security and foreign policies.

Above all, however, the response to the Bali bombings showed how effectively the Australian external policy institutions and coordinating mechanisms were able to manage a complex crisis affecting a large number of Australians under pressure and in the face of adversity. The bombings had a profound effect on Australian society, yet they occurred in another country. Australia's response depended heavily on its diplomatic network and its intelligence agencies. These institutions had well-developed links with Indonesia, and were able to support Australia's response. The bombings also demonstrated the increased salience of consular issues in Australia's diplomacy: the institutions of consular assistance and support that had been enhanced over preceding years played a major role in providing support for the victims of the attacks and their families.

Notes

1   Much of the material in this case study is drawn from interviews with participants. It also draws on a comprehensive chronology of the Australian public service's response to the crisis prepared by *Canberra Times* journalist Verona Burgess. See Verona Burgess, "When Terror Struck: How We Handled the Crisis That Shook the Nation", *Canberra Times*, 5 November 2002.
2   *CPD, House of Representatives*, 10 December 2002, p. 9759
3   Interview with Ian Kemish, December 2002.
4   ibid.
5   For a good analysis of these issues, see the Australian Strategic Policy Institute's report prepared by Aldo Borgu, *Beyond Bali: ASPI's Strategic Assessment 2002*, Canberra: ASPI, 2002.
6   Kevin Rudd, "Arc of Instability, Arc of Insecurity", speech, 23 October 2002. http://www.kevinrudd.com/mediarelease.asp?id=10
7   See, for example, Kevin Rudd, "Body of Evidence", *Weekend Australian*, 21–22 December 2002, p. 23.
8   Alexander Downer, "The Challenge of Terrorism in the Asia-Pacific Region", speech to the Foreign Correspondents Association, 26 November 2002.

CHAPTER 8

The Domestic Landscape

Foreign policy making has long been thought of as an activity that should take place as much as possible in isolation from the passions and controversies of domestic politics. Writers on statecraft have cautioned against involving the passions of the public in the delicate practice of diplomacy, and have regularly counselled the futility of trying to explain the complexities of foreign affairs to the society on whose behalf it is made. In the course of his commentary on *Democracy in America*, Tocqueville observed that "foreign politics demand scarcely any of those qualities which a democracy possesses; and they require, on the contrary, the perfect use of almost all those faculties in which it is deficient".[1] The qualities to which he was referring were the ability to maintain control of a complex undertaking; to persevere with a given policy; to ensure the secrecy of decisions and actions; and to be patient in awaiting the consequences of a decision. Consequently, for Tocqueville, foreign policy should be left to "aristocrats", who remained above the democratic political process. A more recent Australian view was expressed by a former Secretary of the Department of External Affairs, Sir Alan Watt, who wrote, "any private citizen who is sufficiently confident of his own opinions to tell a government precisely what it should do from day to day demonstrates not only his courage but also his rashness and perhaps his vanity".[2]

The horror expressed by many realist writers at the prospect of public interest and involvement in foreign policy making echoes the fulminations of both Tories and Whigs in nineteenth-century Britain at the prospect of the extension of suffrage to the working masses. The masses, it was argued, were not sufficiently educated to understand the policies on which they would vote; they would use the franchise to vote themselves a share in the national wealth they had not earned, and in so doing, would destroy the capacity of society to create ongoing wealth, which was dependent on the efforts of the industrious and thrifty.[3] The coming of universal suffrage brought none of these calamities;

neither is it likely that growing public interest will signal the "end of foreign policy". On the contrary, many argue that because an increasing amount of domestic policy is set by commitments made internationally – giving rise to concerns about a "democratic deficit" – foreign policy making is a realm of government that needs to be subjected to a greater amount of public account-ability and transparency. For Robert A. Dahl, increasing multilateralisation of domestic policy means that citizens are being given increased control of policy that has little effect on their lives, but little control over policies that have major impacts on how they live.[4]

Previous chapters described the foreign policy making machinery in Australia. The central questions in this chapter concern the extent to which foreign policy making in Australia is affected by domestic political processes, which domestic influences are most powerful, and how domestic influences impact on foreign policy making. Our discussion begins with a brief consider-ation of the influence of the political institutions comprising Australia as a federal, Westminster-system democracy: Parliament, Cabinet, the political parties, and the states and territories. We then examine the Australian public in general, and the influence of the media in conveying and influencing public attitudes towards foreign policy. Finally, we examine the role and influence of foreign policy interest groups on Australian foreign policy making.

The influence of Australian political institutions

In Australia, as in the majority of democratic systems, national government is divided between the executive, the legislative and the parliamentary arms. Foreign policy is among the few functions of government to be almost exclu-sively managed by the executive branch: the Prime Minister, portfolio ministers and Cabinet, and the designated bureaucratic departments. This would not be obvious to a casual reader of the Australian constitution. Section 51(XXIX) gives Federal Parliament the responsibility "to make laws for the peace, order, and good government of the Commonwealth with respect to external affairs"; furthermore, Parliament has the power to grant supply and authorise the raising of revenue for foreign affairs, and in the Westminster system the government remains in power so long as it commands a parliamentary majority. Yet in Australia, foreign policy making is a strongly executive function, in terms of the arm of government in which it takes place and – in a useful distinction made by Samuel Huntington – of the nature of the policy process. For Huntington, an executive-type policy process (as opposed to a legislative-type policy process) involves hierarchically arranged participants, between which there is broad agreement on fundamental goals and values, in relation to a limited range of possible policy choices.[5] Huntington contrasts an executive process with a legislative process in which the players participating are roughly equal in power and consequently must bargain; in which important disagreements exist over values and goals; and in which there are many possible alternative choices. He argues that while foreign policy in the US exists in the *executive arm* of government, it can at times exhibit strongly *legislative processes* of policy-making.[6] Our research has found little evidence of such opposition, confrontation and bargaining in the Australian foreign policy making process.

Foreign policy making is concentrated in the executive arm of government for a number of reasons. John Locke, in advocating parliamentary government in his *Second Treatise of Government* in 1689, exempted foreign affairs from the concerns of Parliament, which is only capable of governing through "antecedent, standing, and positive laws":

> For the laws that concern subjects, one amongst another, being to direct their actions, may well enough precede them. But what is done in reference to foreigners, depending much upon their actions, and the variation of designs and interests, must be left in great part to the prudence of those who have this power committed to them, to be managed to the best of their skill, for the advantage of the Commonwealth.[7]

Locke's original insight into the inappropriateness of foreign policy making by Parliament remains compelling. The external realm is not like domestic society, in which policy directives can be authoritatively imposed. Foreign policy making requires the ability to respond to a rapidly changing context with speed, coherence and the greatest possible degree of manoeuvre: qualities that are beyond the capacity of slow parliamentary processes. Foreign policy is thought to be a realm too complex for the simple oppositions of domestic political debate, and often too sensitive for the glare of parliamentary (and public) scrutiny. Only the executive, it is maintained, can guarantee the constant attention, rapid reaction and secrecy required for an effective, clear and consistent foreign policy. What roles, then, if any, are played by other parts of government and the federal system?

Parliament

Under the United States constitution, Congress has important roles in the foreign policy process: treaties made can only be ratified by a Senate vote; Congress has formal roles in the declaration of war and the appointment of diplomatic agents; and both houses have been highly active in setting the parameters for the exercise of executive powers in making foreign policy. The Australian Parliament has none of these formal powers. Rarely does the conduct of Australian foreign policy require enabling legislation; and the debate and discussion of foreign affairs is more often than not relegated behind domestic political issues that call on the legislative powers of both houses of Parliament.[8] Parliamentary debates on foreign policy are relatively rare, and often scheduled around the discussion of domestic matters. Typically, foreign policy debates involve the reading of a prepared statement on Australian foreign policy by the Foreign, Defence or Trade ministers, to which the Opposition responds, also with carefully prepared remarks. A number of commentators have observed the lack of value of such set pieces for the making of informed foreign policy:

> Rarely are positive suggestions made to deal with practical problems. Rarely does one member attempt to convince his opposite number of the wisdom of his argument or the reality of his world view. Rarely is there a true debate in which points made by one side are countered by the other. Rarely will members do other than read from prepared speeches. And rarely does partisan point-scoring give way to constructive criticism and scrutiny.[9]

A less pessimistic view is that Parliament is often used, not to discuss practical details of foreign policy, but to make public, strategic foreign policy statements (see Chapter 2) about general commitments and attitudes shaping the conduct of relations with the outside world. As J.D.B. Miller observes, "debates on foreign affairs are set-pieces for occasional declaration of abstract principle, not for discussion of practical problems".[10]

Debates are not the only occasion on which foreign policy is considered by Parliament. Often foreign affairs issues are raised in parliamentary Question Time, in the form of questions placed on notice and of questions without notice. The preparation of answers to both types of questions occupies significant amounts of the time and resources of the foreign policy bureaucracy, and attracts the close attention of the minister and ministerial staff. In the Australian system, misleading Parliament is a cardinal, and potentially fatal, infraction for a minister.

Questions placed on notice are fed directly to the relevant section of DFAT; often the preparation of the answer will also involve the relevant overseas post. Responses are then cleared through the minister's office. Questions without notice also occupy extensive bureaucratic time, which is spent trying to antici-pate possible questions, and preparing briefing notes for the ministers before and during parliamentary sessions. This requires a close monitoring of the sources that are likely to prompt questions from the Opposition: most often the media, but also international developments that may impact on domestic constituencies. According to many in the foreign policy bureaucracy, the expectations of Parliament and the ministers are steadily rising, demanding more of DFAT's time. Sometimes Question Time will bring an issue to the attention of the minister, who will often make an undertaking to provide a response to the question in a subsequent sitting of Parliament.

None of this, however, should be taken to imply that the discussion of foreign policy in Question Time is significantly more valuable than formal debates.

The most frequent use of Question Time, however, comes in the form of responses by the Prime Minister or ministers to "Dorothy Dixers", prepared answers to known questions asked by government backbenchers under the guise of a question without notice. The term derives from the pseudonymous author of an advice-to-the-lovelorn column in an Australian women's magazine, whose correspondents were widely assumed to be fictional alter-egos of the columnist. "Would the Minister provide an update of Australia's approach to the ongoing conflict in the Middle East?" and "Would the Minister inform the House of what the government has done to advance the interests of Australian farmers in the international trading environment?" are typical examples from one month in 2002. Replies to such questions allow ministers to put on record succinctly (or extensively, if they can get away with it) statements of government policy positions, to outline government achievements or to criticise the Opposition.

Partly to overcome the deficiencies in parliamentary debates and Question Time, and partly to exercise oversight of the use of resources in foreign policy making, a number of parliamentary committees have been established for the consideration of various aspects of foreign policy. Undoubtedly the most powerful of these are the Senate Estimates Committee hearings on the operation of the foreign policy bureaucracy. These have become the primary source of parliamentary scrutiny of the foreign policy bureaucracy, with senators able to ask senior officers of the relevant departments and agencies a wide range of questions, often forensic, about their activities. The seriousness with which the departments and the ministerial offices take these hearings is reflected in the extensive preparations that are made for each round of Estimates Committee hearings.

The other types of parliamentary committee relevant to foreign policy are the joint standing committees established to inquire into specific foreign policy issues. In the current Parliament, the most significant of these are the Joint Standing Committee on Foreign Affairs, Defence and Trade (JFADT), and the Joint

Standing Committee on Treaties. The first Joint Parliamentary Committee on Foreign Affairs was established in 1952, but because of its in camera discussions and direct subordination to the Minister for External Affairs, it was boycotted by the ALP until 1967. Broadened to include consideration of defence in 1972 and trade in 1987, the JFADT currently has thirty-two members: twelve government and eight Opposition MPs from the House of Representatives; and five each from the government and Opposition, and two from the minor parties and independents, in the Senate. The committee is chaired by a government representative. It has four subcommittees, each with a different chair: on foreign affairs, on defence, on trade, and on human rights. Both the full committee and the subcommittees hold hearings and prepare reports on specific issues of current relevance to foreign policy. Each inquiry calls for submissions from government and the public on the issue at hand, and attempts to make use of government and non-governmental expertise on the subject.

It is hard to find evidence of any compelling influence exercised by the JFADT on the foreign policy process. Each report is tabled in Parliament and released to the general public. While governments are committed to responding to each report, rarely do the conclusions of reports impact on the content of foreign policy. In a survey of DFAT officers we conducted in December 2001, 92.9 per cent of respondents listed the JFADT as the least influential on foreign policy of a list comprising the Prime Minister, the Foreign and Trade ministers, ambassadors, ministerial advisers and departmental secretaries. Perhaps the greatest effect of the JFADT is to increase the awareness and interest of parliamentarians in the issues of foreign policy. Depending on the political sensitivity of the committee's reference, the work of the JFADT is often conducted in a spirit of bipartisan inquiry, with genuine exchanges of positions.

Parliament has also gained a greater role in the scrutiny of treaties, primarily through the Joint Standing Committee on Treaties (which currently has sixteen members – nine from the government, six from the Opposition, and one from the Australian Democrats). Parliament has no formal role in ratifying treaties, which are a prerogative of the executive (although if the provisions of treaties are incorporated into Australian law, parliamentary approval for the legislation is, of course, necessary). Over time, however, the convention developed that treaties be tabled in Parliament before ratification. Under the Hawke and Keating governments, the Coalition parties in Parliament became critical of the way in which this was done: often treaties, some of which had already entered into force, were tabled in "job lots" twice a year, limiting MPs' chances to examine and comment on them. Stewart Firth records, for example, that on one occasion in 1994, the government tabled thirty-six treaties together, seven of which had already come into force, and sixteen others that had either been ratified or already acceded to.[11]

With the occasional use of the foreign affairs power by the Federal Government to exercise power *vis-à-vis* the states (see pages 180 to 182), and Australia acceding to several agreements on human rights and the environment in the 1980s and 1990s, the signing of treaties slowly began to become a more salient political issue. This was tied, too, into a wider debate, driven by conservatives, about the alleged loss of Australian sovereignty to multilateral organisations. The Senate and the states and territories each prepared reports suggesting reform of the treaties process in 1995.

On taking power in March 1996, the Coalition Government instituted several changes, mandating a fifteen-day tabling of any treaty, accompanied by a National Interest analysis explaining why Australia has signed it, before it can enter into force. The Joint Standing Committee on Treaties was established, as was a Treaties Council within the Council of Australian Governments (COAG), and an electronic treaties library, available to the public. The Joint Standing Committee on Treaties holds public hearings and prepares its own report on signed treaties.[12] Despite claims that these measures would impose restrictions on the government's freedom of manoeuvre internationally, they do not appear to have had any significant effect either on the numbers or type of international treaties signed by Australia. Perhaps the greatest impact of the new treaties-review process is to occupy yet more DFAT time on parliamentary matters, particularly in compiling the National Interest analyses that must accompany the tabling of any treaty to both houses of Parliament.

Reviewing these processes, it is hard to find any significant role played in the formulation of Australian foreign policy by Federal Parliament. In addition to lacking the capacity to contribute or a formal role in the foreign policy process, Parliament is constrained by the lack of interest (or of incentive to take an interest) in foreign affairs by the majority of parliamentarians. J.D.B. Miller's observation still seems fundamentally apt:

> If [a parliamentarian] wishes to concentrate on foreign affairs in Parliament, he must recognise that this aspect of his work may earn him little electoral advantage and may indeed cause him disadvantage, since, while those who agree with him may not take much notice of what he is saying, those who disagree certainly will.[13]

It is hard to disagree with Indyk's conclusion that Parliament's role in foreign policy is best described not in terms of "positive influence", where direct inputs are contributed to the making of policy, but "negative influence", where it establishes limits outside of which foreign policy cannot range.[14] Because of ongoing deficiencies in capacity, formal role, and incentive, it is unlikely that this situation will change significantly in the foreseeable future.

Cabinet

Cabinet in a Westminster system is, as explained by Bagehot, "a committee of the legislative body selected to be the executive body".[15] In Australia, Cabinet has developed into a powerful mechanism for the collective deliberation of governmental policy, used by both sides of politics. Foremost among its advantages is its capacity to play a broad coordinating role among the various strands of government policy, insuring as much as possible against contradiction, and also serving to resolve, for the most part consensually, the conflicts and competitions that arise between portfolios and ministers. Traditionally, as in Parliament, foreign affairs has not often been a prominent topic of Cabinet discussion. However, this is slowly changing as more and more domestic portfolios acquire international aspects, and particularly as international economic developments play significant roles in shaping Australia's domestic conditions. Details of Cabinet's role in foreign policy making are set out in Chapter 5.

While Cabinet can be a significant influence on foreign policy, particularly in bringing the influence of powerful players such as the Prime Minister and the Treasurer into the policy-making process, its overall impact on the policy process should be kept in context. Cabinet, and its National Security Committee, only consider a fraction of all foreign policy issues confronting Australia. Most of these are considered at the strategic or contextual levels of policy-making. When these caveats are considered, it becomes clear that Cabinet becomes involved in only a narrow slice of all foreign policy, but that in those areas where it does become involved, its influence can be authoritative.

Political parties

The parties of government and opposition in Australia, the Australian Labor Party (ALP) and the Liberal–National Party Coalition, each release foreign and trade policy statements in the course of federal election campaigns. Like most other statements released, the incumbent's document invariably emphasises achievements and ongoing commitments, while the Opposition's usually raises missed opportunities and erroneous policy approaches, and offers a different approach if elected. Increasingly, both the ALP and the conservative parties are also making use of the histories of their parties in terms of achievements in foreign policy. Labor stresses the international activism of figures like H.V. Evatt, Gough Whitlam and Gareth Evans in contributing to international norms and architecture: the UN, engagement with Asia, the opening of relations with China, APEC, and the peace settlement in Cambodia. The conservative parties place pride in the achievements of Percy Spender, Richard Casey and John McEwen in forging foundational agreements with the United States and Japan, and in orienting Australia towards Asia through initiatives such as the Colombo Plan.

As with most historical iconography, these party histories rely to a large extent on myths and questionable assertions: it is particularly difficult in foreign policy terms to authoritatively identify the absolute authorship of any particular policy. Two examples, one from each side, may suffice. The Colombo Plan, a foundational claim in the Coalition's credentials to have oriented Australia towards Asia, was negotiated in January 1950 by Percy Spender, a minister of the Menzies Government, elected in December 1949. It is almost inconceivable that Evatt and John Burton, the previous Foreign Minister and Secretary of the Department of External Affairs respectively, had not played a substantial preparatory role. On the other hand, one of the ALP's great achievements was the creation of APEC in 1989, a development that would have been more difficult without the Fraser Government's commitment to the Pacific Economic Cooperation Council, first established in 1980.

These claims by the major parties have prompted a number of considerations on whether the two main sides of politics in Australia really have developed alternative foreign policy traditions.[16] It is necessary to ask whether the differences between the parties serve primarily as cosmetic means of policy differentiation for political purposes, or whether they signal more profound differences for foreign policy practice. Certainly a broad bipartisanship exists around issues such as the alliance with the United States, the importance of the relationship with Japan, and the Closer Economic Relationship with New Zealand, for example. (Indeed, to find policies genuinely different in substance on these core issues, one must look to the minor parties.) But the lack of genuine, sustained debate on foreign policy issues, and the broad continuities in some areas of foreign policy between changes of government have generated ongoing questions about the extent to which foreign policy in Australia is bipartisan.[17] An important set of distinctions has been made by Matthews and Ravenhill between three possible meanings of bipartisanship: convergence or agreement on policy substance; continuity in policy from one government to another; or an unwillingness to criticise the foreign policy settings of the government for domestic policy reasons.[18] Certainly all of these have strong international rationales, foremost among them the need to assure diplomatic partners of the constancy of Australia's policies and commitments. On the other hand, at times genuine differences have appeared between the parties on foreign policy issues, and have been aired in domestic political debate. The debate over Australia's military involvement in Vietnam and the issue of diplomatic recognition of China in the late 1960s and early 1970s were prominent among them. More recently, it can be argued that since the Asian economic crisis, a measure of bipartisanship in the third sense described above has vanished, with both government and Opposition prepared to attack each other's records, particularly in relation to aspects of Australia's relationship with the East Asian region.[19] The responses of the December 2001 survey of DFAT officers to a question on bipartisanship was interesting: while 44.2 per cent of respondents thought Australian foreign policy is essentially bipartisan and "always has been", 32.1 per cent thought Australian foreign policy is bipartisan, but is becoming "progressively less" so.

Both parties set out their general approaches to foreign policy in party platforms. Such platforms are usually couched in general aspirational terms and are often, especially in the case of the ALP, more revealing of internal political compromises than indications of the way the party will operate in government. Recent Labor foreign ministers have been able to manoeuvre around the strictures of Caucus resolutions on issues such as the US alliance, or the sale of uranium, or policy towards East Timor.[20] This may reflect what a number of commentators see as the declining influence on policy of party organisations on both sides of politics, and a perceptible increase in the independence of the parliamentary wings.[21]

The states and territories

Despite the constitution's clear grant of exclusive powers to the Federal Government for the conduct of external affairs, the Australian states and territories have substantial stakes in foreign policy. "In international relations, for which the Federal Government bears responsibility ... the states stagnate and obstruct", complained a testy E.G. Whitlam.[22]

The Australian states have a long history of separate international relationships, particularly with the United Kingdom. The agents-general of the states in London predated federation, and their right to petition the Crown was enshrined in the Statute of Westminster in 1931.[23] Various of the states and territories have also continued to maintain offices in various cities around the world, mainly to facilitate their own administration and to promote trade and tourism. Premiers, ministers and senior state bureaucrats travel abroad quite regularly in pursuit of these interests. Often the objectives of state offices and missions compete with the interests of other states and territories, especially where economic advantage is at stake, and sometimes clash with interests that the Federal Government is attempting to secure: though rare, this can be a cause of federal–state/territory, or inter-state/territory conflict.

There are other ways in which federal and federal–state/territory interests can come into conflict over foreign policy. Occasionally, the political outlook and interests of state governments can complicate the foreign policy goals of the Federal Government. A good example of this occurred in 1982, when the Victorian Government tried to ban visits by nuclear ships to Victorian ports, a clear potential complication to relations within the ANZUS alliance. Not for the first time, the Federal Government resorted to the constitution to bring the errant state into line: under Section 109, state administration of ports may not be exercised inconsistently with federal control over external affairs.

More commonly, however, federal foreign affairs powers have increasingly enabled the Commonwealth to intrude into areas previously within the domain of the states. One aspect of this trend is tied to the growing multilateralisation of domestic policy issues. As governments negotiate internationally on more and more issues of domestic policy, the Australian states and territories have found issues falling within their jurisdiction subject to international agreements. The other aspect is more intentionally centralising: where federal governments have used the foreign affairs power to enforce state or territory compliance with international agreements signed by the Federal Government. This began in earnest with the Whitlam Government's *Seas and Submerged Lands Act 1973* and its signing of the International Convention on the Elimination of All Forms of Racial Discrimination, which it used to pass the Racial Discrimination Act in 1975. In 1982 the High Court upheld the validity of this legislation against a challenge by the Queensland Government in the course of the *Koowarta Case*.[24] Two other prominent examples involved Tasmania. In 1983 the High Court upheld the validity of the Federal Government's halting of construction of the Gordon-below-Franklin dam on the basis of the government's accession to the UN World Heritage Convention.[25] In April 1994, gay activist Nick Toonen secured a UN Human Rights Commission ruling that Tasmania's laws against homosexuality breached Australia's international human rights obligations.[26]

The increasing impact of foreign policy issues on the Australian states and territories was one of the original reasons given for setting up the Council of Australian Governments (COAG), the mechanism for coordinating discussion between the states and territories and the Federal Government, which replaced the Premiers' Conferences. Consultation and the sharing of information about foreign affairs issues affecting the states and territories continue to be among COAG's functions. One of the major aspects of the reforms of the treaties process was to establish a Treaties Council within COAG. For many state and territory representatives, however, such reforms have not modified the effect of the foreign affairs power on states and territories. Most claim that often the states and territories are informed too late of significant negotiations, and lack the expertise to gauge the full potential impact of such talks. Many are sceptical about their influence on the making of foreign policy that will eventually affect them.

Taken together as a group, these political institutions do play a role in the Australian foreign policy making process, but in a sporadic and less than authoritative way. Their greatest impact is at the strategic and contextual levels of policy-making, but they have little influence on the more reactive and more detailed aspects of the policy process at the organisational and operational levels. At the strategic and contextual levels, their most important influence is to establish broad parameters outside which foreign policy cannot stray without engaging significant opposition. Their other major effect is to inform and to give political expression to the public's reactions to foreign policy issues.

Business groups and foreign policy

Business groups are another element in the domestic landscape seeking intermittently to influence foreign policy. Any government's foreign policy making is, of course, highly attuned to the general economic interests of the country. From the Commerce Agreement with Japan in 1957, through the development of APEC and the Cairns Group of agricultural free-trading countries, to the Howard Government's 2003 support for a free-trade agreement with the United States, economic interests have been a critical driver of Australian external policy. Since the amalgamation of the departments of Foreign Affairs and Trade in 1987, the linkages between trade and foreign policy have been strengthened.

For most businesses, focussed on the domestic market, the government's external policies have limited relevance, but for the growing number of Australian companies actively engaged in overseas markets, either as exporters (the Australian Bureau of Statistics estimates that 32 per cent of large Australian companies are involved in exports)[27] or investors, policy decisions in this area are becoming more important. The interests of these firms lie at two ends of the foreign policy making spectrum – in broad questions of Australia's engagement with the world (for example, opposition to agricultural protectionism or support for access to Asian markets) or at the highly specific points at which their particular business interests intersect with the government's capacity to assist them.

One way in which businesses advocate their views to government is through industry councils such as the National Farmers' Federation, the Australian Industry Group, the Business Council of Australia, or the Australian Services Roundtable. These organisations usually speak for a single industry sector. By means of lobbying and information activities, they seek to influence the government's actions in the international environment (and, more importantly, in the domestic arena) in ways that will broadly serve the interests of their members.

Business interests in external policy are also expressed in a different, country-focussed way. Organisations like the Australia China Business Council or the Australia Indonesia Business Council try to represent the views of all Australian businesses in a particular country. Groups such as these are more important in emerging economies where the role of government is large but processes are opaque, and legal and regulatory structures weak. Such groups have an understandable preference for smooth government-to-government relations that will not impede their commercial objectives. They get nervous whenever bilateral relationships pass through tense periods, as with Malaysia under Labor in 1994, or with China under the Coalition in 1997.

Finally, and most directly, individual businesspeople have their own direct relationships with politicians. These relationships, the inevitable corollary of political life, are often more influential than most public servants understand in providing ministers with outside sources of advice on international issues.

Although they may not constitute "grand foreign policy", many conversations between foreign or trade ministers, or even prime ministers, involve specific, commercially related issues. These can range from expressions of government support for an Australian tenderer, to efforts to secure the removal of barriers facing Australian exporters or investors. An important example was the extensive lobbying and information-sharing between the Federal and Western Australian governments and the Australian gas producers leading up to the 2002 contract to supply 3 million tonnes of liquefied natural gas annually to China over twenty-five years.[28]

Unlike most non-governmental organisations (NGOs), businesses usually prefer to influence policy through private representations to government rather than by engaging in broad public debate. This reluctance has sometimes been a source of frustration to Australian governments, seeking to shore up community support for multilateral trade in the face of anti-globalisation protests, for example. In some cases, as with the coalition of Australian businesses supporting a free-trade agreement with the United States (the Australia

United States Free Trade Agreement Business Group, and its US counterpart the American–Australian Free Trade Agreement Coalition), the government itself has played a catalytic role in encouraging a louder business voice in the public debate.

A group of growing potential importance in influencing external policy is the emerging Australian diaspora – the estimated 950,000 Australians, around 5 per cent of the country's total population, who live offshore.[29] These expatriate Australians, one of the most obvious manifestations of globalisation, have already begun to shape government responses to events overseas. In two of the case studies in this book – the Sandline Affair in Papua New Guinea and the response to the Bali bombings – the impact of policy on the large number of resident Australians in each place was one of the issues at the forefront of government decision-making. Individually, and through advocacy groups like the Southern Cross Group,[30] they have also begun shaping specific policies, such as the Howard Government's agreement in 2002 to permit Australians who deliberately acquire citizenship of another country to retain their Australian citizenship. These influences on policy are likely to intensify as the number of Australians living overseas grows.

The media and public opinion

In modern democracies, in which political and policy processes are increasingly influenced by popular opinion – actual, perceived or anticipated – the mass media have become powerful shapers and conveyors of public attitudes. Without the mass media – newspapers, radio and television – the actors in the political process would have to rely on a variety of difficult and time-consuming direct methods of communication with the electorate: doorknocking by party organisations, public meetings, telephone, mail-outs or the internet. None can compete with the capacity of the mass media to communicate constantly and almost instantaneously with the vast proportion of the public. It is necessary to study the role of the media in relation to foreign policy making as a preparatory step to examining the role of public opinion.

The media and foreign policy making

In countries like Australia, where political power is attained through majority public endorsement, the media, as the prime means of conveying political information and a powerful means of shaping public attitudes, are significant holders of power. However, the nature of this power needs to be properly understood. Media power derives from the role of the media as conduits of information and attitudes: it is a derivative influence that arises from the efforts of governments to communicate with the electorate, and from interest groups' attempts to create and convey certain dispositions to the government through a range of media organs. On the other hand, the media rely on the government for a large part of their material, and hence are a constant audience of most areas of policy-making, including foreign policy. As David Newsom notes, the result is that many foreign policy decisions or initiatives are crafted partly with an eye to how they will be presented to the press:

> the words, written or spoken, are carefully drafted, reviewed, and coordinated ... Briefings are supplemented by periodic press conferences, interviews, statements at ceremonies, speeches, and appearances before ... Committees. Whatever the occasion, the words represent national policy.[31]

Foreign policy makers are further aware that part of the audience of media reporting of Australian foreign policy will be the representatives of other governments, who also maintain a close watch on the Australian media.

But the media do not convey anywhere near all of the material that is prepared for their consumption; and neither are they by any means inert conduits for messages. Much of the power of the media comes from their capacity to select the material they report: choosing which messages to convey, and from whom, the media can determine who can communicate with a mass audience, or from a mass audience to the government, and on what issues. For journalist Ross Gittins, this makes the media unique types of messengers: through a quality loosely defined as "newsworthiness", they choose their messages, the extent to which they will allow the sender to make his or her case, and the prominence the message will be given.[32] The public becomes inescapably reliant on the media to establish criteria of significance and priority among the vast amount of current affairs each day, and consequently the government must work with the media's criteria of relevance also.

However, in determining newsworthiness, the media are by no means autonomous or authoritative actors. The news media are divided into several modes for conveying information – television, radio, newspapers, the internet – each of which in turn is occupied by several different organisations competing in commercial terms for audience patronage, both within the same communications medium and between media. Newsworthiness is therefore a heavily commercial judgement, relying on producers' or editors' assessments of what will be interesting to the public and of what stories competitors are likely to be running. For many critics, calculations of newsworthiness often lead to an unfortunate distinction between what is interesting and what is important.

On the other hand, one should be careful about overstating the role of competition in assuring a non-judgemental selection and presentation of news. The major Australian media outlets – print and broadcast – are controlled by a surprisingly small number of organisations, private and public. Furthermore, different newspapers and television and radio stations target different sections of the public, according to their socioeconomic profile and sets of values. This means that different media organs have more than a little latitude in selecting and shaping news stories according to certain values or preferences, which are often shared by their audience. Whereas Gittins maintains that "news selection is amoral in the search for what people are interested in, not what they should be interested in",[33] it is not difficult to find different slants and ideological positions among Australia's major media organisations. This means that in selecting how to convey stories, the media can often produce a message at odds with the sender's intentions. It also means that the media are not just conveyors of messages; they are powerful shapers and reinforcers of opinion as well.

In an often ambiguous way, the media are therefore both shapers of and responders to the tastes of the public, a trait they share with the political process. It is also important to note that the public is selectively attentive to media reporting. Not only do people select between which media they will pay attention to (if any), but they are also selective in terms of which items they consume. Given personal preferences and attention spans, media studies have found that people tend to pay greater attention to and remember stories that conform to their tastes and pre-existing commitments, while filtering out and forgetting things that do not.[34] This also means that quite often interpretations of news stories, as filtered by values, prejudices and experience, are highly varied between different people, and significantly at odds with the intention of the conveyor of the story.

While it is often unsafe to generalise, there are significant broad trends that can be observed about the different types of media in terms of the types of messages they convey and the audience to whom they convey the message. In discussing print and broadcast media, most media scholars distinguish between the quality and the popular media. The former typically has a smaller, more middle-class audience, the latter a larger, more working-class and lower-middle-class audience. Tiffen distinguishes the quality media as having priorities emphasising domestic and international political and economic developments, and major social institutions, a commitment to more sustained analysis of news stories, and a serious conception of their role. The popular media, on the other hand, have news priorities emphasising crime, political controversy, and scandal, sport, sex and human interest; derive their virtue from their access to a large audience; and see their role more in terms of entertainment.[35] Foreign news is an established segment in both the quality and popular media in Australia, but the consideration of foreign news in the quality media is on the whole more extensive and sustained, more concerned with analysis and context, and less sensationalist. Rosenau, among others, links these qualities directly to differences in public reactions to foreign policy issues: "the popular media contribute to both the passivity and the superficial moods of the mass public, whereas the quality media foster active concern and structured opinion".[36]

Another important distinction to make is that between the print and the electronic media. The print media, and in particular the broadsheet newspapers and news-digest journals such as the *Bulletin*, are able to carry a greater range of news and in much greater depth than any of the electronic media. (Tiffen notes that the transcript of a half-hour news broadcast would not fill the front page of a broadsheet newspaper.)[37] On the other hand, the electronic media – mainly television and radio – are the sole sources of news for the vast majority of the public. Most of this audience relies on the commercial television stations' evening half-hour news broadcast. This has great significance for the amount of foreign policy relevant news available to most of the public. Other than during foreign policy crises, international news is one among six or seven definable segments of the average commercial news broadcast: headlines, state and/or local politics, national politics, international news, finance, sport, and weather. Each broadcast contains fourteen to sixteen stories that run for between one and two minutes each. This means that most members of the public will receive three or four items of international news daily, making a claim on a maximum six minutes of their attention. These figures are, of course, significantly different for those relatively small numbers of people who tune into either SBS world news or ABC news.

A third distinction needs to be made over the level of involvement of the public in the news as it is reported. The majority of the public has a passive relationship to the news as presented on television. However, some media are able to offer different platforms for public involvement with and reaction to the news as it is reported. The print media, particularly the broadsheet media, have the space to be able to feature debate between different positions on a range of issues, as well as to feature opinion pieces by editors and specialists. To this, the public is able to react through writing letters, which may then be printed by the newspaper. This form of debate, in which the exchanges are separated by significant amounts of time, and in which the responses are carefully prepared and placed on view as a part of the public record, is of a very different sort than that featured on talkback radio. This is a form of media that derives its commercial success from its ability to engage its substantial listening public in debate. The immediacy and anonymity of this form of exchange, plus the commercial imperative of talkback radio hosts in stimulating listeners' indignation, gives rise to more extreme opinion and a more hysterical engagement with current affairs. While print media debate often addresses foreign policy issues, it is less significant for political calculations because of the small numbers of people it engages; on the other hand, while talkback radio rarely features foreign policy relevant topics, when it does, its effect on broad public attitudes can be politically highly significant.

This examination of the news media in Australia provides an indication of how influential the media are in shaping public attitudes towards foreign policy issues. The majority of international news stories that are reported are selected according to the perceived interests of Australians, and the values systems shared by media organisations and their publics. For the most part, foreign news reporting is highly Australia-centric: in terms of prioritising issues that either affect Australians, or that occur in places with which significant numbers of Australians feel a connection, or in relation to events that occur in countries or regions near Australia. A story with an Australian "angle" is invariably judged more newsworthy. So are stories related to problems, crises or policy missteps. This has made leaks an important source of media reporting on foreign policy, and an oft-resorted-to mechanism for disgruntled participants in the policy process to support or oppose a position, expose some perceived unethical conduct, or massage egos. DFAT has, at times, faced serious problems from leaks, often resulting in increased secrecy and security measures within the organisation.[38] Apart from leaks, foreign policy reporting is much more reliant on the passage of events for news. The cost of maintaining reporters abroad, and the secretive nature of foreign policy, means that Australian foreign affairs reporters are less able to proactively "make news" than their domestic colleagues; rather, they must resort for the most part to reporting the news from abroad, and relying heavily on the work of overseas media organisations and wire services.[39]

Given the sensitive nature of foreign policy material, the media are often faced with the dilemma of whether publishing certain information will do unacceptable harm to the public interest. On the one hand, the media are defensive of their role as an independent check on government activity, and are outspoken in defence of their freedom of expression. On the other hand, they are aware of a long history of Australia's relationships with regional countries being complicated by media reporting. Perhaps the best-known example was a front-page article by David Jenkins that appeared in the *Sydney Morning Herald* on 10 April 1986, which compared the corruption of the Suharto regime in Indonesia with that of the recently deposed Marcos regime in the Philippines. The reaction of the Indonesian Government included protests, both diplomatic and popular, the sudden removal of visa-free entry to Indonesia by Australians, the cancellation of a ministerial visit, and the refusal of press visas for Australian journalists.[40] The Foreign Minister at the time, Bill Hayden, reacted cautiously, ignoring regional calls to clamp down on the freedom of the Australian media, while pointing out to the media that they had certain responsibilities:

> We can't interfere with what you write, nor would we want to, anyway, but the article has been provocative and there have been clear consequences, and no one can deny that. I leave it to the media to determine whether it is always wise to write those articles and to ask themselves what was achieved by it. In the meantime this country's national interest has been seriously disadvantaged and Australians have been seriously disadvantaged.[41]

Various incidents of media reporting have continued to complicate Australia's regional relations since Hayden's warning. No doubt they will continue to do so, although most journalists we spoke to were very conscious of this occasional tension between the country's foreign policy interests and the interests of the dissemination of information.

From the perspective of foreign policy makers, the media appear to take only sporadic, sensationalist interest in a field with which professionals deal on a long-term basis. There is frequent frustration with the inaccuracy of reporting, its preference for crises and policy mistakes, and the prominence that is given to critical views of Australian foreign policy. However, no less than in any other portfolio, foreign policy makers are highly sensitive to media reporting. Daily the DFAT media office prepares material and briefings for the media, and fields media inquiries. Invariably, each day begins for senior officers with a careful review of foreign policy relevant media reports. Media reporting can determine the work of foreign policy makers by throwing to light possible questions to be asked of the ministers, by raising certain external events to public significance, or by highlighting alleged problems with the conduct of Australian foreign policy. There are several types of news item that are significant for foreign policy makers. In a nominal descending order of priority, they fall into five categories:

1. intensive reporting or a media campaign on major international issues or crises affecting Australia, particularly those that have attracted a broad media audience;
2. analysis or commentary that is highly critical of the content of Australian foreign policy or foreign policy institutions or personnel;
3. developments in which Australians are experiencing difficulties at the hands of foreign governments;
4. international developments with the potential to affect Australia that may prompt parliamentary or media queries concerning the reaction of the Australian Government; and
5. other international or internationally related news items indicating the direction of interest of the media and the public.

On various issues, sustained media attention can create the public-opinion environment within which government policy operates. Continued media attention to Indonesian human rights abuses in East Timor, for example, or to French nuclear testing in the South Pacific, contributed significantly to the policy environment within which foreign policy makers had to operate in relation to those and related issues.

Foreign policy practitioners display a clear conception of the importance of the media to their work. The formidable former Secretary of the Department of External Affairs Sir Arthur Tange complained, "The power of journalists to divert the executive from seriously addressing real national problems is great and destructive".[42] A less irritable assessment was provided by the respondents to our survey: 2.7 per cent assessed the role of broadsheet columnists on foreign policy making as "critical", 30.8 per cent as "important" and 4.9 per cent as "usually irrelevant"; compared with 4.5 per cent ("critical"), 19.9 per cent ("important") and 29.9 per cent ("usually irrelevant") for tabloid columnists; and 8 per cent ("critical"), 22.3 per cent ("important"), and 28.6 per cent ("usually irrelevant") for radio talkback hosts. In general terms, we can conclude that the media have the potential to play an important though sporadic role in the foreign policy process by adding an additional criterion for relevance to policy-makers' existing criteria (as discussed in Chapter 9).

Media reporting on foreign policy – as sporadic and reactive as it is – has the potential to engage the attention of large portions of the domestic electorate. For this reason, even if events do not capture media attention, foreign policy makers and their ministers are aware that they may be asked to respond to breaking events that they have only just heard about. This means that not only must foreign policy makers use the national interest and existing policy commitments as standards of importance and relevance to distinguish between and prioritise international developments, but they must also maintain the capacity to anticipate possible media interest.

Public opinion and foreign policy

Our review of the media, the main source of most of the Australian public's information on international affairs, gives us some idea of the level of broad public engagement with Australian foreign policy. In discussing the role of public opinion in the foreign policy process, however, there are several questions that need to be addressed in detail. To what extent is the Australian public engaged or interested in foreign policy, and what proportion of the public is engaged to a significant extent? Does public opinion affect policy, or does it find more often that its attitudes are affected by policy-makers? Finally, in what directions does public opinion affect policy when it does so, and what are the processes through which this influence is transmitted?

Writing in 1967 on the situation in the United States, Kenneth Waltz observed: "Almost always since World War II, matters of foreign policy have ranked highest among concerns of the people at large".[43] It is impossible to say the same of the Australian public: the weight of public-opinion research conducted on international affairs bears witness to the low relative priority attached to external affairs by the vast majority of the public, other than during significant foreign policy crises.[44] The paucity of information on foreign affairs accessed by the Australian public, plus its low level of interest, leads one in the direction of James Rosenau's famous but somewhat intemperate characterisation of public attitudes to foreign policy:

> The mass public is uninformed about either specific foreign policy issues or
> foreign affairs in general. Its members pay little, if any attention to day-to-day
> developments in world politics. Being uninformed and without initiative, they lack
> structured opinions – that is, they are short of the cognitive and evaluative
> equipment which facilitates comprehension of the ideas or information [relevant
> to foreign policy]. Thus their response to foreign policy matters is less one of
> intellect and more one of emotion; less one of opinion and more one of mood; of
> generalised, superficial, and undisciplined feelings which easily fluctuate from one
> extreme to another – from tolerance to intolerance, optimism to pessimism,
> idealism to cynicism, withdrawal to intervention.[45]

As easy as it would be to do so, it is inaccurate to sum up the nature of Australian public engagement on foreign policy matters with one such rhetorical stroke. In gauging the extent of public engagement in foreign policy matters, it is necessary to make some basic distinctions. There are three identifiable sectors of public opinion: a collection of "issue publics" or interest groups; a small number of "interested generalists"; and the remaining, largely passive majority. Issue publics we will discuss in the next section of this chapter (page 196). Interested generalists, or the "attentive public" referred to in public-opinion literature, are a relatively small minority in Australian society. They are usually tertiary-educated middle-class professionals and regular consumers of the broadsheet print media and quality electronic media. Their interest in international affairs is either prompted by a history of involvement internationally (living overseas, working in an internationally oriented profession, learning a language other than English, the love of another culture), or by a particular normative concern with an aspect of international affairs (human rights, the environment, distributional inequities), or by an intellectual interest in and history of study of international relations. The reactions of interested generalists to foreign policy issues is usually marked by a higher than average understanding of the history and context of the issues, and a set of fairly structured opinions about the nature of international relations and the virtue or otherwise of Australian foreign policy. Interested generalists who are critical of Australian foreign policy and motivated to communicate their discontent to the government usually join one or another of the foreign policy issue publics. Those who either accept government policy or who are disinclined to act over their disagreement remain largely without influence on the foreign policy process, chiefly by virtue of their low numbers.

The vast majority of the Australian public pays intermittent attention to international events, becoming significantly engaged with particular issues only occasionally. For most people in Australian society, foreign policy ranks in importance well below domestic policy concerns for a number of reasons. Foreign policy often seems remote; rarely do foreign policy decisions result in the significant reapportioning of resources within society (and when they do, they become very much a part of domestic politics).[46] Most people seem to take more interest in issues that are closer to their daily lives and interests; it is on these matters that they also tend to feel they have more chance of influencing outcomes.[47] There also appear to be strong tendencies to think that an individual has greater knowledge, capacity and right to form opinions about matters within his or her own society than in others. Related to this is an often-encountered belief that the government's primary responsibility is the well-being of its own society, and that the public should continue to engage its attention in this primary responsibility.

However, there are times when Australian public opinion is aroused, and becomes a significant influence on the policy process. In order to engage the broad mass of public opinion, a foreign policy issue that normally would be remote from the public's interests and concerns needs to touch one or more of several nerves. The most obvious of these is the public's sense of security – especially from possible military conflict or terrorist attack. Other foreign policy issues are more likely to touch diffuse concerns: a sense of national identity or pride (for example, the proposed building of an airport over First World War Australian war graves in France); a sense of collective morality, justice or responsibility (the post-referendum violence in East Timor); issues of cultural or historical continuity or discontinuity (the death of a member of the British royal family); particular ethnic or national questions (concerns over non-European immigration and the issue of Islamic asylum-seekers); and a general sense of national material gain or loss (anti-globalisation protests). It is often hard to predict which issues will touch which collective popular nerve, or in which direction. What is clear is the role played by the electronic media – television and talkback radio – in shaping public attitudes by presenting prominent issues in certain ways. It is also necessary to distinguish between specific public reactions directly on the content of a policy or issue, and derivative opinion, in which the public forms positive or negative opinions on the government's competence and strength of will in handling a particular situation. A good example of the latter is the dive in popularity of Bob Hawke (from 65 per cent to 58 per cent) and the ALP (50 per cent to 43 per cent) after the backdown on cooperation with the US on MX missile tests in February 1985. It is likely that the content of the policy – close cooperation with the US on developing a new weapons system – would have been broadly endorsed; what the public reacted to was perceptions of deviousness and a policy backdown. Sometimes it can be hard to separate these two forms of public reaction, but the different types have obvious effects on policy-makers' latitude of action in relation to foreign policy issues.

To what extent does public opinion, when engaged, affect foreign policy making? In formal terms, public opinion should only directly affect the policy process during election periods, when the electorate is given the chance to endorse or indicate disapproval of a government's policy record and the policy platforms it intends to enact. Only sporadically have Australian federal elections featured foreign policy issues prominently among the matters on which the electorate exercises its primary judgement. With a broad definition of foreign policy issues, one arrives at a figure of perhaps twelve or fourteen of Australia's forty federal elections that have featured strong divisions on and reactions to foreign policy issues. (Those we have counted as "foreign policy elections" are the war and conscription elections of 1914 and 1917; the war elections of 1940 and 1943; the Cold War elections of 1949, 1951, 1954, 1955 and 1958; the Vietnam

War elections of 1966, 1969 and 1972; and the "War on Terror" election of 2001.) Less formally, public opinion sets the essential parameters of the political and policy processes between elections. According to some commentators, government policy-making is becoming steadily more responsive to shifts in the public mood, which is accessed through the continuous use of much more sophisticated opinion polling, often concentrated in marginal seats. Organisations such as Rehame, which is able to track public reactions on talkback radio, also have secured the attention of participants in the political and policy processes. The pervasive effect of this sort of polling is to sensitise the government to the possible domestic political resonances of policy. In this way public opinion can be influential in foreign policy making without being aroused or even aware of the policies being pursued, solely through policy-makers superimposing a "public-opinion filter" on their readings of policy issues.

So far we have reviewed the flow of influence from the public to the government, through the direct engagement of broad public interest in an issue, and in the general anticipation of possible public reactions to alternative policy choices by policy-makers. What should also be acknowledged is the extent to which policy-makers can seek to influence public opinion: to build political support for a specific policy or the government in general; to foreclose the possibilities of critique or opposition; or to circumvent obstruction by colleagues, elites or entrenched interests.[48] The technique of shaping public opinion often requires not only outlining a compelling position for the public to support, but also a counterpart position (often implied) for the public to oppose. Whether or not such strategies actually engage public support depends on a number of issues. One is the way the new issues relate to the pre-existing political commitments of the public, and the enduring positive or negative attitudes of people to the government and Opposition. Another is the success of the strategy in engaging media attention and endorsement, and the capacity of political leaders to respond flexibly to the flow of events.

A third, quite common possibility is the lack of any link at all between public opinion and policy-making. Often political leaders and policy-makers undertake policies that they judge to be in the public interest, despite the beliefs of the electorate. Either the mass of public opinion remains unaware of policies being pursued on its behalf, or governments believe that the policy is important enough to pursue even if it incurs reversals in public opinion. The history of Australian foreign policy is replete with such instances: the signing of the 1958 trade agreement with Japan; the agreement to take large numbers of Indochinese refugees in the late 1970s; the re-engagement of China after the Tiananmen massacre of 1989.

When it does affect policy-making, in what direction does the influence of public opinion work? "The public", observed Henry Kissinger, "has a penchant for choosing the interpretation of current trends which implies the least effort".[49] When aroused, the broad mass of public opinion will most likely coalesce around a general position rather than a specific series of issues. Walter Lippmann observed that, when engaged, the public brings an emotionalism to foreign policy that drives policy to its extremes and removes much of the flexibility from a state's diplomacy.[50] The argument can be made that foreign policy conducted in the light of public attention makes the achievement of positions of clear gain or victory hard to resist, and is ill-disposed towards compromises, patience or self-limitations. Certainly public attention places an imperative on political leaders to emphasise the immediate national benefit, the self-interest advanced in any particular international gesture. For example, Prime Minister Howard defended the extension of Australian aid to Indonesia during the Asian financial crisis in the following terms:

> It is in the national self-interest of Australia to have strong regional economies. It is in the national self-interest of Australia to strengthen an economy as large and potentially as powerful as Indonesia.

Foreign Minister Downer made a similar argument:

> In the last year we had a $1.4 billion trade surplus with Indonesia and it's obviously important to us that countries like Indonesia are able to work their way through their current economic difficulties because it means jobs right here in Australia.

And later: "we are doing this first and foremost in our own interests, and secondly, in their interests, and our two interests happen to coincide".

Even before public opinion is aroused, most policy-makers are aware of the potential costs of misreading public opinion. Perhaps the most salutary recent example was Foreign Minister Gareth Evans's remark that the 1995 decision by France to resume nuclear testing on Mururoa Atoll "could have been worse". The public outcry against both the testing and Evans's response led the Australian Government to adopt a harder line in protests against the tests, and to go further in its response than it otherwise might have done; for example, in setting up the Canberra Commission on the Elimination of Nuclear Weapons.

For the most part, then, public opinion, like the media, becomes significant for policy-making when its interest is engaged, but at other times it retains a potential influence, by engaging policy-makers' anticipations of how the public may react. We can agree with Rosenau that, most of the time, the function of public opinion "is that of setting, through the potentiality of its more active moods, the outer limits within which decision makers and opinion makers feel constrained to operate".[51] The potential arousal of public opinion also increases the importance of political judgement in policy-making, to ensure that the rarefied atmosphere of the executive process of foreign policy making does not breed political misjudgements. A structural change that has resulted is the increased involvement of ministerial offices (for political judgement) and the International Division of the Department of Prime Minister and Cabinet (for whole-of-government contextualisation) in the policy-vetting process. The potential influence of public opinion has also led governments over time to devote greater efforts and resources towards the aspects of foreign affairs that are most visible to the public. These are mainly consular matters: the efficient issue of passports; helping Australians in trouble overseas; providing accessible information on international matters that engage the public's interest.

Foreign policy issue publics

Perhaps the one aspect of the domestic landscape of foreign policy making that remains actively engaged in monitoring and trying to influence the foreign policy process is the range of foreign policy issue publics, more commonly thought of as interest groups. We refer to them as issue publics because this term better conveys the relationship they play to the policy process: these are not groups with defined, enclosed memberships that take sporadic interest in policy; they are sections of the public, often assembled around an organisational core, that maintain regular connections into parts of the policy process. Matthews and Ravenhill have referred to these as "issue networks", or regular conduits of influence, opinion and information that flow along regularised channels of contact between issue publics and participants in the policy process who work on the relevant issue.[52] In assessing how influential issue publics are in the foreign policy process, we need to ask not whether they are the decisive factor in policy-making, but the extent to which their positions are considered in the policy process, and whether these positions inform some of the parameters of a given policy.[53]

A number of distinctions need to be made between different types of issue publics. Most basic is the distinction between permanently functioning issue publics and what Rosenau calls "attention groups", or:

unorganised segments of the mass public, such as ethnic minorities, which are normally passive and disinterested, but which acquire structure as an aroused group when an issue area arises that directly affects their common interests ... Their entrance into public debate is then sudden and impulsive, and confined exclusively to the single issue which provoked them.[54]

Permanently functioning issue publics play a much more effective and sustained role in the policy process. Often their history of activism gives them a political prominence and a set of policy positions that are already established in the minds of policy-makers, the media and the public. They are more likely to have established contacts into the policy process and the media, an institutional memory of successful and unsuccessful activism and strategies, and greater experience in how to engage the policy process effectively.

Australian foreign policy issue publics, other than occasional attention groups, fall into four categories. Economic–utilitarian issue publics are either those that focus attention on Australian foreign and trade policy as it affects a particular sector of the economy, or those that advocate different policy approaches for ensuring the economic well-being of society (for the most part through engaging in multilateral trade liberalisation and economic engagement with East Asia). Ethnic–religious issue publics often combine activism on foreign policy towards a particular state, region or group of people overseas, with a general tendency to support the advance of human rights in general by Australian foreign policy. Normative–cosmopolitan issue publics focus on a general issue in world politics that is thought to be damaging to the well-being of human beings or the ecosphere: human rights, environmental degradation, gender inequality, nuclear disarmament, the maldistribution of wealth. These are groups that are most likely to have international links with like-minded groups, and are much more likely to take part in international campaigns on certain issues. Finally, some issue publics coalesce around various issues of national concern – the welfare and recognition of former and current armed-forces personnel; the campaign to denuclearise Australia – which can have specific foreign policy implications.

Each of these types of issue publics contains its own brand of politics. Often a formal organisation or set of organisations relate not only to the government, but also to a constituency: often the financial support, endorsement and political influence deriving from the claims of such issue publics to represent significant sections of the public are dependent on remaining representative of a constituency that may itself include a broad range of opinion.[55] This can have a powerful effect on the messages that the issue public tries to convey to the government. It also means that the internal politics and the logic of their relation to the policy process can vary widely. One basic distinction has been made by Charles Lindblom: whereas one type of issue public may be dissatisfied with government policy, critical of the government and motivated to try to change an aspect of policy, another type is convinced that current government policy broadly accords with its interests and usually supports the government publicly. The role of the latter is that of a "policy watchdog", ensuring that no adverse change is made to government policy.[56] It becomes immediately obvious that the logic of engagement with the policy process will be very different between these two types. In addition to these broad differences, there are a range of more subtle differences among issue publics, as determined by the specific nature of their concerns and the way they relate to established foreign policy directions.

The capacity of issue publics to influence policy depends on four conditions: access, receptivity, impact and timing. Access relates both to the willingness of the government to countenance public consultation on a particular issue, and to the ability of issue publics to make contact with the policy-makers who are decisive in shaping the policy. While governments are more often than not keen to portray themselves as receptive to messages from the electorate, the consultative mechanisms they develop can function as effectively to filter out unwanted attempts at public influence as they do to convey messages to their intended destination. On the other hand, well-organised issue publics usually make use of a broad range of points of access, direct and indirect. These range from arranging formal meetings with the Prime Minister and the portfolio ministers, sending them letters and formal submissions on particular issues, and accessing particular bureaucrats, to attempting to engage local MPs through constituency representations to bring the issue up in Parliament, networking with other issue publics, regularly publishing newsletters, and directly contacting the media to attempt to publicise a particular issue.

Receptivity governs whether key policy-makers, once they have been contacted, are willing to consider the message conveyed. Many of the NGO representatives with whom we talked argued that the most important factor in the effective transmission of influence was the establishment of interpersonal "chemistry" between NGO representatives and policy-makers, and that significant efforts are therefore devoted to finding and maintaining contacts who are open and sympathetic to the message. According to one NGO representative we talked with, there is a definite process to be followed: "Don't demand; request. Try to see if there is a common understanding of the issues; if there is not, don't make any request. The task becomes one of building shared knowledge and understandings and then making a request in terms of these."

Various factors can impact on how receptive a policy-maker is to a particular group. One set of considerations involves whether the policy-maker under-
stands and is sympathetic to the values and ideological approach of the group,
and has a similar attitude towards the policy in question. Another is the extent
to which the policy-maker believes the group has a legitimate right to try to
influence Australian Government policy in a particular direction. Yet another
factor is whether the policy advocated by the group is judged to be in the interest of the country and the government. Because of the importance of receptivity, most NGOs place great store on their reputation, their credibility, and the
maintenance of trust with policy-makers. The most effective groups carefully
choose non-trivial issues to pursue, and ensure that the evidence they put
forward has passed high standards of proof.

The impact of an issue public's demands depends on whether they can be
couched in ways that significantly affect the relevant policy calculations or the
general political calculus, or both. Sometimes impact is provided by the quality of an idea or a submission, or its capacity to bring to light new information
that is directly relevant to the policy calculus. (Peter Haas and others have
suggested that "epistemic communities", or transnational groups of policy
experts, can be especially influential, not only by offering governments solutions to particular problems, but by ensuring that these are solutions that are
endorsed and shared by the policy communities in other relevant states.)[57]
More often, issue publics try to gain impact by influencing the political calculations of the government: by arguing that a consequence of the message may
be political gain or the avoidance of significant losses. Most NGOs try to couch
their requests in terms of quid pro quo proposals, but whether these are effective depends on a number of factors: the political impact of the issue public's
praise or criticism, endorsement or disendorsement; its ability to mobilise
public and media interest; and the government's sensitivity to the political
calculations involved. Sometimes issue publics are more effective by calling
into question the government's consistency or credibility, by pointing out that
certain commitments are at odds with its public rhetoric and broad policy
commitments. A crucial component here is whether the issue public's request
is within the government's power to grant while maintaining the credibility and
consistency of the rest of its policy and the other commitments it has made.
Milbrath suggests that the less important the issue, and the narrower its impact
on society, the greater chance an issue public has of influencing policy relating
to it.[58] All of this means that representatives of issue publics need to have a
good understanding of the structures and processes of politics and policy;
many have been involved in one form of politics or another, where they have
learnt its basic logic and calculations.

Timing affects issue publics' capacity for influence by determining how quickly they must respond to an issue or policy change, and whether they are dealing with established policy or the process of policy formulation or change. Whether or not the government has set its policy directions, and committed resources and reputation to pursuing them, will obviously greatly affect the capacity of issue publics to change it (or the amount of effort policy "watchdogs" need to devote to ensuring it is maintained). The impact of timing also ensures that issue publics remain closely attentive to international developments that might impact on the sector of government policy of most interest to them. To sum up, different combinations of access, receptivity, impact and timing mean that there is an enormous variation in the ability of different issue publics to influence the calculations of foreign policy makers.

If anything, the foreign policy process is steadily becoming more accessible to issue publics, and more inclined to countenance the development of regular, routinised channels of contact between policy-makers and interests within society. With the increase in the political imperatives to demonstrate the benefits of an often esoteric policy area to the Australian public, foreign policy makers have become increasingly keen to identify and engage the support of constituencies and stakeholders. From their side, issue publics have become no less eager to access policy-makers and try to influence the policy process. One institutional development prompted by this has been the establishment of routine consultations between the foreign policy bureaucracy and the relevant issue publics, both bilaterally, and in the form of regular roundtables such as those on human rights, held several times a year. Within these consultation processes, attempts at influence run both ways: while issue publics attempt to affect a particular policy, policy-makers attempt to convince interested groups of the wisdom of the government's policy, or the real obstacles confronting it. Both sides use such opportunities to collect information: the government to gauge the reception of its policies within significant sections of the community; the issue publics to gain a more detailed knowledge of government policy and emerging issues (the discussions are usually held on a background, non-attributable basis). Another trend has been to include NGO representatives on policy-development panels, and even to include them in delegations to multilateral negotiations. This can have the effect of further ensuring issue publics' sense of "ownership" and participation in relevant aspects of foreign policy.[59] When unsuccessful, however, it can force the government into inflexible policy commitments or end in ruptures followed by bitter NGO criticism of government policy. A good example is the attempt by the Hawke Government to engage environmental groups in the ecologically sustainable development (ESD) consultations. The environmental groups were outraged when the government wrote resource-security guarantees into the ESD process, and threatened to withdraw unless the government adopted the greenhouse-gas abatement recommendations of the June 1988 Toronto Conference on the Changing Atmosphere, of a 20 per cent reduction in carbon dioxide emissions from 1988 levels by the year 2005. Eventually the environmental groups withdrew from the process anyway, in protest at the dominance of economic imperatives in global-warming policy-making, and have since been bitter critics of government policy in this area.

One final aspect of the domestic landscape that comes into regular contact with the foreign policy process is a fairly diverse group comprising academics, foreign policy think tanks, foreign policy interest organisations, and "second-track diplomacy" groups. Academics engage with the policy process at a number of levels. Many foreign policy practitioners have received some sort of formal training in academic international relations. Of the respondents to our survey, 23.7 per cent listed politics or international relations as their principal field of academic training; the next highest fields were history (17.4 per cent) and economics (16.5 per cent). While in general there is little communication between international relations academics and foreign policy practitioners, area or issue specialists do regularly contribute to the policy process. (There is a regular if informal process of consultation particularly between DFAT and Defence and Asia specialists and economists from the Australian National University; Senate and parliamentary committees also make regular use of Canberra-based academics.) A number of senior academics have also been invited onto the Foreign Affairs Council, established by Alexander Downer, which meets several times a year for a general dialogue on foreign policy issues.

Several foreign policy think tanks have been established over time, mostly relating specifically to Australia's integration with the East Asian region. These have developed a variety of formal and informal relationships with the institutions of foreign policy making and the portfolio ministers. Often these are forums also to engage foreign policy practitioners, interested businesspeople, the media and academics in ongoing discussions, again particularly on Australia's relationships with its region. Slightly different are the foreign policy interest organisations, prominent among which is the Australian Institute of International Affairs (AIIA). Founded in 1933, the AIIA seeks to promote interest in and understanding of international affairs among the Australian public, by providing a forum for the debate and exchange of views. Ministers and senior diplomats sometimes use forums provided by the AIIA to publicise strategic policy statements.

There remains a collection of organisations that involve foreign policy practitioners and other interested parties – usually academics or businesspeople – that undertake semiofficial dialogue with similar groups in other countries on a particular aspect of foreign policy. These range from the Pacific Economic Cooperation Council (PECC) and the Conference for Security Cooperation in the Asia–Pacific (CSCAP), to a variety of bilaterally focussed organisations, like the Australia China Business Council (ACBC). Often these engage in second-track diplomacy, or the use of non-official dialogues to explore diplomatic initiatives and solutions to sensitive issues. While taking place under the auspices of non-official organisations, such arrangements often involve officials participating in an ostensibly non-official capacity. Often these occasions are used to explore the reactions of other states' representatives to certain initiatives. The actions and resolutions of such conferences do not carry official consequences, but are reported back to home governments and can be subsequently built on by states. For their part, non-governmental participants can use these conferences to feed ideas into official thinking and to maintain access to such thinking.

Conclusion

The domestic influences on foreign policy making are highly varied in terms of their sources and their potential impact. For the most part they are dormant, significant only in terms of their potential to be aroused and to set the parameters of foreign policy makers' freedom of action. Thus the ongoing effect of these parts of the domestic landscape is to set limits and to impose additional criteria of judgement on policy-makers' reactions to international developments. Other aspects of the domestic landscape, such as issue publics, have been drawn into consultation as much as possible, as a consequence of what some would see as the developing politicisation of foreign policy. In such areas as the routinised consultation with issue publics and the use made of second-track diplomacy, real departures have been made. For the most part, however, there is no significant change in the relationship of foreign policy making to the domestic environment. This allows the great bulk of foreign policy to be formulated and carried out beyond the attention of all but its practitioners.

Notes

1 Alexis de Tocqueville, *Democracy in America*, Oxford: Oxford University Press, 1946, pp. 161–2.
2 Alan Watt, *The Evolution of Australian Foreign Policy 1938–1965*, London: Cambridge University Press, 1967, p. 363.
3 Ironically, it was an arch-realist, Kenneth Waltz, who first made this observation; see Kenneth N. Waltz, *Foreign Policy and Democratic Politics: The American and British Experience*, Boston: Little, Brown, 1967, p. 265.

4 Robert A. Dahl, "A Democratic Dilemma: System Effectiveness Versus Citizen Participation", *Political Science Quarterly*, Vol. 109, No. 1, 1994, pp. 23–34.

5 Samuel P. Huntington, *The Common Defense: Strategic Programs in National Politics*, New York: Columbia University Press, 1961, p. 146.

6 ibid.

7 John Locke, *Two Treatises of Government*, ed. Mark Goldie, London: J.M. Dent, 1993, p. 190.

8 Brian L. Hocking, "Parliament, Parliamentarians, and Foreign Affairs", *Australian Outlook*, Vol. 30, No. 2, August 1976, p. 301.

9 Martin Indyk, *Influence without Power: The Influence of the Backbench in Australian Foreign Policy 1976–1977*, APSA/Parliamentary Fellow Monograph No. 1, Canberra: Parliament of Australia, 1977, pp. 28–9.

10 J.D.B. Miller, "The Role of the Australian Parliament in Foreign Policy", *Parliamentarian*, Vol. 50, No. 1, January 1969, p. 3.

11 Stewart Firth, *Australia in International Politics: An Introduction to Australian Foreign Policy*, Sydney: Allen & Unwin, 1999.

12 "Australia and International Treaty Making Information Kit". http://www.austlii.edu.au/au/other/dfat/reports/infokit.html

13 Miller, "The Role of the Australian Parliament in Foreign Policy", p. 3.

14 Indyk, *Influence without Power*.

15 Walter Bagehot, *The English Constitution*, London: Fontana, 1963, p. 66.

16 See Henry S. Albinski, *Australian External Policy under Labor: Content, Process and the National Debate*, Brisbane: University of Queensland Press, 1977; David Lee and Christopher Waters (eds), *Evatt to Evans: The Labor Tradition in Australian Foreign Policy*, Sydney: Allen & Unwin, 1997. A similar consideration of the Liberal tradition in foreign policy has been carried out by David Lowe and Joan Beaumont, and will be published as an edited collection in 2003.

17 See, for example, Henry S. Albinski, "The Role of Foreign Policy in Australian Electoral Politics: Some Explanations and Speculations", *Australian Outlook*, Vol. 28, No. 2, August 1974, pp. 118–41; Trevor Matthews and John Ravenhill, "ANZUS, the American Alliance, and External Threats: Australian Elite Attitudes", *Australian Outlook*, Vol. 41, No. 1, April 1987, pp. 10–21; T.B. Millar, "Emerging Bipartisanship in Australian Foreign Policy", *Asia–Pacific Community*, Winter 1985, pp. 1–15.

18 Trevor Matthews and John Ravenhill, "Bipartisanship in the Australian Foreign Policy Elite", *Australian Outlook*, Vol. 42, No. 1, April 1988, pp. 9–20.

19 See Michael Wesley, "Australia and the Asian Economic Crisis" in James Cotton and John Ravenhill (eds), *The National Interest in a Global Era: Australia in World Affairs 1996–2000*, South Melbourne: Oxford University Press, 2001, pp. 320–2.

20 See Bill Hayden, *Hayden: An Autobiography*, Sydney: Angus & Robertson, 1996, pp. 376–7.

21 David W. Lovell, Ian McAllister, William Maley and Chandran Kukathas, *The Australian Political System*, Melbourne: Longman, 1995, pp. 272–3.

22 Quoted in P.J. Boyce, *The International Relations of Federal States,* Perth: Royal Australian Institute of Public Administration, 1984.

23 G. Campbell Sharman, "The Australian States and External Affairs: An Explanatory Note", *Australian Outlook*, Vol. 27, No. 3, December 1973.

24 *Koowarta v Bjelke Petersen* (1982) 153 CLR 168.

25 *Commonwealth v Tasmania* (1983) 158 CLR 1.

26 *Toonen v Australia* UN Doc CCPR/C/50/D/488/1992 (8 April 1994).

27 Figure quoted in Tim Harcourt, "Australian Exporters – A Vital Minority in a World of Opportunity", 28 June 2002. http://www.austrade.gov.au/articlespeech/

28 Tony Walker, "How Howard Helped Crack China", *Australian Financial Review*, 10 August 2002, p. 12.

29 Kate Legge, "Reversing the Diaspora of the Hyper Mobile", *Weekend Australian*, 7–8 December 2002, p. 3; Richard Smith, "Australia and Asia: the Impact of Globalization", 34th Alfred Deakin Lecture, Melbourne University, 2000.

30 http://www.southern-cross-group.org

31 David D. Newsom, *The Public Dimension of Foreign Policy*, Bloomington: Indiana University Press, 1996, p. 20.

32 Ross Gittins, "The Role of the Media in the Formulation of Economic Policy", *Australian Economic Review*, 4th Quarter, 1995, p. 6.

33 ibid.

34 Rodney Tiffen, *News and Power*, Sydney: Allen & Unwin, 1989, p. 4.

35 ibid., p. 16.

36 James N. Rosenau, *Public Opinion and Foreign Policy*, New York: Random House, 1961, p. 82.

37 Tiffen, *News and Power*, p. 22.

38 See, for example, Craig Skehan, "Secret Talks on Plan to Crack Down on DFAT Leaks are ... Leaked", *Sydney Morning Herald*, 9 December 1996.

39 Bernard C. Cohen, *The Press and Foreign Policy*, Princeton, NJ: Princeton University Press, 1968, pp. 57–9.

40 See Hamish McDonald, "Press War Continues", *Far Eastern Economic Review*, 24 April 1986; for broader regional reactions to the Jenkins article, see "Overstepping the Mark", *Far Eastern Economic Review*, 8 May 1986.

41 Quoted in Michael Maher, "The Media and Foreign Policy" in P.J. Boyce and J.R. Angel (eds), *Diplomacy in the Marketplace: Australia in World Affairs, Volume 7: 1981–90*, Melbourne: Longman Cheshire, 1992, p. 58.

42 Quoted in Tiffen, *News and Power*, p. 1.

43 Kenneth N. Waltz, "Electoral Punishment and Foreign Policy Crises" in James N. Rosenau (ed.), *Domestic Sources of Foreign Policy*, New York: Free Press, 1967, p. 263.

44 See for example Henry S. Albinski, "The Role of Foreign Policy in Australian Electoral Politics"; David Campbell, "Australians and National Security Issues: An Analysis of Public Opinion and Policy" in Hugh Smith (ed.), *Australians on Peace and War: Proceedings of a Conference on "Perspectives on War and Peace in Australian Society" Held on 26–27 June 1986 by the Australian Study Group on Armed Forces and Society at the Australian Defence Force Academy*, Canberra: ADSC, University College, UNSW, ADFA, 1987; Peter Trickett, "What Australians Think About Overseas Aid", *Focus*, Vol. 3, No. 3, July 1989, pp. 9–10; Graeme Cheeseman and Ian McAllister, "Popular and Elite Support in Australia for Overseas Military Intervention", *Australian Journal of International Affairs*, Vol. 48, No. 2, November 1994, pp. 247–65; Graeme Cheeseman and Ian McAllister,

"Australian Opinion on International Trade and the Security Link with the United States", *Pacific Review*, Vol. 9, No. 2, 1996, pp. 265–74; Murray Goot, "How Much? By Whom? In What? Polled Opinion on Foreign Investment, 1958–1990", *Australian Journal of International Affairs*, Vol. 44, No. 3, December 1990, pp. 247–67; Ian McAllister and John Ravenhill, "Australian Attitudes towards Closer Engagement with Asia", *Pacific Review*, Vol. 11, No. 1, 1998, pp. 119–41.

45 Rosenau, *Public Opinion and Foreign Policy*, pp. 35–6.

46 James N. Rosenau, "Foreign Policy as an Issue-Area", in Rosenau (ed.), *Domestic Sources of Foreign Policy*, pp. 44–5.

47 Gabriel A. Almond and Sidney Verba, *The Civic Culture: Political Attitudes and Democracy in Five Nations*, Princeton, NJ: Princeton University Press, 1963, pp. 184–5.

48 Rosenau, *Public Opinion and Foreign Policy*, pp. 21–6.

49 Henry A. Kissinger, *The Necessity for Choice*, New York: Harper, 1961, p. 7.

50 Walter Lippmann, *The Public Philosophy*, Boston: Little, Brown, 1955.

51 Rosenau, *Public Opinion and Foreign Policy*, p. 36.

52 Trevor Matthews and John Ravenhill, "ANZUS, the American Alliance, and External Threats", p. 11.

53 Lester W. Milbrath, "Interest Groups and Foreign Policy", in Rosenau (ed.), *Domestic Sources of Foreign Policy*, p. 232.

54 Rosenau, *Public Opinion and Foreign Policy*, p. 37.

55 A good example is presented by the National Farmers' Federation; see Tom Connors, *To Speak With One Voice: The Quest by Australian Farmers for Federal Unity*, Canberra: National Farmers' Federation, 1996.

56 Charles E. Lindblom, "The Science of 'Muddling Through'", *Public Administration Review*, Vol. 19, Spring 1959, pp. 79–88.

57 See, for example, the special issue of the journal *International Organization* on epistemic communities, edited by Haas (Vol. 46, No. 1, Winter 1992).

58 Milbrath, "Interest Groups and Foreign Policy", pp. 249–50.

59 See, for example, the account of the involvement of the Australian Food and Grocery Council in the Australian delegation to the December 1996 Singapore WTO Ministerial, and subsequently in the development of Australian policy on the APEC EVSL initiative, in Michael Wesley, "The Politics of Early Voluntary Sectoral Liberalisation in Australia", IDE–APEC Study Centre Working Paper Series 2000, Japan External Trade Organisation, February 2000.

CHAPTER 9

The International Policy Landscape

At any given time, the Australian Federal Government divides its responsibilities among fifteen to twenty-five bureaucratic departments. While different governments may combine their various functional responsibilities in different ways, the same set of responsibilities tends to recur from government to government, conservative or Labor. A glance at the structure of the federal bureaucracy is a good way to gain a quick overview of how the government defines its responsibilities and work. Each department's policy "brief" – the discrete portion of the government's responsibilities assigned to it – is fairly apparent from its name: Agriculture, Fisheries and Forestry; Education, Science and Training; Finance and Administration; Industry, Tourism and Resources; and so on. Most Federal Government departments relate to clearly defined interests, activities and aspirations in society, and the boundaries of their responsibilities are established by the societal interests and activities to which they relate, as well as by the government's policies in relation to those interests and activities.

This may initially appear to be the case for the Department of Foreign Affairs and Trade also. In its 2000–01 Annual Report, the department announces it is "responsible for the protection and advancement of Australia's international interests". However, it soon becomes apparent that this is a department that is not able to identify clearly a set of societal interests and aspirations that remain its brief. Foreign Affairs is a portfolio defined by the *location* of its policy responsibilities rather than by a given set of activities, interests or aspirations within society. (The states of early modern Europe had no separate foreign ministries: foreign affairs was seen as an intermittent subject for all departments of government when their primary responsibilities assumed an international aspect. Great Britain was an early pioneer of a separate foreign ministry when it formed separate Foreign and Home offices in 1782.)[1] Potentially, any functional responsibility of the Federal Government can become part of DFAT's brief if it is affected by sources external to Australia or if it can be addressed at sites external to Australia. The simple answer to the question, "What is DFAT's policy brief?" is the international system, in all its complexity and dynamism.

In this chapter, we explore the nature of the foreign policy maker's policy brief. In dealing with such a vast area of responsibility, foreign policy makers impose a structure of priorities on the international system to make their brief more manageable. This chapter examines the conceptual ordering systems of Australian foreign policy makers in terms of three superimposed intellectual frameworks. The most basic and fixed framework – the way the world's states are ranked in terms of priority and therefore attention – is discussed in the first part of this chapter. The second framework is the subject of part two: the trends and forces that have the potential both to impact directly on Australian foreign policy interests, and to change the prioritisation of states under the first framework. Part three is concerned with the governing framework: the network of Australian foreign policy interests at any given time, which establishes the patterns of significance and priority of the other two frameworks. These three frameworks establish which developments in world politics are determined to be "events" of significance for Australian interests, and which are not. It is therefore necessary to examine the nature of "foreign policy events", and how they are established as such by the pattern of Australia's foreign policy interests.

The conceptual ordering of world politics

The need to establish conceptual frameworks to order and make sense of the vast complexity of everyday experience is a basic reality of all human existence. For all of us, these conceptual frameworks enable an intellectual organisation of the daily flow of events, distinguishing between them on the basis of priority, significance and causality. Without such a capacity to distinguish between and order events in terms of significance, human existence would be directionless, chaotic: either frantically reactive to all stimuli irrespective of their origin, nature or impact, or passively overwhelmed by the sheer volume of events. A foreign policy maker has just as urgent a need for a conceptual ordering of his or her policy brief: the vast, complex, and ever-changing arena of world politics. The task of monitoring and responding to a terrain populated by 189 states, thousands of international organisations and agreements, hundreds of ethnic or religious movements pursuing a political program of some nature, and an array of international non-governmental organisations (INGOs) and multinational corporations would be beyond the capacity of any foreign policy bureaucracy. Even if large and well-resourced enough to monitor all events in world politics, a foreign policy bureaucracy would find the task of coordinating its responses to each of these events almost impossible. Such conceptual frameworks are the major influence at the contextual level of policy-making, assisting foreign policy makers to assess the seriousness of international developments and to determine responses that do not damage other foreign policy interests. They are by no means formal or even, at times, conscious. They are, nevertheless, real; a powerful and permanent sifting and prioritising mechanism. Our first task in surveying the policy brief of foreign policy makers, then, is to examine the conceptual frameworks they use to order events in world politics in terms of significance and priority.

The most basic component of the conceptual framework for foreign policy making is the identification of the most significant actors in world politics; that is, those with the greatest capacity to affect societal interests or aspirations within Australia. The majority of foreign policy makers would agree that the most significant actors are states. Even in the age of globalisation, global social movements, and civilisational and/or religious conflicts, few foreign policy makers would deny that the state remains the basic unit of world politics. States retain an overwhelming predominance, if not an absolute monopoly, of the means of coercive force in the world. They remain significant holders of economic and financial power, and the ongoing source of the necessary conditions for the existence of other units of economic power. They remain compelling locators for non-familial loyalty for most humans on earth. States are the basic units of international organisations, the main subjects and formulators of international law, and the predominant means through which other influences on world politics operate, be they economic, religious or ideological. The policy brief of the foreign policy maker, then, is predisposed to concentrating on the actions of states. The main exceptions to this focus are the major international and regional organisations.

While this narrows the field somewhat, monitoring the foreign policies of 189 states across a range of relationships and international organisations would still be a massive task. Therefore the next level of the foreign policy maker's conceptual framework is to order these states according to their importance to Australia. States are prioritised according to their capacity to influence Australian society and affect its desired foreign policy outcomes. States accorded higher priority are given greater attention, and more resources are devoted to relationships with them.

The highest priority is accorded to states with a significant capacity to impact on Australia's national interests. Australia has fairly consistently identified its core national interests as security and economic prosperity,[2] and these interests select the most important relationships for Australian foreign policy. The states that are significant to Australia's security interests include its partners in formal security agreements (especially the United States), states to which it has security commitments (such as Papua New Guinea, Singapore and Malaysia), and important neighbouring countries like Indonesia or regional powers like China, which have the potential to disrupt Australia's security environment.

Australia's major economic interests focus initially on its major trading partners, particularly its major export markets. Table 9.1 shows that the list of major export markets has changed little over time, establishing a clear list of economic priorities. With the exception of Germany, these priorities reinforce those established by Australia's security interests. Another set of economic relationships of major importance are sources of critical resources for Australia's economy and society that cannot effectively be produced within Australia. Australia is lucky in that it is resource-rich and agriculture-rich and has a reasonably diverse economy: perhaps the only resources for which it is truly dependent on the outside world are defence equipment (overwhelmingly supplied by the United States and the United Kingdom) and high-technology equipment, much of which is produced by its major trading partners. Also of importance to Australia's economic interests are major players in the world economy: the world's largest economies, and those states with control over critical resources and with the capacity to influence the fortunes of the world economy generally. This adds to the list of Australia's priorities the principal states of the European Union, other large economies in the Organisation for Economic Cooperation and Development (OECD), and major resource-producing countries with a significant capacity to affect the global economy.

Australia's interests and diplomatic endeavours are also strongly affected by the major international organisations and significant caucus groups of which it is a member, or which have a major potential to affect it. Global as well as regional in scope, these are, in rough order of priority: the United Nations, the World Trade Organisation (WTO), the International Monetary Fund (IMF), the Asia–Pacific Economic Cooperation group (APEC), the Association of Southeast Asian Nations (ASEAN), the South Pacific Forum, the ASEAN Regional Forum, the World Bank, the Asian Development Bank, the European Union, the OECD, the Commonwealth of Nations, the Cairns Group, and the Valdivia Group. While some of these organisations are significant enough to count as key actors and relationships for Australia's foreign policy in their own right, states wielding considerable influence within these organisations assume a major priority for Australia's foreign policy makers. This adds the leaders of major coalitions or caucus groups to the list of priority relationships – South Africa,

Table 9.1   Australia's major export markets (September quarter)

Year	Countries (listed in descending order)
2001	Japan, US, RoK,[1] PRC,[2] NZ, Singapore, Taiwan, UK, Hong Kong, Indonesia
2000	Japan, US, RoK, NZ, PRC, Singapore, Taiwan, Hong Kong, UK
1999	Japan, US, RoK, NZ, Taiwan, PRC, Singapore, UK
1998	Japan, US, RoK, NZ, Taiwan, Hong Kong, UK, PRC
1997	Japan, RoK, NZ, US, PRC, Taiwan, Singapore, Indonesia
1996	Japan, RoK, NZ, US, PRC, Taiwan, Singapore, Hong Kong
1995	Japan, RoK, NZ, US, Singapore, Taiwan, PRC, Hong Kong
1994	Japan, US, RoK, NZ, Singapore, Hong Kong, Taiwan, PRC
1993	Japan, US, RoK, UK, NZ, Singapore, Taiwan, PRC
1992	Japan, US, RoK, Singapore, NZ, Taiwan, Hong Kong, UK, PRC
1991	Japan, US, RoK, NZ, Singapore, Taiwan, UK, Germany
1990	Japan, US, RoK, Singapore, NZ, Taiwan, UK, Germany
1989	Japan, US, NZ, RoK, UK, Hong Kong, Taiwan, Germany
1988	Japan, US, NZ, RoK, Taiwan, UK, PRC, Germany
1987	Japan, US, NZ, UK, RoK, PRC, Taiwan, Germany

Notes: 1. Republic of Korea, or South Korea.
          2. People's Republic of China.
Source: Australian Bureau of Statistics Annual Reports, 1987 to 2001.

Nigeria, Brazil, Egypt, Argentina, India – as well as influential players in their own right, such as Sweden.

Less direct but still pervasive in their effect on Australia's foreign policy interests are the general alignments in global politics. It follows then that states that are major shapers of global alignments, along with their key interests and commitments, are important to Australia. These include the global powers – the United States and formerly the Soviet Union – along with the major regional powers: the United Kingdom, France, Germany, the Russian Federation, China, Japan, India, Pakistan, Nigeria, South Africa and Egypt. Their key role in regional developments brings to the list states such as Israel, Iran, the states of the former Yugoslavia, and the main Latin-American countries. Once again, many of these priorities duplicate those established by other foreign policy interests.

States in significant geographic proximity also assume greater importance as foreign policy priorities. Generally, states that are closer have a greater impact on security calculations, are more important trading partners because of lower transport costs, share greater mutual population flows and have similar regional interests. Consequently, most proximate states have already established their importance according to the priorities discussed above. Those not already named but whose proximity gives them an importance are Brunei, Cambodia, Laos and Myanmar.

Then there are some countries with which Australia has affective links, reflecting significant ethnic and/or cultural continuities and shared historical experiences. The former add significant sources of Australian immigration to the list of relationships: Ireland, Greece, Poland, Turkey and Malta. Shared historical experiences include alliances, commitments, and engagements in major wars (Cyprus, Turkey), as well as the continuing links established by membership in the British Commonwealth or shared British colonial history (Uganda, Sri Lanka, Kenya and Zimbabwe).

Finally, there is a group of countries that think about the world in more or less the same way as Australia and with which Australian policy-makers can freely debate the issues on the international agenda. This includes allies like the United States and Britain, but, more importantly in this context, other liberal-democratic middle powers like Canada, the Netherlands, New Zealand and the Scandinavian countries. This group is known in United Nations parlance as "like-minded" countries.

These relationships and interests establish a rough order of priority for Australian foreign policy makers. It becomes apparent that the priority of many relationships is reinforced from category to category, developing into a fairly clear hierarchy. This hierarchy of important relationships is reproduced in the internal organisation of DFAT, and in the pattern of resource and personnel distribution of Australia's diplomatic missions. The department is divided into functional and geographical divisions. In 2003 its geographical divisions were: South and Southeast Asia Division; South Pacific, Africa and Middle East Division; Americas and Europe Division; and North Asia Division. The high priority of North and Southeast Asia for Australian foreign policy, as established by our review of states with a major impact on Australia's national interests, is reinforced by the devotion of two of the department's four geographic divisions to this region. Furthermore, these are the two most heavily staffed geographic divisions. This pattern of resourcing and staffing is reproduced in the pattern of diplomatic postings. Table 9.2 shows that Northeast, South and Southeast Asia together account for 42.2 per cent of all overseas staff, and 38.9 per cent of all posted Australia-based staff.

The world of states and international and regional organisations thus falls into a reasonably clear order of priorities for Australian foreign policy makers. At the top of this conceptual ordering, many of the categories establishing states' importance for Australian interests and foreign policy repeat the nomination of

Table 9.2   DFAT postings by region, 2000–01

Region	Australia-based staff	Locally engaged staff	Total staff	% of total overseas staff
Northeast Asia	66	175	241	11.8
South and Southeast Asia	138	484	622	30.4
Americas	72	209	281	13.8
Europe	134	379	513	25.1
New Zealand and South Pacific	60	135	195	9.5
Middle East and Africa	54	137	191	9.3

Source: DFAT Annual Report 2000–01, Appendix 3

those states established as being of importance in other categories, thus rein-forcing the priority of these states for foreign policy makers. For example, the United States, Japan and China appear as major security and economic inter-ests, key players in important international and regional groupings, major shapers of global and regional alignments, and so on. The ordering of states of importance is clearer at the higher end of the priority scale than at the lower. Patterns of interlocking security and economic interests emphasise the clear priority of states in the Asia–Pacific region for Australian foreign policy. At the lower reaches of the priority scale, the ordering becomes less clear: while Australia has maintained well-staffed diplomatic missions to priority states for a long time, many lower-priority states and regions have had posts withdrawn or staffed on a very limited basis.

Overlaying the conceptual framework that prioritises states in terms of greater or lesser importance to Australia is an interests-based framework that sees international relations as an interlocking pattern of the foreign policy priorities and dispositions of crucial states. The tradition of viewing interna-tional relations in this way is very old, going back at least to Kautilya, a fourth-century BCE Brahmin counsellor instrumental in the expanding empire of Chandragupta Maurya. In his *Arthashastra*, Kautilya developed, among other things, a Mandala-wheel-type "interest map" of his prince's enemies, and enemies of enemies.[3] Meinecke dates the modern tradition of developing interest maps to Samuel von Pufendorf (1632–1694), a political theorist and historian best-remembered for his contributions to the develop-ment of the early modern theory of international law. In his histories, he devel-oped the concept of the interests of the kingdoms and realms of Europe as a set of interlocking and impersonal interests, which it was the duty of statesmen to follow objectively, and the duty of the historian to interpret and report on objectively.[4]

Most foreign policy makers carry a mental map of the international system as a context for foreign policy: the international environment of states is partially understood as a system of interlocking – competing and coinciding – interests. Important states' dispositions and aspirations in relation to various issues – their major security challenges, attitudes to trade and development, human rights, major alliances and rivalries – are characterised and related to those of other important states. Part of the exercise of monitoring international developments involves determining whether the responses of these states conform to what was expected of them according to what were understood to be their interests. These mental maps of interests are relied on by foreign policy makers to predict how crucial states will react to certain developments in international relations, and to anticipate probable reactions to Australian foreign policy initiatives. They are thus vital to the contextualisation and strategic planning of Australian foreign policy: allowing adverse reactions to be anticipated and forestalled; facilitating the beneficial linkage of foreign policy initiatives; and permitting the building of coalitions of states behind foreign policy ventures.

Monitoring change and trends

A foreign policy apparatus that concerned itself solely with the actions and dispositions of certain important states, regions and organisations would soon be overtaken by unforeseen developments. Even though states remain the primary actors in international relations, world politics is an arena of constant, often surprising change. Developments that are system-wide or that pervade societies can be missed if attention is fixed only on the governments of states. Even if these changes eventually alter the actions of states and the calculations of their governments, a foreign policy apparatus unable to anticipate and track these changes can be caught short. Therefore, the foreign policy maker's conceptual framework is also attuned to monitoring trends and systemic or societal changes that may alter their policy brief in ways significant for Australian interests or the conduct of Australian foreign policy.

Shifts in global polarity and power hierarchies

Australia's tradition of maintaining close relationships with predominant global powers – first Great Britain, then the United States – has developed among its foreign policy makers a sensitivity towards monitoring developments in the international system's structure, polarity and power hierarchies. Kenneth Waltz seemed to have been echoing the anxiety with which Australian foreign policy makers had often watched challenges to the global power hierarchy when he wrote:

> A structural change [that is, a change in the polarities and hierarchies of the international system] is a revolution, whether or not violently produced, and it is so because it gives rise to new expectations about the outcomes that will be produced by the acts and interactions of units [that is, states] whose placement in the system varies with change in structure.[5]

There is a strong historical tendency for Australian foreign policy makers to think of Australia's security and foreign policy interests as ultimately bound up with the global order. Even if the challenge to its global power ally seemed to have taken place far from Australia and its immediate interests, there was a recurring belief that the challenge to the global order would eventually translate to a disruption of calculations and a recalibration of interests closer to Australia. Australia's foreign policy history is replete with statements along the following lines:

> we must altogether get rid of the idea that we have different interests to those of the rest of the Empire, and we must look at the matter from a broad common stand-point. If the British nation is at war, so are we ...[6]

While such statements would not be expressed like that today, the sentiments underlying them have remained constant in Australia's contributions to the 1991 and 2003 Gulf conflicts and the 2001–02 war in Afghanistan.

Yet while they may be thought to be of critical importance to Australia, transitions in the global power hierarchy and structures of polarity are notoriously difficult to see. Most are apparent only in the long sweep of history, although the last major power transition – the end of the Cold War – was immediately obvious and caught practitioners and academics of international relations by surprise.[7] Few foreign policy makers would dispute that Australia's international position is intimately tied up with the fortunes and tenure of the United States as the predominant global power. Most international relations theorists suggest that all great powers wane, although a sharp and unresolved debate raged from the 1960s to the late 1980s and early 1990s over whether the United States also will be surpassed by other global powers. Robert Gilpin argued that any hegemon's economic and technological superiority will eventually diffuse to its competitors, while internally the social expectations of its citizens and the privileging of consumption will sap its ability to maintain its external predominance.[8] Torbjorn Knutsen agreed, adding that social consensus within the hegemon fragments, while externally the legitimacy of its power is challenged by rising competitors.[9] Mancur Olsen suggests internal economic scleroses eventually hobble the lead of economic powers, and they are soon overtaken by competitors,[10] while Robert Cox predicts the inevitability of contradictions arising in the dialectical relations of power and production within the hegemonic power and the structures of world order it creates.[11] Paul Kennedy coined the term "imperial overstretch" for the tendency for a great power's international commitments to degrade and outstrip its economic capacity to service those commitments: "if a state overextends itself strategically … it runs the risks that the potential benefits from external expansion may be outweighed by the greater expense of it all …".[12] Raymond Aron argued that even without any internal weakening of the great powers, it is the international system's tendency towards equilibrium that assures the rise of competitors that tend to balance and restrict their global influence.[13] Christopher Layne agrees, arguing that the "unipolar moment" enjoyed after the Cold War by the United States will prove fleeting as new great powers arise.[14]

The years since these debates of the 1980s and 1990s, which have witnessed the highest rates of economic growth in decades in the United States, plus the demonstration of US military might in the Gulf War, Kosovo and Afghanistan, seem to have vindicated Joseph Nye's case that those predicting the decline of the United States from global pre-eminence were wrong. Not only was such analogising from history mistaken, but it was dangerous, leading to the sort of panicked retrenchments in military spending and international commitments that would make the prediction of US decline self-fulfilling. Nye argued that while the United States may have slipped in some of the indices of power, the nature of global power itself has changed, and the US alone remains predominant across all of the major indices of power. Nye coined the term "soft power" to suggest that the lure of US culture, values and institutions was an important lever of influence in world politics.[15] Australia, so dependent on US primacy for its own military and intelligence capacities, and so comfortable with the US-supported global market and international institutions, appears to have little to worry itself about in relation to global power structures. Yet it is unlikely that foreign policy makers will become complacent about possible changes in power hierarchies. While Australia's only two experiences of global power transitions – from British regional dominance in a global balance of power to US regional dominance in a bipolar global system, and thence to US dominance in a unipolar system – have been benign from the point of view of Australia's alliance preferences, the next power transition may not be. It is likely that the next challenger of US predominance will not share such continuities of values and interests with Australia. If such a challenger becomes predominant in Australia's region, it could seriously complicate the choices of Australia's foreign policy makers.

Patterns of alignment and enmity

Another set of trends monitored consistently by foreign policy makers are patterns of alignment and enmity, global and in Australia's region. While related to global polarities and power hierarchies, patterns of alignment and enmity need to be monitored independently. Not only can they affect Australia's security interests directly, but they can also change the calculations underpinning a range of Australian diplomatic initiatives. Barry Buzan defines patterns of amity as structures of interstate relations embodying "relations ranging from genuine friendship to expectations of protection and support".[16] Broadening this definition into the non-security realm, we would include relations including sponsored economic integration and significant permanent commitments between states. Buzan defines patterns of enmity as "relationships set by suspicion and fear",[17] to which we would add relations characterised by competition for power or influence, on either a regional or a global basis.

Patterns of alignment and enmity can either be relatively fixed, arising from ethnic and/or cultural affinities or animosities, ideological competition or historical grievances, or more fluid, relating to calculations of power balances. It is important to note that patterns of amity and enmity are often mutually constituting, particularly with enmities often creating alignments of expedience as states align on the basis of their opposition to or fear of other states. Global and regional patterns of amity and enmity can be so tightly interrelated that change in a central competitive relationship can see the rapid unravelling and reconstitution of a range of other relationships. One only needs to contemplate the effects of the end of enmity between the United States and the Soviet Union on relationships in the Asia–Pacific region to see how fast and profound such reorderings can be. The relationship between fixed and fluid patterns of amity and enmity can be difficult to predict: at times the considerations of more fluid patterns are so powerful that they overshadow or mask more permanent grievances; at other times, fluid patterns can accentuate fixed enmities or can be limited by the boundaries of such enmities.

Navigating among such patterns of alignment and enmity is a crucial task for Australian foreign policy makers. The most important patterns that need to be monitored are regional, because these have the greatest potential to affect Australian interests and the conduct of its foreign policy. The recent history of Australia's foreign policy in the Asia–Pacific demonstrates some of the difficulties posed by such terrain. For example, then Foreign Minister Bill Hayden found his attempts in the mid-1980s to bridge the main fault line of animosity in Southeast Asia between Vietnam and the ASEAN states to have seriously complicated Australia's amicable relations with ASEAN. Despite the end of the Cold War and the disappearance of such clear regional antipathies, the task of navigating among competitive and often acrimonious regional relations has not eased for Australian foreign policy makers. Arguably, the task has become even more difficult because the antipathies and competitive relationships are masked by ostensibly amicable relations and webs of mutual commitments. For Australia, its relationship with the United States presents one such complication for its relations with some Southeast and Northeast Asian states. At times some of these states have raised suspicions that Australian policy may be designed to reinforce US interests in the Western Pacific, where many of the states have complicated relationships with the US, combining dependence and competition, admiration and animus.

Yet such a situation is preferable to the re-emergence of clear fault lines of enmity in the region. One scenario never far from policy-makers' minds and extensively discussed by foreign policy commentators, is the difficult position in which Australia would find itself if a serious confrontation developed between China and the United States. Not only does Australia have crucial interests bound up with both major protagonists, but it is not clear how the other states of the region, also important to Australian economic and security interests, would align along the new patterns of animus and amity. It is hard to overemphasise the effect on Australian interests of such a scenario coming to pass in the Asia–Pacific.

New actors in global politics

An important set of influences on the domain of Australian foreign policy are the emergence of new states, or the assumption of different roles by states, or the emergence of significant non-state actors in global politics. The second half of the twentieth century saw a dramatic multiplication in the number of states in the international system; as a measure of this growth, the United Nations' membership of 51 in 1945 had expanded to 189 by 2000. Figure 9.1 shows that

Figure 9.1   Growth in United Nations membership, 1945 to 2000

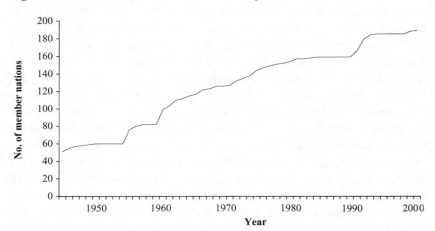

while UN membership has expanded steadily during this period, the two major periods of membership growth came between 1955 and 1965, and 1990 and 1994. The first high-growth period was the result of the rapid decolonisation of large parts of Africa, Asia and the Middle East, the second of the break-up of former Soviet-bloc states: the Soviet Union, Yugoslavia and Czechoslovakia.

These trends represent more than just a change in the number of actors in the international system: they brought new types of states into the system. Both trends continue to have a major impact on global politics and economics. Decolonisation saw the entry of the post-colonial state to the realm of international relations, more inclined to be sceptical of the western world order, highly sensitive to issues of racial hierarchy, colonialism, hegemony and domination, plagued by issues of economic development and dependency, and highly critical of the international distribution of wealth and power. It is no accident that the 1960s and 1970s saw what many commentators termed a major "radicalisation" of politics within the United Nations and other international institutions.

The end of the Cold War saw the entry of post-Communist states onto the international stage. It is yet to be seen what long-term effect these states will have on the international system. The regions of the post-Communist world have supplied a significant proportion of the conflict and instability in the post-Cold War world, in the Balkans, southern Africa, the Caucasus and Afghanistan. Many post-Communist states have serious ongoing ethnic tensions. While many such states have attempted to move towards liberal democracy and the rule of law, in most the status of the transition is not beyond doubt, while in some the tendency to revert to a form of authoritarian populism has emerged. Post-

Communist states have had a significant effect on the global economy as major competitors for development aid and international investment, and, according to some, as major sources of potential instability in the global economy. The most immediate impact of post-Communist states may be the effect of their alignments on regional balances of power, especially in Eastern Europe and Southeast Asia.

From the early 1970s, Australia's foreign policy makers have adjusted aspects of foreign policy to accommodate these new types of actors. From 1972 the Whitlam Government began to realign its foreign policy on a series of issues "to express a greater sympathy for and identification with the causes espoused by the majority of the Afro-Asian world".[18] Whitlam's change of direction went beyond principle. By the early 1970s, post-colonial states held a majority in the UN General Assembly. After Britain's 1968 decision to withdraw its military forces east of Suez and the 1969 US announcement of the Nixon Doctrine (President Nixon's declaration, to be applied to the situation in Vietnam, that in future the United States would "furnish military and economic assistance when requested in accordance with our treaty commitments. But we shall look to the nation directly threatened to assume the primary responsibility of providing the manpower for its defense"), Australian foreign policy makers realised that they would have to assume greater responsibility for relations with states in the region, and most of these were post-colonial. (Indonesia was a leader of the Non-Aligned Movement and host to its first meeting.) Furthermore, Whitlam and Fraser after him were aware that the history of the White Australia Policy and the continued mandate relationship with Papua New Guinea could be complicating factors for foreign policy in an international community roused to great passion by colonialism, apartheid and the 1965 unilateral declaration of independence by the white minority regime in Rhodesia. Ever since, the presence of post-colonial states of significant importance to Australia in global and regional politics has required foreign policy makers to be sensitive to the resonances of actions and statements, aware that it is all too easy for Australia, to the detriment of its interests, to be placed on the wrong side if an issue is framed in post-colonial terms. The sharp Asian reaction in 2002 to speculation by John Howard about Australian pre-emptive strikes against regional terrorists was an example.

A more contemporary set of issues concerning post-colonial states are beginning to confront Australian foreign policy makers (as well as those of other countries and the United Nations) with a different sort of problem. Many former colonies in Australia's vicinity – in Southeast Asia and the South Pacific – have begun to manifest a series of symptoms that can be grouped under the general diagnosis of serious crises in the post-colonial state form. In 1999, the term "the arc of instability" was coined for a group of states, from Indonesia and Papua New Guinea to Australia's northwest and north, to the Solomon Islands and Fiji to the northeast and east, all experiencing crises of internal governance. These range from brutal internal conflicts arising from ethnic or religious divisions or competition over resources, to conditions of chronic economic non-viability, serious breakdowns in internal law and order, and political instability ranging from rioting to coups to political assassination. Clearly the western-derived model of the secular sovereign state with supreme authority over and responsibility for all in society, acting impartially towards its citizens, and expected to deliver a range of policy outcomes from security to education and health, is severely tested in some of these states. These issues have the potential to fall directly within the purview of Australian foreign policy makers. Indonesia is a large and crucial neighbour, and Papua New Guinea is Australia's former mandate territory, while Australia is a major power and aid donor to the Pacific states. Australia would also be likely to be the destination of large numbers of refugees if the crises developed further in any of these states. Here is a set of issues that may deeply challenge Australian foreign policy makers into the future.

Australia's need to maintain relations with Communist states in the Asia–Pacific dates from the early 1970s. In 1972 and 1973, relations were established with the People's Republic of China, the Democratic People's Republic of Korea and the Democratic Republic of Vietnam. China's move away from its command economy in 1978, followed by Vietnam's in 1986, opened the two to more rapid economic growth. Dealing with regional Communist and post-Communist states poses a different set of challenges for Australian foreign policy makers. They are important relationships in security, economic and regional terms, yet they are potential sources of instability. North Korea, beset by internal economic collapse and with a developing nuclear capacity, is perhaps the greatest source of regional instability. Tensions across the Taiwan Straits remain unresolved. Unprepared to match economic with political liberalisation, China has resorted to nationalism as a tool for maintaining state authority, yet nationalism may be a force in Chinese foreign policy that the leadership finds difficult to control. The effect of the alignments of Vietnam, Cambodia and Laos with ASEAN on the regional balance of power *vis-à-vis* China remains to be seen, as does the extent of China's challenge to the United States for regional predominance.

While it seems unlikely at this stage that significant numbers of new states will be added to the current number, it would be naive to cease monitoring for new types of actors. Revolutions within states, changing their basic principles of social, political or economic order, can be profoundly destabilising to international relations.[19] Filled with what Edmund Burke called a "malignant charity",[20] such states often try to export the principles of their revolution to other states, and often repudiate the conventions of diplomacy and the commitments entered into by the previous regime. Raymond Aron's observation of a homogenising tendency in international relations[21] can create significant competition and enmity between revolutionary and status quo states, each seeing the other as a profound threat to the structure of its own state and society, and each striving to impose on the other a similar system to its own. Martin Wight described three major revolutionary periods in modern international relations – 1517 to 1648 (Protestantism, or religious diversity as the revolutionary force), 1792 or 1871 (nationalism as the revolutionary force), and 1914 to 1989 (Communism as the revolutionary force) – each characterised by profound instability and extensive warfare in the international system.[22] (Wight actually had the last of these periods covering the years between 1917 and 1960, the latter date being the time of his writing, but no doubt he would have agreed that the period would have extended to the end of the Cold War.) A more contemporary revolutionary period can possibly be added to the list, beginning with the 1979 Iranian revolution, driven by the revolutionary force of fundamentalist religious conviction and a rejection of the modernist, secular values of the majority of other states and societies. The theocratic revolutions have generated significant instability and international enmity, and may generate significant interstate hostilities beyond the 2001–02 war in Afghanistan. Their potential to generate conflict will most likely extend beyond the current "war on terrorism". Australian foreign policy makers remain aware of the vanguard of this revolution in some of its closest neighbours.

While as yet unable to challenge the predominance of states in international relations, several types of non-state actors, rising to the global stage in the late twentieth century, have a growing effect on world politics through influencing the calculations of states. One type of influential non-state actor is economic – the multinational corporation (MNC), a firm based across several countries or with its production processes distributed internationally. Despite early precursors such as the British East India Company, MNCs are predominantly the product of the post-Second World War liberal trading system, which established the conditions enabling firms to maximise market access and internalise transaction costs transnationally. Their proliferation and size have been assisted also by the growth of international private finance, the technology and communications revolutions, and the development of modern management techniques. So dominant have such entities become that it is estimated that one-third of all international trade now takes place within companies. As states become ever more responsive to the demands of competition in a globalised economy, MNCs have become very powerful *vis-à-vis* states, as potential providers (or withholders) of foreign direct investment, technology, industrial capacity and employment. Competition has grown between states vying to attract MNCs.

The rise of MNCs has had a major effect on the world view of Australian foreign policy makers. Such organisations take their place alongside major Australian export industries as significant "clients" of Australia's foreign policy machinery. Australia's diplomatic network has assumed a major role in seeking access to foreign markets for Australian firms, and in dealing with the strategies of other governments seeking to maximise their own trade access and foreign direct investment in Australia. As discussed in Chapter 8, business is a politically powerful client for foreign policy makers, and has a significant input into Australian foreign policy. The influence of MNCs, however, remains confined to a narrow range of foreign policy issues. For the most part, MNCs only become interested in those aspects of foreign policy that can or do impact directly on their business interests.

Another type of influential non-state actor has arisen in the political–social realm: the international non-governmental organisation (INGO). These are internationally linked "networks, movements, and organisations of non-profit interest groups which form to assert interests, identities, or causes outside state-based and controlled institutions",[23] and have developed into major challengers to governments and political parties for the loyalties and political commitment of citizens. Their growth since the 1970s has been spurred by the communications revolution; by rising living standards and what Inglehart called the postmaterialist shift in values;[24] by spreading education and access to media reporting; and by what some would argue are the increasingly conservative economic and social agendas of governments. Most of the largest and most influential INGOs (the top eight INGOs in the world have an annual budget of US$500 million or more) are organised around issues of social justice, ecology or ethics that are often seen to be ignored or exacerbated by the actions of states: environmental degradation, poverty, human rights, refugees, women's rights and disarmament.

The years since the 1970s have seen a rise in the willingness and capacity of INGOs both to support and to contest the mechanisms of global governance. For some time, they have played an important role in the United Nations system (despite the most fleeting of mentions in the UN Charter), supporting and complementing the work of relief and development agencies, and playing a crucial role in monitoring and publicising abuses of human rights, environ-mental standards and other issues in which the UN has an interest, but is constrained from acting because of the restrictions on domestic interference established by Article 2(7) of its Charter.[25] More recently, however, INGOs have managed to challenge the activities and objectives of states and interna-tional organisations with some effect. Some have begun to copy the multilat-eral diplomacy of states in organising summits at the same time and in the same place as major intergovernmental summits, in order to press the state delegates to take certain human and environmental interests into consideration along with state interests. Other loose networks of INGOs have mounted successful global campaigns that have shifted state policy on core security and economic issues, such as the campaigns against landmines[26] and against the OECD's Multilateral Agreement on Investment (MAI).[27] The latter campaign, along with extensive anti-globalisation protests at the site of international economic summits, points to a rising wave of resistance to certain aspects of global governance, particularly those associated with the structures of the interna-tional economy.[28] Arguably, oppositional INGOs have registered a growing rate of success, ranging from the abovementioned campaigns against landmines and the MAI, to greater acknowledgement in the work and consultation proce-dures of the World Bank and the Asian Development Bank.

Parallelling their role in world politics, INGOs have assumed a similar double role in the world views of Australian foreign policy makers, sometimes seen as valuable organisations enhancing the objectives of Australian foreign policy, while at other times seen as irritating obstacles to the conduct of interna-tional diplomacy. (The influence of interest groups on foreign policy is discussed in Chapter 8.)The former role has assumed prominence particularly in the after-math of the Asian economic crisis as the Australian Government pursues strate-gies of promoting governance and democratisation in Southeast Asia especially. In this line of foreign policy, INGOs are seen as valuable allies in campaigns against corruption, human rights abuses and ethnic violence; some of those participating in this work have attracted Australian Government funding. The latter category includes a range of INGOs critical of various aspects of Australian foreign policy: its global-warming diplomacy; its support for institutions of economic globalisation; its stance on refugees; and various aspects of its aid policy. In the past, groups critical of Australian foreign policy have had limited influence (the exception being the very broad coalition of groups opposed to the Indonesian control of East Timor). Yet the successes of the INGO campaigns mentioned above have kept the attention of foreign policy makers on INGOs as possible significant complicators of regional and global diplomacy.

One final type of non-state actor in world politics is international terrorist groups, an entity particularly prominent in foreign policy makers' minds since the 11 September 2001 attacks on New York and Washington, DC, and those of 12 October 2002 on Bali. While these attacks showed that terrorists' techniques and weapons have not developed significantly (from a tactical point of view, passenger jets were used in the United States in the same way as car bombs), they signal an important advance in terrorists' capacity to affect world politics. What is significant about the al-Qaeda network, which has been accused of planning and carrying them out, is its global objectives.[29] Rather than targeting the immediate objects of grievance in a local conflict, they have targeted the broad strategic role of the United States and its sponsorship of a particular regional and global order. In simple terms, one of the general settings of world politics has been targeted.

Trends affecting world politics

A number of general trends affecting the nature of international relations in various ways are included in the watching briefs of foreign policy makers. These trends are often less pervasive or obvious than those discussed above, while their effects on international relations generally are hotly debated by foreign policy practitioners and international relations academics alike. Yet they remain prominent to observers of world politics, and if they do have the effects predicted by some, their impact on international relations will be profound indeed.

Perhaps the defining trend of the post-Cold War period has been globalisation: the growth in the extent and intensity of international economic exchange, and financial and communications flows. Arguably the greatest effect of globalisation on governments has been to shift their attention more urgently towards the international. For foreign policy makers, globalisation signifies both an intensification of their role and a broadening of the policy issues with which they are required to deal. It also raises the stakes of their work, not only by increasing the competitiveness of certain aspects of international relations, but also as significant signs of instability and fragility begin to appear in certain aspects of the global economy.

The effects of globalisation on Australian foreign policy making will be more fully explored in Chapter 10; here we will confine ourselves to a few comments on how it affects the policy brief of foreign policy makers. It is important to note at the outset that despite what its name implies, globalisation has an uneven effect on world politics. By far the states most deeply affected by globalisation are those in the developed world, along with the rapidly developing states of East and Southeast Asia, Latin America and Eastern Europe. Parts of Central Asia, Africa and the South Pacific have little or no experience of some of the defining processes of globalisation. Globalisation has increased the intensity of interactions and social relations among some states and societies, but it has not challenged the basic power hierarchies of international relations; if anything, globalisation has entrenched these structures. The United States and its developed allies, which sat atop the power hierarchy during the Cold War, continue to do so in the age of globalisation. In the contemporary world, the less-developed, powerless, internally fragile states seem even weaker than they did thirty years ago. Nor has globalisation changed the inclusiveness or extensiveness of international relations, with the priority relationships of the developed world remaining largely the same as during the Cold War.

Yet it tells us something significant about international relations that globalisation is nevertheless a defining process. It exists in a mutually reinforcing dynamic with the major international and regional institutions, which have not only established the conditions for the advancement of globalisation, but are increasingly the sites through which states address the externalities arising from its processes. Globalisation has sponsored the rise of many "non-traditional" issues into the realm of foreign policy making, as well as a growing awareness (at least among national elites) that many contemporary problems facing states are shared problems. Arguably, globalisation has given aspects of the international system – particularly the global economy – a much greater place in domestic politics and society. Consequently, foreign policy is now more public, more implicated in other areas of government policy, and attended by higher political stakes. The lasting effects of globalisation on international relations as the realm of responsibility of foreign policy makers are yet to be seen. Yet there is little doubt that it is an important set of trends to be monitored and potentially responded to by foreign policy makers.

A different type of trend, both more transient and easier to discern, is also important to foreign policy makers: alternating periods of fluidity and rigidity in global and regional politics. Following the long period of rigidity of the Cold War, contemporary international relations is undergoing a period of relative systemic fluidity. Systemic fluidity is a three-faceted condition: it combines a multiplication of foreign policy possibilities for a greater number of states with the resolution or de-intensification of large numbers of seemingly intractable conflicts or enmities, and a more intensive phase of creating and reforming the norms and institutions of international relations.[30]

As discussed earlier, the late 1980s and early 1990s became a period of quite rapid change in world politics. The UN Security Council became for a period completely free of vetoes; after 1994, vetoes have returned but are used at only a fraction of the rate seen during the Cold War. Conflicts, civil wars and internal divisions were resolved at an unprecedented rate – Iran–Iraq, USSR–Afghanistan, Namibia, Nicaragua, Cambodia, El Salvador, Mozambique, East and West Germany – while apartheid was brought peacefully to an end in South Africa. Remarkable progress, if not resolution, was made in peace processes in Northern Ireland and Israel–Palestine, and between the Koreas. Previously poisonous bilateral relations thawed: China–Taiwan, China–Russia, Japan–Russia. "New Regionalism" gained momentum, and not only in economic terms: in Europe with the Single European Act and Maastricht; in the Pacific with APEC; and in the Americas with NAFTA and Mercosur.[31] A range of multilateral agreements and organisations came into being: the WTO, the Comprehensive Test Ban Treaty (CTBT), the Montreal Convention on the Protection of the Ozone Layer, the Rome Statute for the International Criminal Court, the Ottawa Convention against Landmines, and the Chemical Weapons Convention (CWC), to name only the most prominent.

Australian foreign policy during the 1990s has been influenced by the effects of this increased international fluidity. In no realm is this more evident than in the development of Australia's foreign policy towards the Asia–Pacific region. The end of the Cold War enabled Australian foreign policy makers to play a crucial role in resolving the war in Cambodia, as we describe in the case study on page 88. Into this new environment, Australian diplomacy helped inject visions of a regional economic organisation that developed into APEC, and a regional security dialogue that became the ASEAN Regional Forum. Beyond the region, Australian diplomacy played crucial roles in bringing agricultural trade within the ambit of consideration of the new WTO; in renegotiating an agreement between the trustees of Antarctica; and in bringing to conclusion the CTBT and CWC.

In the early years of the twenty-first century, the international system seems to be still in a state of relative fluidity, but not to the extent it was in the early 1990s. No permanent alignments have emerged – globally or regionally – but the phase of frantic conflict resolution, rapprochement and institution-building that occurred between 1987 and 1994 has not endured. If anything, the years since have seen something of a rationalisation and consolidation of those earlier developments, with some institutions, such as the CTBT and the Statute on an International Criminal Court, continuing to be rejected by important states. In regional relations, the 1997–98 Asian financial crisis has introduced some fluidity, but fluidity that seemingly is not as conducive to the conduct of Australian foreign policy as previously. The regional institutions of which

Australia is part – APEC and the ASEAN Regional Forum – have moved some-what from the centre of the region's politics, while alternative nascent institu-tions, of which Australia is not a member, have developed, such as ASEAN + 3. As shown by the Asian financial crisis, fluidity can also bring inauspicious change, yet times of fluidity seem preferable to times of rigidity for foreign policy makers, if only for the opportunity they provide to put in place new structures and relationships in anticipation of a return to times of rigidity. The current period continues to hold a greater range of choices for foreign policy makers than many periods before 1989. The challenge to the strategic vision and diplomatic creativity of foreign policy makers is how to make the most of times of international fluidity.

Two partial trends remain to be discussed, the impact of which on the policy brief of foreign policy makers remains unclear and hotly debated. The first can be loosely termed changes in the human and social capabilities of large sections of the world's population. The second half of the twentieth century has seen a general improvement in the health, nutrition and education of a large proportion of the world's inhabitants. Democratisation has occurred at a much more partial, but still significant, rate. As mentioned above, a truly global popular culture has emerged, with simultaneously cosmopolitanising and fragmenting effects on social attitudes.[32] The extent to which this partial trend will affect the domain of international relations remains to be seen. One possibility is that all of these trends will increase the interest of more societies in the foreign policy of their state, in the way that Hamilton and Langhorne argue that spreading literacy and democracy in Western Europe after the First World War changed foreign policy for those states forever.[33] In many states, growing public engagement in foreign policy settings has decreased the flexibility of foreign policy makers, making deals seen by the population as humiliating (such as perceived acquiescence to US hegemony) less possible. On the other hand, spreading literacy and access to information may strengthen the influence the United States can wield through "soft power" as more populations are attracted by perceived US ideals, which are increasingly disseminated through US popular culture. One need only scan the list of Hollywood movie releases between 2000 and 2002 to find a gamut of war and foreign policy films designed to present American ideals in positive ways: *Saving Private Ryan*, *Thirteen Days*, *Behind Enemy Lines*, *Black Hawk Down*, and so on.

The second debatable trend that needs to be noted can be termed significant shifts in norms governing the legitimacy of different forms of international actions. Some academics and former practitioners of international relations have hailed what they see as the development of the norm of legitimate humanitarian intervention in the 1990s. Citing the "no-fly zones" in Iraq, the Unified Task Force (UNITAF) intervention in Somalia, and the NATO operation over Kosovo, they suggest that a significant development in the norms and rules governing international society has been a growing acceptance of the proposition that "states that massively violate human rights should forfeit their right to be treated as legitimate sovereigns, thereby morally entitling other states to use force to stop the oppression".[34] Others have observed that the 1990s saw intervention that was both non-violent and less overt, but almost as compelling in forcing weaker states to accede to powerful states' conceptions of legitimate domestic behaviour, in the injection of norms governing labour and environmental standards into trade diplomacy, particularly by the United States.[35] Yet it remains unclear whether this is an enduring or defining development. While the evidence of the above cases is undeniable, it cannot be said either that "states that massively violate human rights should forfeit their right to be treated as legitimate sovereigns" has been applied anything but selectively, or that the "moral entitlement of other states to use force to stop the oppression" is one that is recognised by many states other than the US and its closest allies. In November 2002, the Australian Defence Minister, Robert Hill, asked whether

> international law has kept pace with the changed circumstances that have evolved in the world since the end of the Cold War as it relates to today's conflicts – crimes against humanity, genocide, religious, ethnic and communal conflicts, global terrorism and the like.[36]

It was now more difficult, Hill suggested, for states to deal with issues like self-determination and pre-emption, the status of combatants and rights of human-itarian intervention.[37]

The changes and trends that we have identified have the potential to cause important shifts in the international policy environment with which Australian foreign policy makers must work. Yet maintaining attention to these trends and changes is not always a straightforward task: it becomes readily apparent that many of the changes we have discussed are qualitative, and manifest them-selves through the actions of various agents in world politics. However, they remain important in both informing and constraining the policy calculations of most states in international relations, and as such become attendant conditions that are factored into Australian foreign policy makers' diagnoses of significant developments in their policy brief. It remains for us to discuss the nature of these "significant developments" in the work of Australian foreign policy makers; specifically, to examine what constitutes a foreign policy "event".

Foreign policy events

In our discussion on the nature of foreign policy in Chapter 2, we argued that foreign policy making is for the most part events-driven. We defined foreign policy "events" as developments that caused significant disturbance to those social values deemed the responsibility of the foreign policy apparatus to promote or protect, or that could interfere with the achievement of important foreign policy goals. The everyday flow of such events through the foreign policy "space" is constant: each week sees the development of a range of potentially significant foreign policy developments. Some of these are public and self-evidently important – such as a coup in Fiji – while others are barely noticed by the media or the public, and yet others are not at first thought to be of significance for Australian foreign policy interests, but in time prove crucial. In what remains of this chapter, we discuss what makes a foreign policy event, and how foreign policy makers respond to significant developments in the international policy environment.

In the previous two sections, we described two of the fundamental conceptual frameworks used by foreign policy makers intellectually to order and prioritise the international system in terms of actors and events of importance to Australia. The first was a prioritising of states of greater or lesser importance; the second was the identification of significant changes or trends to be monitored according to how they affected the prioritising of states and Australian foreign policy generally. There is a third conceptual framework that is superimposed on these other two: at any given time, senior foreign policy makers can glance at the international system and see the array of Australian foreign policy interests. This framework is not the same as the two just described: while the previous two indicate what *should* be important to Australian foreign policy makers, the one we are about to discuss covers what *is* important at any given time. Australian foreign policy is limited by what it can address at any one time: on any day of the week one can look at the world and nominate a handful of foreign policy priorities of the moment from among the range of potentially important interests. This governing framework of overriding priorities gathers together Australia's commitments, undertakings, and crucial relationships and memberships, and its policy initiatives, goals and aspirations. This network of interests is constantly monitored and promoted by Australia's foreign policy machinery. Each significant interest either relates to a situation imminently or actually affecting social values or welfare in Australia (such as a major export access agreement) or constitutes the contemporary "state of play" in a diplomatic initiative designed to promote Australian interests, values or welfare, or to forestall the possibility of negative developments. It is not hard to see that this third conceptual framework gives shape to the other two: it is the crucial yardstick for determining what is important and what is not in relation to those aspects of international relations monitored by the other two.

At any given time, therefore, Australia has a range of different foreign policy positions, each relating to a societal interest or to a diplomatic initiative. Each of these foreign policy positions can develop in one of three possible ways: existing commitments, relationships or memberships can be maintained and consolidated; further progress can be made towards a diplomatic objective; or the capacity to protect social values or advance a diplomatic objective can be degraded. Foreign policy events, then, are developments that can have a significant impact, for better or worse, on a given foreign policy position. No development in international relations is *per se* a foreign policy event: that status is conferred by the consequences of the development for Australia's network of foreign policy interests and positions. Conferring the status of foreign policy event can often be straightforward and obvious; at other times it can be a subjective and contested process. In 1995, for example, the then Foreign Minister Gareth Evans was initially disinclined to view the resumption of French nuclear tests in the South Pacific as a significant foreign policy "event" with domestic ramifications, an opinion that was vigorously contested by other parts of the government, the Opposition and the majority of public opinion.

Given the range of possible developments that can become "events" demanding some sort of foreign policy response, it is necessary to order and classify them. Once again, the map of Australia's interests is used to establish the importance of events. Some foreign policy events, such as political crises or changes in government portending a significant shift in policy commitments in important states, affect fixed interests and priorities of Australian foreign policy. Shifts in policy dispositions of important states are invariably treated as significant events. A rise in levels of hostility between states that can affect global or regional alignments, or significant alliances or collaboration among states affecting vital foreign policy settings, invariably gain the status of events. Events that are more time-bound but equally important can include the launch by other states of new international initiatives or policies that can have a significant impact on Australian interests. Similarly, significant reactions to Australian foreign policy initiatives can challenge or enhance unilateral, bilateral or multilateral interests, thereby gaining the status of foreign policy events.

Beyond these general observations, it is impossible to classify foreign policy events without descending into exhaustive and detailed dissections of actual happenings in Australian foreign policy. It is enough to observe that an international development becomes an event according to its capacity to impact on Australian foreign policy interests. The same measure is used to prioritise among foreign policy events according to the urgency and resources that must be devoted towards a response. The peaceful dissolution of Czechoslovakia into two successor states is an enduring international development, but one with relatively minor implications for Australia's foreign policy interests, whereas the sudden heightening of tensions between China and Taiwan may be less enduring but has much greater implications for Australia's foreign policy interests.

The general map of Australia's foreign policy interests not only determines whether international developments are foreign policy events, but also serves as a crucial guide in determining the scale of the response to be made. Initially, the different interests affected by the event can be arranged in such a way as to determine whether the event is a positive or a negative development. The interest map informs policy-makers of what is at stake in terms of a hierarchy of foreign policy interests and settings as a consequence of any given event; some developments can have positive effects on some interests and negative effects on others. The interest map is a guide in helping them to determine what foreign policy positions should be enhanced or salvaged (depending on whether it is a positive or negative event), and whether certain minor interests or positions can be safely degraded or sacrificed in order to advance or salvage a crucial interest. The interest map also informs the objectives of the response: in the case of a negative development, it supplies a conception of the foreign policy position before the event as a guide to approximating what position should be salvaged or returned to; in the case of positive developments, it provides a clear idea of the diplomatic aspiration guiding the initiative.

The flow of foreign policy events and the strategic map of Australian interests thus interact constantly through time: while the interest map determines and prioritises foreign policy events, the constant flow of events continually changes the interest map. The interest map in turn has a crucial reciprocal relationship with the other two conceptual frameworks of foreign policy makers: the priority states and relationships, and significant changes and trends. All combine to form a complex and carefully tuned system of monitoring the policy brief of foreign policy makers in ways that give them the greatest capacity to anticipate events of importance to Australia's foreign policy interests.

Conclusion

The international system, the policy brief of Australia's foreign policy makers, is almost an impossibly complex and varied domain to deal with without frameworks to simplify and classify all that occurs there. Whether or not they do it consciously, foreign policy makers in Australia utilise an extremely effective system of three interlocking and mutually reinforcing frameworks: a strategic network of foreign policy interests, positions and initiatives; a prioritisation of important relationships, states and memberships; and a catalogue of important changes and trends affecting both interests and orderings. These conceptual maps are replicated in the minds of foreign policy makers, in the socialisation and organisational culture of the foreign policy bureaucracy, and in the internal organisation of the foreign policy machinery. They are affirmed or challenged as much in the hierarchical processes of reporting and instruction-giving as in general judgements of policy successes and failures. The ongoing challenge for these frameworks that order the international policy landscape is to maintain a viable balance between imbuing them with enough authority to act as a guide in monitoring developments and reacting to events, and ensuring they are flexible enough to adapt to the constantly changing policy environment itself. Policy failures or misjudgements are often blamed on policy-makers' preconceptions or prejudices; yet as we have seen, these are crucial to any effective monitoring of the international policy landscape.

Notes

1 See Keith Hamilton and Richard Langhorne, *The Practice of Diplomacy: Its Evolution, Theory and Administration*, London: Routledge, 1995, p. 73.
2 A classic statement of this is, of course, Department of Foreign Affairs and Trade, *In the National Interest: Australia's Foreign and Trade Policy*, White Paper, Canberra: Commonwealth of Australia, 1997.
3 See Adda Bozeman, *Politics and Culture in International History*, Princeton, NJ: Princeton University Press, 1960.
4 See Friedrich Meinecke, *Machiavellism: The Doctrine of Raison D'État and Its Place in Modern History*, trans. Douglas Scott, New Brunswick, NJ: Transaction Publishers, 1998.
5 Kenneth N. Waltz, *Theory of International Politics*, New York: McGraw-Hill, 1979, p. 70.
6 Australia's first Defence Minister, Sir John Forrest, quoted in Gordon Greenwood and Charles Grimshaw, *Documents on Australian International Affairs 1901–1918*, Melbourne: Nelson, 1977, p. 115.
7 For an investigation of the failure of international relations academics to anticipate the end of the Cold War, see John Lewis Gaddis, "International Relations Theory and the End of the Cold War", *International Security*, Vol. 17, No. 3, Winter 1992–93, pp. 5–58.
8 Robert Gilpin, *War and Change in World Politics*, Cambridge: Cambridge University Press, 1981.

9 Torbjorn Knutsen, *The Rise and Fall of World Orders*, Manchester: Manchester University Press, 1999.

10 Mancur Olsen, *The Rise and Decline of Nations*, New Haven, CT: Yale University Press, 1982.

11 Robert Cox, *Power, Production, and World Order*, New York: Columbia University Press, 1987.

12 Paul Kennedy, *The Rise and Fall of the Great Powers*, London: Fontana Press, 1988, p. xvi.

13 Raymond Aron, *Peace and War: A Theory of International Relations*, trans. Richard Howard and Annette Baker Fox, London: Weidenfeld and Nicolson, 1966.

14 Christopher Layne, "The Unipolar Illusion: Why New Great Powers Will Rise", *International Security*, Vol. 17, No. 4, Spring 1993.

15 Joseph Nye, *Bound to Lead: The Changing Nature of American Power*, New York: Basic Books, 1991; "Soft Power", *Foreign Policy*, Vol. 80, 1990, pp. 153–71.

16 Barry Buzan, *People, States, and Fear: An Agenda for International Security Studies in the Post-Cold War Era*, New York: Harvester Wheatsheaf, 1991, p. 189.

17 ibid., p. 190.

18 T.B. Millar, *Australia in Peace and War: External Relations 1788–1977*, Canberra: Australian National University Press, 1978, p. 412.

19 See Fred Halliday, "'The Sixth Great Power': Revolutions and the International System" in *Rethinking International Relations*, Houndmills: Macmillan, 1994.

20 Edmund Burke, *Reflections on the Revolution in France*, London: Penguin, 1986, p. 136.

21 Aron, *Peace and War*, pp. 373–402.

22 Martin Wight, *Power Politics*, Harmondsworth: Penguin Books, 1979, p. 92.

23 Diane Otto, "Non-Governmental Organisations in the UN System: The Emerging Role of International Civil Society", *Human Rights Quarterly*, Vol. 18, No. 1, February 1996.

24 Ronald Inglehart, *The Silent Revolution: Changing Values and Political Styles among Western Publics*, Princeton, NJ: Princeton University Press, 1977.

25 See Allan Gyngell and Michael Wesley, "Interweaving of Foreign and Domestic Policy: International Policy" in Glyn Davis and Michael Keating (eds), *The Future of Governance: Policy Choices*, Sydney: Allen & Unwin, 2000, pp. 212–13.

26 See Korinna M. Georghiades, "The Ottawa Convention: Meeting the Challenge of Anti-Personnel Mines?", *International Relations*, Vol. 14, No. 3, December 1998, pp. 51–70.

27 See Stephen J. Kobrin, "The MAI and the Clash of Globalisations", *Foreign Policy*, Fall 1998, pp. 97–109.

28 See Robert O'Brien, Anne Marie Goetz, Jan Aart Scholte and Marc Williams, *Contesting Global Governance: Multilateral Economic Institutions and Global Social Movements*, Cambridge: Cambridge University Press, 2000.

29 I am indebted to a series of conversations with, and a paper by, Joanne Wright for this observation.

30 The concept of "international fluidity" was first developed in Gyngell and Wesley, "Interweaving of Foreign and Domestic Policy", pp. 214–16.

31 See Louise Fawcett and Andrew Hurrell (eds), *Regionalism in World Politics*, Oxford: Oxford University Press, 1995.
32 A wonderful discussion of some of these paradoxes of globalisation can be found in Benjamin R. Barber, *Jihad vs McWorld*, New York: Times Books, 1995.
33 Hamilton and Langhorne, *The Practice of Diplomacy*, pp. 136–48.
34 Nicholas J. Wheeler, *Saving Strangers: Humanitarian Intervention in International Society*, Oxford: Oxford University Press, 2000, pp. 12–13.
35 John Gerard Ruggie "At Home Abroad, Abroad at Home: International Liberalisation and Domestic Stability in the New World Economy", *Millennium*, Vol. 24, No. 3, Winter 1995, pp. 507–26.
36 Robert Hill, John Bray Memorial Oration, University of Adelaide, 28 November 2002.
37 ibid.

CHAPTER 10

Conclusion: The End of Foreign Policy?

In September 2001 the attacks by Al-Qaeda terrorists on the World Trade Centre in New York and the Pentagon in Washington shook world politics deeply. They signalled an end to the uncertainty of the "post-Cold War" era.[1] By generating within the United States an unexpected and profound sense of vulnerability and a determination to prevent such attacks in future, they led the world's only remaining superpower to adopt a much more assertive unilateralism in its policy approaches. Military action followed in Afghanistan and, outside a United Nations framework, in Iraq. In parallel, US policymakers showed a new determination to resist any multilateral constraints on their capacity to act in a number of social as well as political and military areas. These events all struck a dramatic opening chord for early 21st century international relations. In our view, however, another, deeper, more reverberating, note was sounding underneath and through this chord. This was the impact in all its various manifestations of globalisation.

The form, origin and destination of globalisation are all contested. Despite disagreement on its form, origins and destination, a majority opinion within the vast and burgeoning literature on the subject suggests that globalisation is a process, or series of processes, that manifested itself most vigorously in the years after 1990, and is advancing, gaining in momentum, broadening in scope. As the terrorist attacks showed, a globalising world is by no means homogeneous, and it is not necessarily more secure. But just as the terrorists were motivated by hostility to aspects of globalisation's social impact and their actions made possible by its easy and rapid communications and the growing movement of people between countries, so actions and reactions within the world have been powerfully shaped by the economic, technological and social forces whose combined momentum has driven globalisation on.

Writers on the subject have predicted a range of effects of globalisation on world politics. Many of these forecast or imply the end of the state or its eclipse as the sole authoritative actor on the international stage. Such perspectives pose a serious question for what we have written in this book: precisely, does understanding the processes, institutions, actors and environment of foreign policy making matter so much if the foreign policy machinery, along with the state, is about to be downgraded or even swept away as an international actor?

Perhaps predictably, we are firmly of the opinion that the institutions, processes and actors of Australian foreign policy making will continue to be important long into the future. However, this does not mean that we are of the (small) group that asserts that nothing has changed at all. Rather, we suggest in this concluding chapter that the forces of globalisation are indeed changing international relations, thereby posing significant challenges to the foreign policy institutions of all states, including Australia. In what follows, we address three central questions: What is the significance of globalisation for the foreign policy machinery of a state like Australia? How have the forces of globalisation altered the subject matter of foreign policy and the environments in which it is conducted? And to what extent have the processes and institutions of foreign policy making in Australia changed to cope with the challenges posed by globalisation?

Globalisation and the institutions of foreign policy making

For some writers, "globalisation" is a word that is now so overused to discuss such a broad variety of phenomena that it risks being drained of any fixed meaning or analytical usefulness. The word has been used to refer to a number of linked but distinguishable processes. Jan Aart Scholte names five: (communications) internationalisation, (economic) liberalisation, (cultural) universalisation, westernisation and deterritorialisation.[2] Baylis and Smith collect eight main types of globalisation most prominently discussed in the literature on globalisation: the growing economic interdependence of the world economy; the transnationalisation of popular modes of communication, which "alters our notions of the social groups we work and live in"; the increasingly pervasive spread of a highly Americanised global popular culture; an advancing homogenisation of differences between people and societies; the collapse of ideas of chronological time and geographic space before the advance of communications and media technology; the emergence of a "global polity" of transnational social and political movements, and the transference of allegiance away from the state; the development of a cosmopolitan culture of local action for global causes; and the emergence of a global "risk culture" in which people regard the greatest threats that face them as global ones that overwhelm the state's responses.[3]

These various manifestations of globalisation suggest a number of ways in which the state and its policy instruments may be affected, but do not lead to any firm conclusions. One of the central debates within the globalisation literature is over this very question: how the globalisation-led transformations in world politics will affect the state. At one end of the scale are those who predict a fundamental reordering of world politics, for whom globalisation represents the gathering momentum of an "empire of speed", collapsing the time–space boundaries of the modern states system into a postmodern system of "intensified world-wide social relations" unmediated by hierarchic social or political structures.[4] Then there are those who suggest that the state will not be washed away, but will lose its primacy in international relations, becoming just one of many actors shaping global outcomes. This general position covers the "governance" school, whose members foresee the development of consensus-based partnerships between states, civil society groups, international organisations and private companies to address "functions that have to be performed in any viable human system irrespective of whether the system has evolved organisations and institutions explicitly charged with performing them".[5] Also in this school are the inheritors of Hedley Bull's conception of a "new medievalism":

> If modern states were to come to share their authority over their citizens, and their
> ability to command their loyalties, on the one hand with regional or world
> authorities, and on the other hand with sub-state or sub-national authorities, to
> such an extent that the concept of sovereignty ceased to be applicable, then a neo-
> medieval form of universal political order might be said to have emerged.[6]

Moving towards the other end of the scale are those who argue that the state will remain, but will be changed by the pressures of globalisation. These views tend to coalesce around arguments that government authority has shifted in one or more of three directions. Some argue it has shifted downwards, to regions, localities, particularistic identities.[7] Some claim it has shifted upwards to international organisations – global, regional and functional – as the responsibilities of states are broadened and their control over outcomes weakens, forcing a new type of international relations based on negotiation and cooperative action.[8] As noted earlier, others suggest the state's authority is disaggregating laterally,

> into its separate, fundamentally distinct parts. These parts – courts, regulatory
> agencies, executives, even legislatures – are networking with their counterparts
> abroad, creating a dense web of relations that constitutes a new trans-
> governmental order [which is] rapidly becoming the most widespread and
> effective mode of international governance.[9]

Yet others claim that globalisation has seen not the sweeping or withering away of the state, but its growth in power and size. Dani Rodrik observes that state budgets have grown during the age of globalisation;[10] Linda Weiss argues that the state has lost none of its regulatory power and has indeed extended its regulatory scope,[11] while Charlotte Bretherton argues that the same technological revolution that has intensified global social relations has also enhanced the state's control over its own society.[12]

Each point along this scale of opinions, of course, carries implications for how one views globalisation's implications for Australia's foreign policy making instruments. The different views in turn derive from a deeper disagreement over the relationship of the state to globalisation. For those who see globalisation as a "secular and unstoppable trend", independent of and antagonistic to the state, the structures of government that are currently feebly struggling to respond to globalisation's many challenges will be eventually swamped. On the other hand, for those who see it as the product of purposive choices made by states to lay the foundations for globalisation's many manifestations, the processes are open to manipulation by states themselves, and states actually gain power from globalisation. While endorsing aspects of both of these arguments, we tend to agree with Ian Clark's more sober assessment, that "globalisation must be understood as something, which, in addition [to transforming relations *between* states,] happens *to* and *within* states but which states, in turn, can encourage or resist".[13] Far from being a helpless victim of globalisation, the Australian state is an active participant in the process, by turns shaping, resisting, exploiting and insulating against the forces of globalisation with purposive public and foreign policies for a range of expected benefits to society.

Another element in the controversy is the aspect of the state on which one chooses to concentrate. The bases of the great majority of these debates centre on one of two modalities of the state. The first is a view of the state as an instrument of control over outcomes within society, and a holder of certain capacities to determine certain outcomes authoritatively. If the state is viewed this way, then it is certainly possible to argue that globalisation is degrading (some of) the state's capacities and authority over social outcomes, such as various macroeconomic settings. The other view is of the state as an important locator of citizens' identities and loyalties, and as the ultimate object for their political activities. If the state is viewed this way, then the rise in the number of people joining international civil society groups or identifying with supranational religious groups, and the decline in membership of the major political parties and the proportion of the electorate that votes in non-compulsory systems can be taken as evidence for the decline of the state. However, neither of these aspects of the state is centrally relevant to foreign policy, which is that arm of the state that seeks to advance and protect societal interests by wielding influence *vis-à-vis* other states and societies. Notwithstanding the intensification in global social relations and the rise of international civil society groups, transnational corporations and terrorist movements, the state remains an institution unmatched in its capacity to access the decision-makers in other states and wield influence over international outcomes. To justify this claim, one need look no further than the fact that most of these alternatives to the institution of the state regularly seek to influence, coopt or intimidate the state as a crucial part of their strategies to influence global outcomes.

A number of pieces of evidence buttress this argument. Even if one takes the toughest case against which to test this proposition – the supposedly "postmodern"[14] states of the European Union that are advancing "beyond territoriality"[15] – one can find efforts to coordinate foreign policies, but not even the beginnings of a process of dismantling a foreign ministry.[16] Furthermore, while they are yet to manifest themselves decisively in Australia, concerns in Europe and North America about the "democratic deficit" – the tendency of more and more areas of public policy to be determined by diplomatic negotiations and bureaucrats in multilateral settings rather than by electorally accountable representatives of national parliaments – are testament to the abiding influence of states' international policy institutions. While, as we have argued in Chapter 4 and will argue below, the foreign policy bureaucracy in Australia has been subject to cuts in staffing and budget, we have been able to find no evidence that this has been due to governmental or societal beliefs that these institutions are no longer necessary or useful. Rather, it is one of the conclusions of our research that expectations of the foreign policy machinery have risen; it is simply expected to perform its traditional roles, plus additional ones, more cost-effectively. Before we can assess whether it has risen to this challenge, however, we need to gauge how globalisation has affected the subject matter and environments in which foreign policy is made.

The challenges of globalisation

Globalisation's main effects on the subject matter and policy environments of foreign policy making can be discussed under four headings: diffusion, enmeshment, contradiction and transformation. Each of these not only has consequences for the range and type of issues that foreign policy is required to address, but it also alters the contexts within which such issues are addressed and the mechanisms by which it is done. All, in turn, place additional challenges in front of Australia's foreign policy machinery, requiring it to evolve and change in certain significant areas.

Diffusion

Globalisation has resulted in an international policy environment that has become much more diffuse in a number of ways.[17] The development of international dimensions to more and more aspects of society's activities and aspirations has multiplied the number of areas of public policy with which the government must deal. It is now difficult to identify a Federal Government policy portfolio without an occasional or enduring international dimension. With the diffusion of the subject matter of international policy has come the end of familiar foreign policy "logics", derived from an era when foreign policy supposedly involved a clear hierarchy of a small number of concerns (usually headed by security). With advancing diffusion, not only does each policy area possess its own slightly different "logic", but also there is no longer any clear and immutable hierarchy among the concerns of foreign policy. Increasingly, these issue areas also have crosscutting concerns, adding layers of complication to policy-making. To use one example, trade policy within multilateral settings has recently acquired aspects of environmental and social justice concerns, requiring policy-makers to have an understanding of the linkages between these issues simply in order to be able to pursue their multilateral trade agendas.

Diffusion in a different sense is a direct consequence of diffusion in the sense discussed above. The expansion of the number of policy domains with international aspects has brought with it a proliferation of the parts of government that are conducting some aspect of Australia's international policy. This diffusion affects not only different parts of the Federal Government, but also, as we discussed in Chapter 8, different *layers* of government, with the Australian states and even to some extent some parts of local government conducting their own international policy. The respondents to our survey of DFAT policy officers endorsed this observation strongly: 75 per cent either agreed (60.7 per cent) or agreed strongly (14.3 per cent) that foreign policy is no longer the preserve of "specialist" international departments of government.

A third way in which diffusion has affected foreign policy has been that a much greater array of societal interests have become involved with international concerns in the calculus of foreign policy making. As areas of social activity internationalise, they bring a range of new interest groups into the foreign policy arena. Thanks to the communications revolution, such groups have developed increasingly effective linkages with like-minded groups outside Australia. Consequently, they are better organised and better informed. We asked a senior member of one of the major industry groups in Canberra what the principal changes had been in the way he performed his work over the past five years. His response was that "DFAT can't put anything over on us any more". He explained that whereas the interpretation of any given international development proposed by the government would once have been accepted, at least initially, by his organisation, now he could call up instant information on the internet and test the government's account with like-minded organisations elsewhere in the world by email, and all in time to react during the first news cycle.

These social groups, as well as internationalising Australian business, have considerably multiplied the number of strands linking Australian society with the outside world. At one time or another, all of these groups make requests or demands of the Australian foreign policy machinery, usually in relation to their international goals, thereby adding to the complexity of both the domestic and the international environments of the foreign policy institutions. Among the foreign policy makers responding to our surveys, 33.9 per cent strongly agreed that "there is a greater need to interact with actors other than other states' foreign ministries", while 58.5 per cent agreed.

Enmeshment

Globalisation and multilateralism are symbiotic processes. While economic and communications globalisation have been underpinned by a series of multilateral agreements and organisations creating the conditions for global markets and communications networks, the forces of globalisation have also multiplied the number of policy externalities for states, which are most effectively managed through multilateral action. The late twentieth century saw a massive expansion in the number of multilateral agreements and international organisations in world politics. As the process has advanced it has led to the multilateralisation of more and more policy areas. In its most basic sense, multilateralism involves the exchange of policy undertakings by three or more states. In making increasing numbers of such policy commitments, states have affected their policy capacities in a particular way. While many multilateral agreements enhance individual states' capacities to deal with transnational issues, at the same time such agreements have the effect of constraining states' freedom of action within the bounds of their mutual commitments.

Australia no less than any other state has become increasingly enmeshed in multilateral agreements at the global, regional, transregional and subregional levels since the end of the Second World War.[18] This in turn has slowly expanded the number of policy domains that are subject to international agreements, adding an external influence to the relationship between the government and its policy constituents. From a foreign policy perspective, the sheer number of international organisations and agreements that have to be monitored and serviced each year continues to rise. Many multilateral commitments are not fixed agreements, but involve participation in organisations with evolving policy agendas of their own, all of which must be monitored and responded to by Australia's foreign policy bureaucracy, and which have regular meetings that have to be attended either by ministers or officials. The expanding number of international commitments also increases the complexity of, and potential for, contradiction in Australian foreign policy. Policy initiatives must be audited to ensure that they do not compromise any of the strands of the growing web of Australia's multilateral commitments.

Contradiction

The forces of globalisation not only place more international policy demands on foreign policy makers, but many of these demands have a tendency to contradict each other. Not all the consequences of globalisation have the same implications for Australia and its society: some may be positive, others may be negative. Of course, such judgements ultimately depend on society's own conceptions of what is beneficial and what is to be avoided. While the facilitation of Australia's export trade and the greater access of Australian industry to international invest- ment are seen by many as positive aspects of economic globalisation that must be acted on to Australia's benefit, others regard the prospect of increased labour movements as part of a globalising economy as less attractive. Similarly, while the globalisation of communications and travel enhances the welfare of Australian society in a number of ways, these same developments also generate new, or magnify existing threats to the security and well-being of the national community: terrorism, drugs, HIV/AIDS, organised crime.

Such contradictions are not always immediately obvious to policy-makers. The more subtle the consequences of different globalising trends, the harder it is to see their implications for Australian foreign policy on other issues. Obvi- ously, such developments add greatly to the complexity and difficulty of foreign policy making, especially as globalisation adds to the rate of change in the foreign policy environment. In this sense, globalisation is a process that needs constantly to be monitored and evaluated for its effects on Australian society.

Transformation

Globalisation has also wrought a series of transformations to the nature of inter- national relations, contributing to a number of traits that distinguish contemporary international relations from previous periods. At a basic level, the realm of economics has been raised to a new level of importance in world politics. In terms of dominant conceptions of international relations, power relativities are now almost universally acknowledged as being tied to relative economic performance.[19] Economic competition between states has moved to the highest levels of international relations.[20]

As the ideological basis of Cold War strategic competition evaporated, to be replaced by economic competition, international relations was being transformed because the logic of economic competition differs from that governing strategic competition. That brought a different mix of imperatives towards competitive and collusive behaviour among states. On the other hand, the post-Cold War years have demonstrated an intriguing tendency for international economic relations to become, at times, prey to competition between states and blocs over "ideologies" of free-market organisation: first between the United States and the "Asian tigers", and more recently between the United States and the European Union.

Another transformation has occurred to the nature of the state as the subject of international relations. The late twentieth century has seen the dominant conception of the state change, in developed economies at least, from that of the welfare state, concerned to intervene in order to shield society from the shocks inherent in the national and global economy, to the "competition state", determined to transform society in order for it to be maximally responsive to fluctuations in the global economy.[21] In Australia, this transformation took place during the period of the Hawke and Keating governments, which saw the dismantling of the "Australian Settlement", established at federation and based on an interlocking system of industry protection behind high tariff walls, wage arbitration and state paternalism.[22] As a consequence, many more areas of public policy are compared between different states, and policy settings are increasingly made with an eye to international "market opinion".[23] The competition state has specific requirements of its foreign policy, involving not only monitoring the institutional underpinnings of the global economy for their conduciveness to national economic performance, but also using diplomatic connections to advance the international endeavours of national firms. It is, however, increasingly difficult to determine what a "national firm" is. In Australia's case, is it one like News Limited, which is headquartered in Australia but operates principally overseas? Or Rio Tinto, which operates locally but is headquartered overseas? Or Holden or Mitsubishi, which are owned overseas and manufacture locally? Or Amcor or Foster's Group, which are owned locally but manufacture overseas? Or any of the innumerable other available variations?

The general rule-of-thumb answer on the part of governments seems to be that if it has tangible benefits locally, we will support it.

International economic and strategic objectives are being joined by a range of different issues at the higher levels of importance in international relations. Internationally operating terrorist groups, international environmental issues, competition for and preservation of resources and energy, refugees and asylum-seekers, and the transnational spread of epidemics are issues that are rising steadily to the level of serious concern.[24] States have to relate to each other in much more complex ways; no longer do they need only to factor a few, fairly simple calculi into their international relations. Therefore, Australia's most important contemporary bilateral relationships are a series of strands of complementary and conflicting interests, a situation posing challenges to the management of those relationships and to foreign policy more broadly.

Each of these effects of globalisation on international relations raises significant challenges for Australian foreign policy making. In the section that follows, we will assess how Australia's foreign policy making machinery has changed to deal with these challenges.

Australian foreign policy making: Rising to the challenge?

Globalisation is a topic that seems inevitably to promote disagreements. Among the many foreign policy makers with whom we talked, there was great disagreement about whether the basic foreign policy making institutions and processes in Australia are still fundamentally the same as they were when the first recruits entered the Department of External Affairs in 1941, or whether they have changed profoundly. Those of the former opinion focus on the basic structural characteristics of institutions and processes: diplomatic reporting; information storage and retrieval; hierarchic organisation; functional and geographic differentiations; and the centrality of bilateral diplomacy. Those of the latter viewpoint to the merger of Foreign Affairs and Trade; the effect of the information revolution on what can be done via communications with overseas posts; the increasing sophistication and demands of interest groups; and the added intrusiveness of the media. Both approaches contain important truths. For our part, we see Australian foreign policy making facing a task expansion: it must add a range of new tasks added by globalisation to its traditional responsibilities. In this final section, we examine the nature of these tasks, and the demands for change they have placed on the foreign policy making institutions, processes and actors in Australia.

The diversification of foreign policy

The most obvious way in which new demands have been placed on foreign policy makers is simply the range of issues that now falls either permanently or sporadically within their policy space. This has been brought about by the effects of diffusion, contradiction and transformation discussed above. No longer able to concentrate solely on bilateral political, strategic and trade relations, foreign policy makers are now required to address environmental, financial, legal, health, policing and many other issues. They are joined in addressing these issues by other federal departments, and are brought into contact with a range of additional interest groups and societal concerns. Consequently, as we discussed above, the number of strands of official policy stretching between the Australian Government and the outside world have multiplied, quite often complicating each other and adding new layers of considerations to the making of foreign policy.

Australian posts in developed countries like the United States, Canada and Britain find that they are being called on to provide reporting and information to the Australian Government relating to its domestic policy agenda almost as often as on traditional foreign policy issues.

The diversification of foreign policy work has necessitated a number of changes in the way policy is made. In terms of policy processes, it has raised the importance of the contextual level of policy-making to an even higher level of importance, as issues need to be assessed for their significance across a broader range of policy considerations and commitments, and as policy responses need to be closely vetted against whether they complicate other strands of policy. This in turn puts greater pressure on processes of communication, reporting, and information storage and retrieval within the foreign policy machinery. It has increased the pressures on, and the number and importance of, institutions of foreign policy coordination, from the level of the Cabinet National Security Committee, to the Department of the Prime Minister and Cabinet, the Secretaries Committee on National Security, the Strategic Policy Coordination Group, the International Economic Coordination Group, to interdepartmental committees and task forces. (Australia's Westminster system of Cabinet government would not make a comprehensive control and coordination mechanism like the United States National Security Council possible.)

In terms of the actors involved in foreign policy making, it is less easy to see much change. Twenty-five years ago, Hedley Bull predicted that the rising "technicality" of foreign policy and diplomatic work would necessitate the greater recruitment of people with specialist skills into the foreign policy machinery.[25] It is hard to find any evidence of a significant rise in recruitment of people with specialist skills relevant to the new policy issues. Our survey, as well as recent DFAT annual reports, show that the profile of DFAT recruits remains broadly the same as always: the majority have studied the humanities, law and economics (see Chapter 4), although the department is undertaking specialist recruitment in areas such as accountancy. The absence of the more specialist recruitment patterns Bull foresaw may reflect the increasing direct involvement of specialists from other departments, such as Environment, with their overseas counterparts or with multilateral institutions. But the nature of foreign policy work and the structure of diplomacy continue to lead inevitably, in any case, to generalist approaches rather than narrow specialisation. The capacity to make comparisons and draw connections across a range of issues and countries, including for the purposes of understanding and negotiating trade-offs, are more useful skills at the senior levels of the foreign policy bureaucracy than subject specialisation.

Domestic politics

The diffusion and enmeshment effects of globalisation have brought Australia's international relations into the realm of domestic politics in a number of different and mutually reinforcing ways. The accretion of international aspects to a greater number of domestic policy areas has given governments the tactical capacity to use the international and domestic policy arenas as interchangeable political domains. Ikenberry has suggested that increasingly governments are able to shift policy action to the international realm when faced with serious domestic policy problems and political costs; similarly, when faced with demanding policy constraints internationally, they can make use of the domestic political arena to achieve desired objectives.[26] There is some evidence that Australian governments have been adept at this for some time. Higgott argues that the Cairns Group initiative in the 1980s was a response in the international arena of a government facing a domestic "rural revolt", and with limited options for dealing with it domestically.[27]

The government is not the only organisation to have utilised international structures for domestic policy reasons. The communications revolution has given large numbers of domestic interest groups the opportunity to establish international linkages, which are often used to leverage their domestic policy influence. For instance, angered by their exclusion from influence in making Australia's global-warming strategy, Australian environmental groups used their considerable international linkages to bolster the level of critique of government policy on the issue. In a different way, domestic interests unable to gain a favourable hearing by the government or courts in Australia have appealed to international organisations of which Australia is a member, or made reference to international conventions to which Australia is a signatory, in order to gain redress on issues that concern them. It is likely that the tactic of using international forums and commitments to place pressure on the Australian Government by domestic groups will gain further momentum, bringing Australia's network of multilateral commitments into the domestic political process in a range of different ways. Events such as this, as well as each successive invocation of the foreign affairs power by the Federal Government to override state legislation, place Australia's international commitments under ever greater scrutiny.

The international has become a more significant part of the domestic political process in other ways. Successive governments have used the globalising world economy as an external imperative to help them introduce unpalatable policies into domestic politics. In this sense, the globalising international market becomes a resource for political rhetoric, as in the argument that without certain painful policy commitments, Australia will lose its competitive edge in the global economy. This was an important element in the arguments in favour of the introduction of the goods and services tax in 2001. In this and other ways the perception has spread that the global market is affecting the lives of ordinary Australians in ever more insistent ways. "Globalisation" has become a much-used word in domestic politics, used both to critique and to justify government policies. One of the consequences of globalisation has been the stimulation of a significant transnational anti-globalisation movement. Even outside the economic area, the acquisition of international aspects by other policy areas has often brought vocal sets of interest groups into the domain of international policy. Perhaps most obviously, issues with significant international aspects and implications were made part of domestic electoral competition during the 2001 federal election campaign.[28]

All of these developments have subjected Australia's relationships with the outside world to much broader and more sustained public scrutiny. Whether through the greater frequency of the Australian public's travel and work overseas, or the incidence of foreign policy commentary in the news media, international issues are much more prominent (if still not gaining significant attention – see Chapter 8). For governments and oppositions ever more finely attuned to opinion-poll fluctuations, foreign policy has become as much a part of electoral calculations as other areas of policy. This has affected different strands of foreign policy in different ways. There are some ways, however, in which the pressures of politicisation have affected foreign policy making generally.

At the most obvious level, increasing amounts of foreign policy makers' time and resources are being devoted to the management of its relations with the Australian public and monitoring its public image. DFAT's efforts on this front are taking place at several levels. In various ways, DFAT has reshaped its relations with the Australian public as the "stakeholders" to which it must provide services. Greater efforts (and more resources) are being made to provide the most effective service possible to the interface where the majority of the Australian public come into contact with DFAT: in its passport and consular services to Australians overseas. The department and its ministers are increasingly attempting to explain the settings of foreign policy to the broader community: through the DFAT website, publicity materials, and accessible explanations of Australian foreign policy from Evans's and Grant's *Australia's Foreign Relations: In the World of the 1990s*,[29] to the 1997 and 2003 foreign and trade policy White Papers and *East Timor in Transition 1998–2000*.[30]

More and more of the time of departmental officers is being spent preparing material for possible questions asked of DFAT's ministers in parliamentary Question Time. Each year, substantial time is spent preparing for the gruelling sessions before the Senate Estimates Committee, arguably the most intrusive parliamentary forays into the opaque world of Australia's foreign policy bureaucracy. And while parliamentary committees such as the Joint Standing Committee on Foreign Affairs, Defence and Trade and the Treaty Review Committee have not significantly increased their influence on the foreign policy process, their regular reports and public hearings generate parliamentary and public interest in the foreign policy process. The department is highly sensitive to media reporting: a dedicated media unit deals with the media interface, while the daily routine of most senior DFAT staff begins with a careful reading of the foreign policy related news, prepared by an external clippings service. According to our survey, 32.9 per cent of DFAT policy officers reported spending between 10 and 40 per cent of their time each week to preparing material for ministers in parliamentary Question Time and responding to media and public inquiries

As more international policy issues resonate with sensitive constituencies in the electorate, foreign policy questions are subjected more often to political judgements. This has resulted in greater involvement in the way policy is packaged by the staff in the ministers' offices. Appointments to ministerial advisory positions and even senior diplomatic postings are increasingly closely scrutinised in terms of the political leanings of the possible candidates.

In all of these ways foreign policy making is being exposed to a different and more intense set of demands and requirements from the domestic political arena. These tendencies are unlikely to fade.

The information revolution

The communications revolution has fundamentally affected foreign policy making in ways impacting on all of the effects of globalisation: diffusion, enmeshment, contradiction and transformation. Not only has it changed the amount and type of information with which the foreign policy machinery must deal, but it has also altered the context of DFAT's information function, by making it one of many providers – and increasingly one of many competing interpreters – of information about the international system. The communications revolution thus poses twin problems for foreign policy makers: one internal, in analysing and managing a much greater amount of information; the other external, in increasingly contesting other sources of information and opinion on world politics from within Australian society itself.

The foreign ministry's diplomatic network was for centuries rivalled only by large international bureaucracies such as the Catholic Church as the sole effective gatherer and storer of information about the world outside of the state. Now, Australia's foreign policy institutions and diplomatic networks face a range of "real-time" competitors, delivering international news almost simultaneously to ministers and the public. Naturally, no foreign policy maker likes to be "scooped" with the news of a significant international development. Invariably, ministers, the media and the public want immediate contextualisation and reaction to these developments. Diplomats are forced therefore to monitor both the news and the news media as part of their new, expanded information role.

Internally, the communications revolution has changed the ways in which information can be transmitted and stored between Canberra and the posts, and between the different parts of the foreign policy bureaucracy in Canberra. Telegraphs and telexes have been replaced by efficient telephone and fax systems, and secure internal email systems such as the original ADCNet and the current SATIN. This has eased the process and lowered the costs of maintaining contact, but it has also vastly increased the volume of information transmitted between Canberra and the posts, and within Canberra itself. Some within the department lament the effect of the ease of communication on diplomatic reporting, suggesting that the old methods of carefully composing cables in crisp, spartan prose, when each document had to be encoded by hand, added a layer of quality control to the information system. Overseas posts now also confront new challenges in collecting information: the communications revolution and the multiplication of the media now present diplomats with new avenues of material that must be monitored and commented upon.

This greater volume of information puts greater pressure on the analytical capacities of Australia's foreign policy machinery. As Keohane and Nye observe,

"A plenitude of information leads to a poverty of attention. Attention becomes the scarce resource, and those who can distinguish valuable signals from white noise gain in power".[31] It is an operational imperative that policy-makers not be paralysed by greater volumes of information: they must retain their capacity to sort information and direct attention to that which is urgent or important, while retaining and storing that which is potentially significant. One coping strategy in increasing use has been to impose reporting guidelines on posts: many less-important posts are issued instructions not to report unless major developments occur. In Canberra, however, the greater volumes of information place even greater emphasis both on the strategic level of foreign policy making to define frameworks for analysing and prioritising information, and on collective under-standings in the department of what are important issues and relationships.

The communications revolution has eroded the foreign ministry's position as one of the few authoritative sources in society of knowledge about the outside world. Many interest groups that deal with DFAT have access to high-quality information about international developments of interest to them. This has had the effect of increasing the contestation of knowledge about international rela-tions, and opening foreign policy makers' reasonings and actions to much greater public and media scrutiny.

This leads to yet another imperative for the information role of the foreign policy machinery: to monitor international information sources for issues that could become significant in domestic politics. Now that a vast range of sources of international information are available to Australian society, in areas of rele-vance to Australia, the government needs diplomats on the ground at the source of the information, to explain, analyse and contextualise information flowing into Australia. In a foreign policy process that is increasingly prey to the inter-pretations of domestic politics, the maintenance of DFAT's independent capac-ity to analyse and contextualise such information seems essential to the job of sober and balanced international policy-making.

Routinisation

Another trend we have discerned, very much related to the pressures of global-isation, is a growing tendency for the domestic and international consultation procedures of foreign policy to be regularised and routinised. Domestically, the advent of more, better-informed and better-organised interest groups, plus the sensitivity of foreign policy makers to domestic controversy or disapproval, has led to a regularisation of contact between the foreign policy institutions and various interest groups. The regular human rights roundtables, held several times annually, are one example. Similar forums take place in trade policy, the environment and arms control. Both sides to these consultations have an incentive to meet and talk regularly. Foreign policy makers are increasingly seeing interest groups as either "stakeholders" or potential critics within society; the chance to meet with them, to learn from them, but also potentially to coopt them, is useful. Interest groups in their turn appreciate regular access to policymakers; they like being "taken seriously", and they see benefits in being able to "see what government is thinking". The result, at the domestic interface of foreign policy, is a series of contacts, with a range of domestic interests, that has become more regular and predictable for both sides.

Internationally, a parallel process seems to be occurring. As Australia becomes increasingly enmeshed in a range of global, regional, transregional and subregional organisations, its work is increasingly regularised and structured by the pressures of servicing these institutions. Similarly, bilateral relations are to a new degree shaped around ministerial meetings (United States, Indonesia, Japan, China, Papua New Guinea, and so on), government–private-sector forums (Korea), and a very wide range of regular consultations on human rights (Vietnam, China), politico-military affairs, policy planning, and so on. Not only is the foreign policy machinery's collective diary heavily committed long into the future by these meetings, but much of its work involves preparing for them. Australian foreign policy makers have a culture of taking multilateral commitments seriously. They devote substantial resources to analysing developments, responding to initiatives, and conducting policy in international and regional organisations. One vignette may illustrate this. When the concept of early voluntary sectoral liberalisation (EVSL) was proposed for the APEC forum by Canada at the November 1997 Vancouver meetings, DFAT responded by compiling an econometric analysis of the benefits for regional trade of early liberalisation in various nominal sectors. When the results were bound and distributed (and came to be known as "the red book") to other APEC economies early in 1998, it led to a widespread perception that EVSL had been an Australian initiative.

This devotion of resources adds to the demands of servicing multilateral commitments (11.2 per cent of survey respondents agreed strongly that "servicing commitments to international organisations is placing greater demands on DFAT resources", while 45.5 per cent agreed). Such commitments also take up increasing amounts of time in the context of bilateral diplomacy, as attempts are made to persuade fellow members of organisations to support or oppose particular initiatives.

One effect of routinisation on the processes and institutions of foreign policy making may be to act as a countervailing effect to the rise of information and time pressures. By making foreign policy demands somewhat more predictable, some of the pressure is taken off foreign policy makers, and the planning of policy work and the marshalling of resources at the organisational level of policy-making are made somewhat easier.

Resource pressures

At the same time as the demands on foreign policy makers are expanding, they are being asked to do more with less. Globalisation and the rise of the competition state have resulted in a broad commitment to reduce the size of government and the resources it uses. While most parts of government have been subject to efficiency drives, DFAT has been more affected by resource-cutting than most. It presents a tempting target for government cost-cutting. The costs of maintaining overseas missions has grown, particularly with a low Australian dollar, and have had to be accommodated within the same or smaller budget allocations. Second, as mentioned above, DFAT has no powerful, permanent domestic constituency willing to contest any attempt to cut its budget, as do the Health and Education departments (and, for other reasons, Defence). Third, and less tangibly, resentment at the perceived elitism and perks of DFAT's personnel still make it harder to marshal intra-bureaucratic sympathy when the bureaucratic battles are fought.

The department has responded to resource constraints in a number of ways. Unlike that of some other areas of government, the confidential nature of its work has made it unable to outsource most of its core activities. Therefore, it has had to resort to a number of other measures. One is reducing the number of staff: between 1995 and 1999 it shed 20 per cent of Australia-based staff serving in Canberra and overseas. Another tactic has been to expand the responsibilities of locally engaged staff at overseas posts. Some departmental reforms have contributed to resource savings: the commitments to multiskilling and breaking down old structural divisions between Foreign Affairs officers (diplomats) and administrative staff have assisted in the process of reducing the department's administrative "tail", concentrating staff resources as much as possible in policy areas. Increasing use has been made also of non-resident accreditation and post-sharing arrangements with Canada and New Zealand in order to save on the costs of maintaining the overseas network. In addition, the department has become more active in cultivating constituencies within the broader community, among internationalising business, interest groups, the travelling public, and the general public interested in international affairs.

Conclusion

Whatever the scale of the changes globalisation brings to the international system, for as far ahead as we can usefully see the Australian people will require some arm of the national government to grapple directly with its challenges. The social and economic forces that act on Australians – the collective sense of isolation from natural regional groupings, of limited power and population, of national prosperity and wealth that needs to be carefully managed – all project high expectations onto the institutions of government that interact with the outside world.

In this, the first sustained external examination of the processes, institutions and actors involved in making Australian foreign policy, we have shed light on a series of highly developed, interlocking components that are unique among foreign policy making machineries. The result of historical development, altered inheritances, and intangibles such as national culture, Australia's foreign policy making machinery has several distinctive features.

First, it is relatively small and highly collegial. At the officials level (and even at the executive level, where former officials are well-represented in ministerial offices) there is substantial interaction and movement between senior staff in different agencies, and considerable bureaucratic continuity between governments. Inter-agency conflict on policy is surprisingly rare. The world view of most of the policy-makers is heavily realist, and this seems to be a position to which their experience drives them, rather than an attitude with which they are recruited (see pages 74–5). This is not to suggest, however, that ministers are in thrall to a foreign affairs establishment. Our evidence shows that Australian officials are highly responsive to conceptual direction from the political leadership (see page 275).

Second, the executive seems to be steadily increasing its influence over foreign policy making. The growth in the Prime Minister's power is greatest. In part, that is because more foreign policy issues (illegal people movement, terrorism and international trade agreements, for example) have a domestic political aspect to them and involve a wider range of departments.

Third, and in contrast to the bureaucratic level, foreign policy making at the political level in Australia seems to be operating with less consensus than at any time since the early 1970s. One example was the division over participation in the Iraq conflict in 2003. This reduction in consensus is not necessarily a bad thing: pro forma bipartisanship about foreign policy can be stultifying, but what seems to be happening is not more vigorous debate about the future of policy, but a sharpening of points of disagreement on a narrowing range of issues. That may partly be the result of the particular approaches of individual politicians at any given time, but it also seems to reflect two other consequences of globalisation. One is the already noted greater interaction of domestic policies with foreign policy. The other is the increasingly active and effective role in foreign policy of advocacy groups, operating with fuller access to information than ever before and using such issues specifically to highlight political causes. The debates over greenhouse-gas emissions, or international instruments such as the Multilateral Agreement on Investment (MAI) or the UN Convention on the Rights of the Child, are examples of such dramatising impacts.

Fourth, Australian foreign policy institutions operate with a high degree of professionalism. Whatever debate may be had about the policy being pursued at any given time, these institutions show effective advocacy and implementation skills. This effectiveness is greatest when the bureaucracy and the executive are working closely together (see the case studies on the Sandline Affair and the Cambodia Peace Process, pages 1 and 88). Two recent comparisons of DFAT's capacity to change and manage to pressures of globalisation – one internal to DFAT,[32] and one external[33] – have concluded that in most respects, DFAT has responded more effectively than foreign ministries in other states.

Australia's foreign policy making institutions now face a series of new challenges, however, and it is to these that we want finally to turn. To examine them, we will refer back to the four interrelated levels of foreign policy making we set out in Chapter 2.

The first challenge is at the *strategic* level. The sort of world in which Australian foreign policy is made, and to which it must react, is changing again. Past Australian foreign policy makers have had to respond to two great transformations of the international system. First came the wave of decolonisation after the Second World War, in which the European colonies around Australia were replaced by newly independent states. Many of the issues that preoccupied Australia for the following twenty-five years, including the Suez crisis, the Malayan Emergency, Confrontation (*Konfrontasi*) with Indonesia, the Vietnam War and the Indonesian incorporation of East Timor stemmed from that process. Then the end of the 1980s brought the unexpected end of the bipolar system, facilitated by the transforming power of economic globalisation and the information revolution. The development of APEC, the Cambodia Peace Settlement, the development of the World Trade Organisation and the consequences of the Asian financial crisis of 1997–98, among other issues, all flowed from that second change.

As we noted at the beginning of this chapter, globalisation's implications for the international system have by no means played themselves out. Two of its continuing consequences are already causing policy-makers to rethink the strategic level of foreign policy. One is the emergence of China as a regional power in East Asia; the other, the reinterpretation of concepts of security after the end of the Cold War, and especially after the terrorist attacks of September 2001 and October 2002, and the war against Iraq in March 2003.

China will not be a global peer competitor of the United States in the foreseeable future, but it is already exercising a combined political, economic and strategic influence on East and Southeast Asia, greater than any regional power before it. Australian policy-making, used to an environment in which the country's major ally – first Britain, then the United States – has also been the dominant external power in the region, will now find it an often more sensitive and a sometimes more difficult task to balance its political and its security interests. Determining that balance will be further complicated as the strategic level of Australian foreign policy making grapples with the adjustments in foreign policy as well as defence policy, required to respond to substate security threats like terrorism. Two signs of these difficulties at the strategic level were the extended delay, presumably for rethinking and rewriting, of the second of the Howard Government's White Papers on foreign policy, originally promised for 2002 and finally issued in 2003, and the February 2003 revisions to its own December 2000 defence White Paper, issued as *Australia's National Security: A Defence Update 2003*.

At the *contextual* level, foreign policy now needs to influence and deal with a wider range of targets than the governments of nation-states. These include multilateral organisations, global markets, transnational businesses, advocacy and lobby groups (from aid organisations to environmental groups), specific sections of other communities (like potential people-smugglers in Indonesia), terrorist and other substate groups, and broad public opinion in other countries.[34] As government departments and intelligence agencies have found, networked organisations are particularly difficult for hierarchies to target and to influence. For example, when the International Campaign to Ban Landmines shared the Nobel Peace Prize in 1997, no legal entity existed to claim the prize: the ICBL was simply an amorphous network of interest groups.[35]

The incentives and means of persuasion for non-state actors are very different from those for state actors. Traditional forms of diplomatic persuasion and of threat do not work. So foreign policy makers will need to draw on different skill sets and to find different ways of delivering policy. This will mean, among other things, drawing more effectively on Australia's "soft power" resources, to use Joseph Nye's phrase – its cultural and social strengths and influences.

In some cases, the government will want to form specific coalitions of interest with non-government actors. Non-governmental organisations, for example, have been drawn on in support of arms-control initiatives (such as the British Government's work on conflict diamonds with the group Global Witness), and business organisations in support of trade proposals.

On the other side of the same contextual coin, we have already noted how the increasing interrelationship between domestic and foreign policy, reinforced dramatically by the impact of terrorist attacks, has resulted in a more politicised foreign policy and one that focuses on the immediate at the expense of the longer term. The glitter of short-term political rewards always has for ministers an allure with which the sober analysis of long-term interests can find it hard to compete. Policy-makers at all levels will have to work harder to get that balance right.

Some of the largest future challenges will occur at the *organisational* level. The collegiality of the Australian foreign policy making machinery is a strength: any set of institutions lubricated with large amounts of trust and "social capital" will almost always be highly effective and resourceful in responding to new challenges. However, the cultural distinctiveness that marks foreign ministries and intelligence organisations alike can easily become inward-looking and self-absorbed, increasing the danger of what Irving Janis famously termed "groupthink", a condition of dogmatic thinking that tends to discount contrary evidence in the interests of maintaining consensus.[36] It will be a particular challenge for the institutions of foreign policy making to preserve openness to divergent views and new approaches.

It will also become increasingly hard for governments to preserve the traditions of secrecy that have cocooned foreign policy and national security policy for so long. Secrets will still be held, but the balance will change. Pressures will increase on governments to justify those secrets rather than on the public to justify their release. An early example of this challenge was the debate after the Bali bombings, about how much the government should reveal about its sources in developing travel warnings for Australian tourists.

At the *operational* level, the challenges will relate to ways of maintaining the capacity of the Australian policy machinery in an atmosphere of continuing resource constraints and changing patterns of work. Neither DFAT nor the intelligence agencies should have difficulty recruiting staff, but keeping them could become harder as attitudes towards lifetime careers change and as overseas employment becomes less unusual. Most important will be the challenge of providing the policy space and time in which people can operate effectively. In the struggle between the immediate and the important, in which the odds so heavily favour the immediate, foreign policy makers will need to carve out more time to give attention to the important.

As we observed in the introduction to this book, many periods have been defined as unpredictable and challenging for Australia's foreign policy makers. To these must be added the first decades of the twenty-first century. But lack of predictability and complex challenges are inherent to the work of foreign policy makers everywhere. Here, the capacity of Australian foreign policy making to respond creatively and flexibly to emerging challenges and old dilemmas will continue to be tested. Some of the cultures, institutions and practices we have discussed in this book will be of great assistance in the coming years, while others may cause difficulties or impede Australia's foreign policy performance. One observation is hard to deny: foreign policy making, and the positive and negative consequences that can flow from it, will have no less an impact on Australian society. In an uncertain environment, and with such high stakes, making effective and far-sighted Australian foreign policy is one of the country's most pressing continuing tasks. No factor will be more important in determining the success of the enterprise than the engaged attention of an informed Australian public.

Notes

1 See "What Comes After the 'Post-Cold War' World?", *Foreign Policy*, Vol. 119, Summer 2000.

2 Jan Aart Scholte, *Globalisation: A Critical Introduction*, Basingstoke: Palgrave, 2000.

3 John Baylis and Steve Smith, *The Globalisation of World Politics*, Oxford: Oxford University Press, 2001, p. 9.

4 See, for example, R.B.J. Walker, *Inside/Outside: International Relations as Political Theory*, Cambridge: Cambridge University Press, 1993; Anthony Giddens, *The Consequences of Modernity*, Cambridge: Cambridge University Press, 1990; Ronald J. Diebert, "Harold Innis and the Empire of Speed", *Review of International Studies*, Vol. 25, 1999, pp. 273–89.

5 James N. Rosenau, "Governance, Order, and Change in World Politics" in James N. Rosenau and Ernst-Otto Czempiel, *Governance without Government: Order and Change in World Politics*, Cambridge: Cambridge University Press, 1992, p. 3.

6 Hedley Bull, *The Anarchical Society: A Study of Order in World Politics*, Basingstoke: Macmillan, 1977, pp. 254–5.

7 For example Jan Aart Scholte, "The Globalisation of World Politics", in Baylis and Smith (eds), *The Globalisation of World Politics*, p. 24.

8 Baylis and Smith, *The Globalisation of World Politics*, p. 7.

9 Anne-Marie Slaughter, "The Real New World Order", *Foreign Affairs,* September–October 1997.

10 Dani Rodrik, *Has Globalisation Gone Too Far?* Washington, DC: Institute for International Economics, 1997.

11 Linda Weiss, *The Myth of the Powerless State*, Ithaca, NY: Cornell University Press, 1998.

12 Charlotte Bretherton and Geoffrey Ponton (eds), *Global Politics: An Introduction*, Oxford: Blackwell, 1996.

13 Ian Clark, *Globalisation and Fragmentation: International Relations in the Twentieth Century*, Oxford: Oxford University Press, 1999, p. 6 (emphasis in original).

14 Robert Cooper, *The Postmodern State and the World Order*, London: Demos, 1998.

15 John Gerard Ruggie, "Territoriality and Beyond: Problematising Modernity in International Relations", *International Organization*, Vol. 47, 1993, pp. 139–74.

16 See the studies on the foreign ministries of a number of EU states in Brian Hocking (ed.), *Foreign Ministries: Change and Adaptation*, London: Macmillan, 1999.

17 ibid.

18 For figures, see Allan Gyngell and Michael Wesley, "Interweaving of Foreign and Domestic Policy: International Policy" in Glyn Davis and Michael Keating (eds), *The Future of Governance: Policy Choices*, Sydney: Allen & Unwin, 2000.

19 See Robert Gilpin, *War and Change in World Politics*, Cambridge: Cambridge University Press, 1981; Paul Kennedy, *The Rise and Fall of the Great Powers*, London: Fontana Press, 1988.

20 John M. Stopford and Susan Strange, *Rival States, Rival Firms: Competition for World Market Shares*, Cambridge: Cambridge University Press, 1991.

21 John Gerard Ruggie, "At Home Abroad, Abroad at Home: International Liberalisation and Domestic Stability in the New World Economy", *Millennium*, Vol. 24, No. 3, Winter 1995, pp. 507–26.

22 See Paul Kelly, *The End of Certainty,* Sydney: Allen & Unwin, 1992.

23 Dani Rodrik, "Sense and Nonsense in the Globalisation Debate", *Foreign Policy*, Spring 1998.

24 For an account of these threats in Australia's region, see Alan Dupont, *East Asia Imperilled: Transnational Challenges to Security*, Cambridge: Cambridge University Press, 2001.

25 Bull, *The Anarchical Society*, 1977, p. 177.

26 G. John Ikenberry, "The State and Strategies of International Adjustment", *World Politics*, Vol. 39, No. 1, October 1986, pp. 53–77.

27 Richard Higgott, "The Politics of Australia's International Economic Relations: Adjustment and Two-Level Games", *Australian Journal of Political Science*, Vol. 26, 1991, pp. 2–28.

28 Michael Wesley, "Perspectives on Australian Foreign Policy, 2001", *Australian Journal of International Affairs*, Vol. 56, No. 1, April 2002.

29 Gareth Evans and Bruce Grant, *Australia's Foreign Relations: In the World of the 1990s*, 2nd ed., Melbourne: Melbourne University Press, 1994.

30 Department of Foreign Affairs and Trade, *East Timor in Transition 1998–2000: An Australian Policy Challenge*, Canberra: DFAT, 2001.

31 Robert O. Keohane and Joseph Nye Jr, "Power and Interdependence in the Information Age", *Foreign Affairs*, Vol. 77, No. 5, September–October 1988, p. 89.

32 Foreign and Trade Ministry Best Practice Review, Report to the Secretary by R.C. Smith, August 2000, Restricted.

33 Hocking, *Foreign Ministries*.

34 Gyngell and Wesley, "Interweaving Foreign and Domestic Policy", p. 226.
35 For an interesting account of the campaign, see Motoko Mekata, "Building Partnerships toward a Common Goal; Experiences of the International Campaign to Ban Landmines" in Ann M. Florini (ed.), *The Third Force: The Rise of Transnational Society*, Washington, DC: Carnegie Endowment for International Peace, 2000.
36 Irving Janis, *Victims of Groupthink*, Boston: Houghton Mifflin, 1983.

The Perceptions of Australia's Foreign Policy Makers

In December 2001 we sent a forty-two-part questionnaire to more than 800 Department of Foreign Affairs and Trade policy officers, posted in Canberra and overseas. It was our intention to try to gauge their opinions on a range of issues, from their optimal career path and choices of postings, to their perceptions of the nature of contemporary world politics. Two hundred and forty-two officers responded to the questionnaire. The analysis of their responses is presented below.

What is your age group?

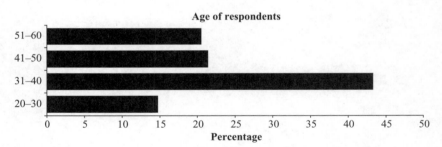

How long ago did you join DFAT?

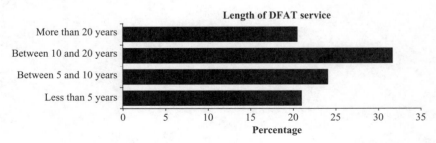

What was your principal area of academic study?

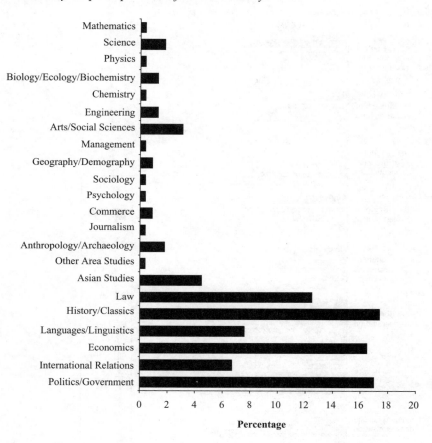

What is your work location?

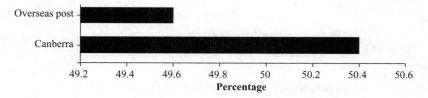

Rank the following issues from most to least important for Australian foreign policy.

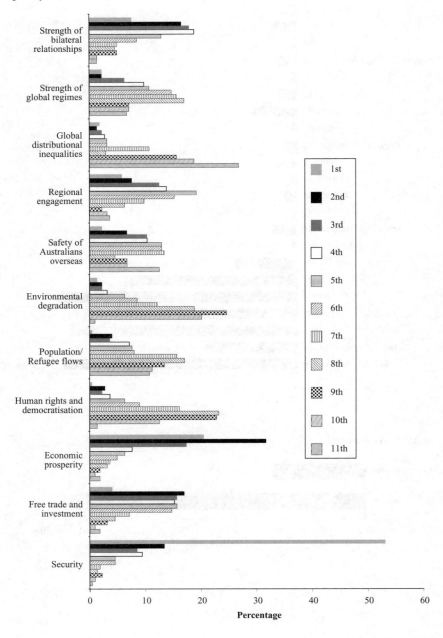

Has the nature of world politics changed since you joined DFAT?

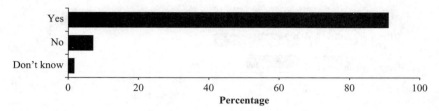

Which of the following has had the greatest effect on the "subject matter" of foreign policy making? Has it affected it substantially, somewhat, or negligibly?

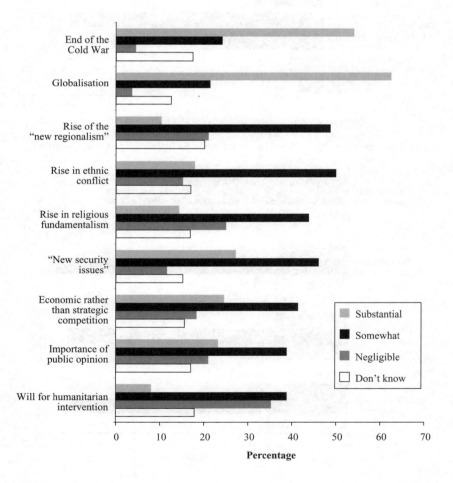

How profound are the changes you nominated for the nature of world politics?

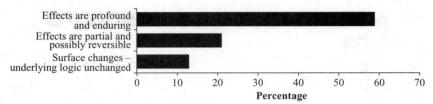

Which of the following statements most closely reflects your understanding of the general nature of world politics?

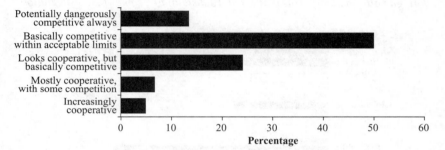

To what extent are the following actors gaining influence in world politics?

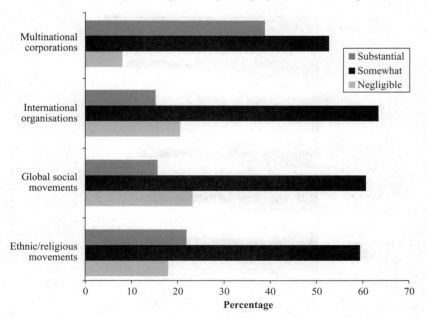

Please indicate the extent to which you agree or disagree with these assessments about Australia's role in the world.

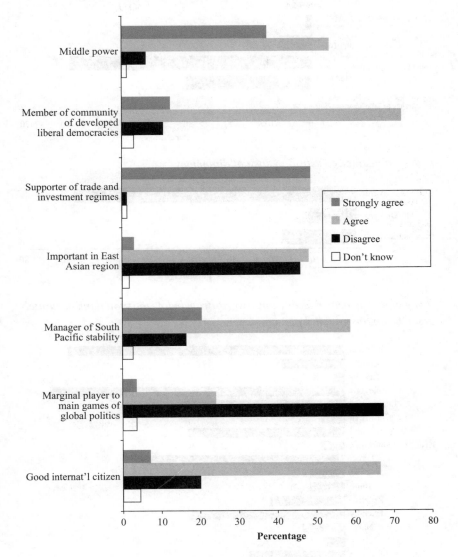

How much freedom of choice and initiative do Australia's foreign policy makers have in world politics?

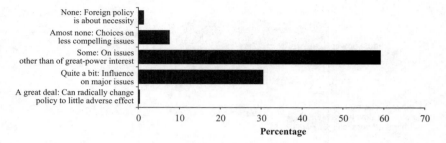

Is there a distinctly Australian style of diplomacy?

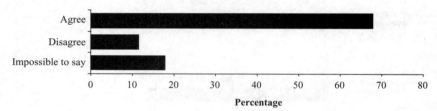

If you agree, please underline three words from below that you think accurately describe an Australian diplomatic style.

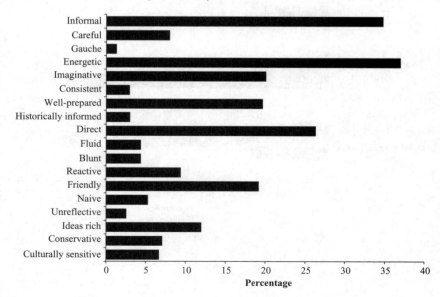

Is Australian foreign policy essentially bipartisan?

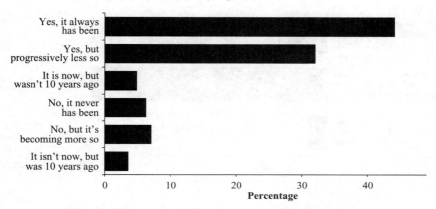

Do you think that principles demonstrating concern for human well-being in other societies conflict with foreign policy goals formulated in accordance with Australia's national interest?

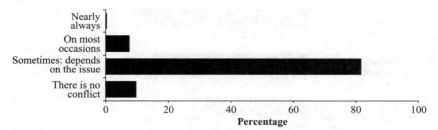

"The only time principles demonstrating concern for human well-being in other societies should be a determining factor in foreign policy is when it enhances the effectiveness of that policy." Do you (a) agree in all situations; (b) think it depends on the stakes involved; or (c) disagree – concern for the human impact of policy should never be subordinate to other policy goals?

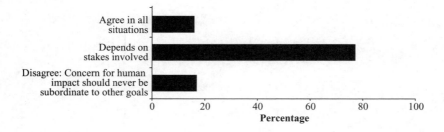

How much influence do you have on foreign policy?

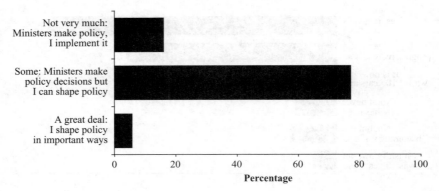

Which values do you think it is most important to inject into policy-making?

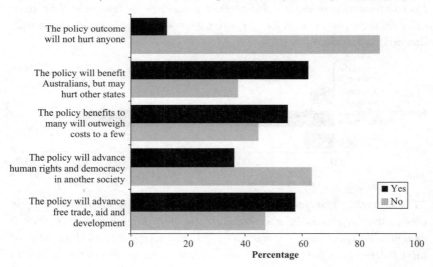

Do you agree or disagree with the following statement, or can't say?

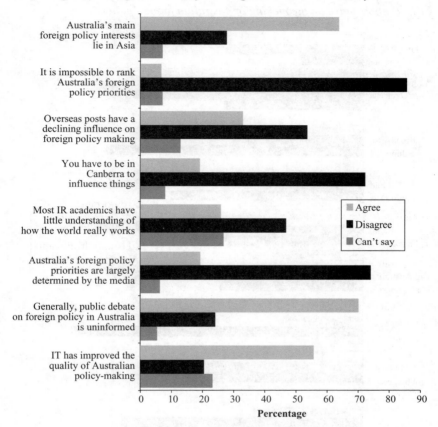

On a day-to-day basis, how much influence do you think the following positions or institutions have on the making of Australian foreign policy?

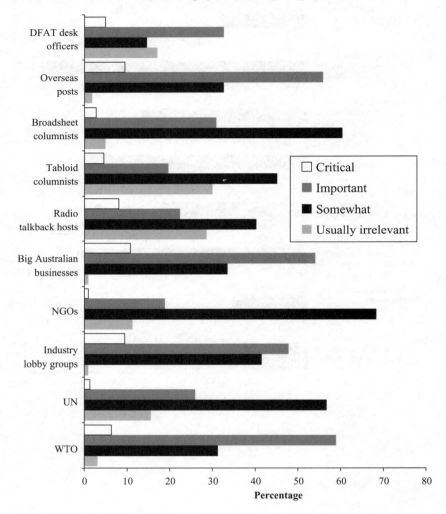

What are the main sources of your information on foreign policy?

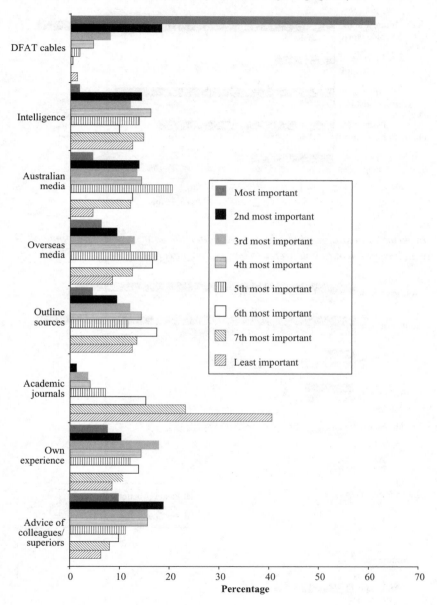

Why did you join DFAT?

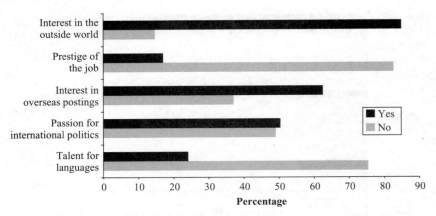

In terms of postings, what regions are better for your career development? To which region would you prefer to go on your next posting?

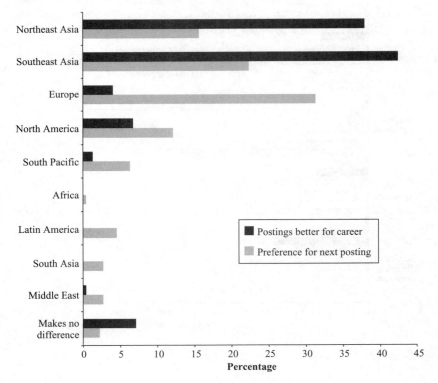

In terms of promotion, which sections/areas/divisions in Canberra are better for your career? (See the Glossary for an explanation of the initials.)

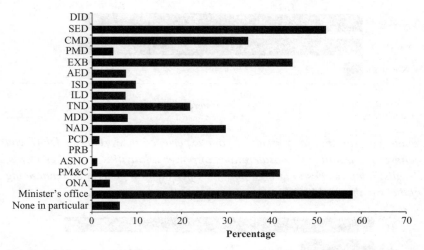

On the whole, how would you describe your professional contacts with officers in other Federal Government departments or agencies?

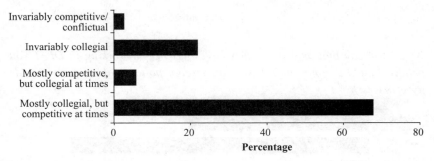

How would you describe the range of opinion among DFAT officers on most issues in world politics?

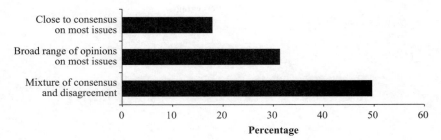

*Would you say that as a result of your experience in working in DFAT your
views on the way the world operates have changed?*

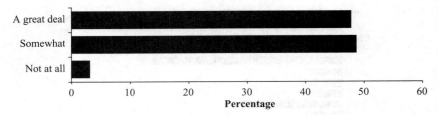

*Would you say that as a result of your experience in working in DFAT you
believe that traditional considerations of power relativities – in other words,
"realist" approaches to foreign policy – offer the best general understanding
of the way the world works?*

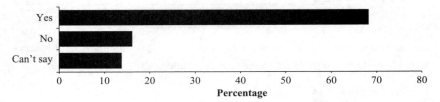

*Would you say that as a result of your experience in working in DFAT you
believe that the inputs into Australian foreign policy making from outside
government:*

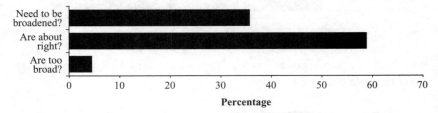

Please rank from 1 to 8 the following positions in terms of their influence on a serious, principally bilateral Australian foreign policy issue: Foreign/Trade ministers; ambassador at post most affected; the Secretary of DFAT; the Prime Minister; Secretary of PM&C; Prime Minister's international adviser; Foreign Minister's senior adviser; member of the Joint Parliamentary Committee on Foreign Affairs, Defence and Trade.

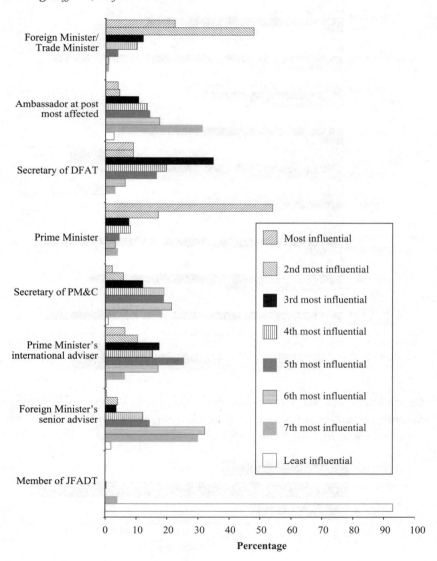

Compared with the time you joined DFAT, would you say that the following groups or institutions have more influence or less on the content of Australian foreign policy?

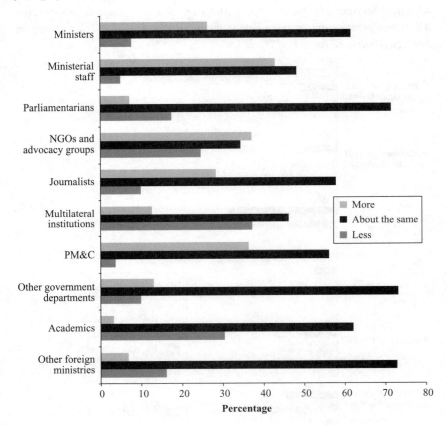

On the whole, how do you think regular Management Reviews, Performance Reviews, Output Pricing Reviews, and efficiency measures generally impact on the effectiveness of foreign policy making?

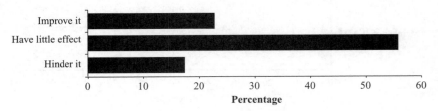

Is globalisation changing foreign policy making? Do you agree strongly, agree, disagree with the following statements, or can't say?

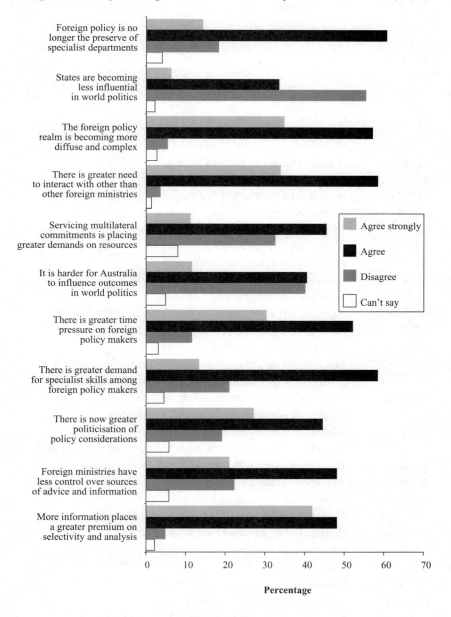

Glossary

ACBC	Australia China Business Council
ADB	Asian Development Bank
ADCNet	Former internal encrypted email system of DFAT
ADF	Australian Defence Force
AED	Americas and Europe Division, DFAT
AFP	Australian Federal Police
AIC	Australian intelligence community
AIIA	Australian Institute of International Affairs
ALP	Australian Labor Party
ANZUS	Australia, New Zealand, United States Security Treaty
APEC	Asia–Pacific Economic Cooperation group
ARF	ASEAN Regional Forum
ASEAN + 3	Meetings of the ASEAN states plus Japan, the People's Republic of China, and the Republic of Korea
ASEAN	Association of Southeast Asian Nations
ASIO	Australian Security Intelligence Organisation
ASIS	Australian Secret Intelligence Service
ASNO	Australian Safeguards and Non-Proliferation Office, DFAT
AusAID	Australian Agency for International Development
Austrade	Australian Trade Commission
BHP	Broken Hill Proprietary Limited
CHOGM	Commonwealth Heads of Government Meeting
CIA	Central Intelligence Agency (United States)
CMD	Corporate Management Division, DFAT
CNN	Cable News Network
COAG	Council of Australian Governments
ConOps	Consular Operations Centre, DFAT
CPD	Commonwealth Parliamentary Debates (Hansard)

CSCAP	Conference for Security Cooperation in the Asia–Pacific
CTBT	Comprehensive Test Ban Treaty
DAFF	Department of Agriculture, Fisheries and Forestry
DEH	Department of Environment and Heritage
DEST	Department of Education, Science and Training
DFAT	Department of Foreign Affairs and Trade
DID	Diplomatic Security, Property and Information Management Division, DFAT
DIGO	Defence Imagery and Geospatial Organisation
DIMIA	Department of Immigration and Multicultural and Indigenous Affairs
DIO	Defence Intelligence Organisation
DoD	Department of Defence
DSB	Defence Signals Bureau
DSD	Defence Signals Directorate
EMEAP	Executive Meeting of East Asian and Pacific Central Banks
EU	European Union
EXB	Executive, Planning and Evaluation Branch, DFAT
FAS	First Assistant Secretary
FBI	Federal Bureau of Investigation (United States)
FIPD	Foreign Intelligence Planning Document
FPDA	Five Power Defence Arrangement
GCHQ	Government Communications Headquarters (United Kingdom)
GDP	gross domestic product
HIAM	Heads of Intelligence Agencies Meeting
HIV/AIDS	Human Immunodeficiency Virus/Acquired Immunodeficiency Syndrome
HUMINT	human intelligence
ICC	International Criminal Court
IDC	interdepartmental committee
IECG	International Economic Coordination Group
IGIS	Inspector-General of Intelligence and Security
ILD	International Organisations and Legal Division, DFAT
IMF	International Monetary Fund
INGO	international non-governmental organisation
IR	international relations
ISD	International Security Division, DFAT
JFADT	Joint Standing Committee on Foreign Affairs, Defence and Trade

MAI	Multilateral Agreement on Investment (OECD)
MDD	Market Development Division (now Trade Development Division), DFAT
Mercosur	Common Market of the South (Mercado Comun del Sur)
MI6	Secret Intelligence Service (United Kingdom)
MNC	multinational corporation
MP	Member of Parliament
NAD	North Asia Division, DFAT
NAFTA	North American Free Trade Agreement
NATO	North Atlantic Treaty Organisation
NFF	National Farmers' Federation
NFIAP	National Foreign Intelligence Assessment Priorities
NGO	non-governmental organisation
NICRC	National Intelligence Collection Requirements Committee
NSC	National Security Committee of Cabinet
OECD	Organisation for Economic Cooperation and Development
ONA	Office of National Assessments
PCD	Public Diplomacy, Consular and Passports Division, DFAT
PECC	Pacific Economic Cooperation Council
PM&C	Department of Prime Minister and Cabinet
PMD	South Pacific, Africa and Middle East Division, DFAT
PNG	Papua New Guinea
PNGDF	Papua New Guinea Defence Force
PRB	Protocol Branch, DFAT
PSCC	Protective Security Coordination Centre, Attorney-General's Department
RAAF	Royal Australian Air Force
SATIN	DFAT's internal encrypted email system
SCNS	Secretaries Committee on National Security
SED	South and Southeast Asia Division, DFAT
SES	Senior Executive Service
SIGINT	signals intelligence
SPCG	Strategic Policy Coordination Group
SPEC	South Pacific Economic Commission
SPF	South Pacific Forum
TND	Trade Negotiations Division, DFAT
UAV	uninhabited aerial vehicle
UK	United Kingdom

UKUSA	Cooperative arrangement between the SIGINT organisations of the United States, Britain, Canada, Australia and New Zealand
UN	United Nations
UNTAC	United Nations Transitional Administration in Cambodia
US	United States
USSR	Union of Soviet Socialist Republics
WTO	World Trade Organisation

Index